Andrew Flower was born in Rothwell near Leeds and after a brief apprenticeship joined the Royal Electrical Mechanical Engineers at the age of 18. After serving 22 years in Germany, Canada, Northern Ireland, Bosnia and Saudi Arabia, he left the Army and worked as a Trials and Development engineer, for a large defence company, working on armoured vehicles until retirement. His main hobbies are camping, swimming and playing the guitar. He has two children and four grandchildren and lives with his wife in Telford, Shropshire.

This book is dedicated to C Company fitter section REME and the Staffordshire and Cheshire Regiments I served with during the conflicts I have recorded.

Andrew Flower B.E.M.

AN ARTIFICER'S TALE

AUSTIN MACAULEY PUBLISHERS
LONDON * CAMBRIDGE * NEW YORK * SHARJAH

Copyright © Andrew Flower B.E.M.2025

The right of Andrew Flower B.E.M.to be identified as the author of this work has been asserted by the author in accordance with sections 77 and 78 of the Copyright, Designs and Patents Act 1988.

All rights reserved. No part of this publication may be reproduced, stored in a retrieval system, or transmitted in any form or by any means, electronic, mechanical, photocopying, recording, or otherwise, without the prior permission of the publishers.

Any person who commits any unauthorised act in relation to this publication may be liable to criminal prosecution and civil claims for damages.

All of the events in this memoir are true to the best of author's memory. The views expressed in this memoir are solely those of the author.

A CIP catalogue record for this title is available from the British Library.

ISBN 9781035873661 (Paperback)
ISBN 9781035873678 (ePub e-book)

www.austinmacauley.com

First Published 2025
Austin Macauley Publishers Ltd®
1 Canada Square
Canary Wharf
London
E14 5AA

Table of Contents

Chapter 1: Ramblings	9
Chapter 2: Where Shall I Start?	14
Chapter 3: You're in the Army Now	19
Chapter 4: Stand Back, I'm in Charge	30
Chapter 5: The Poetry Corner Part One	35
Chapter 6: Introduction to the Action Bits	47
Chapter 7: Operation Granby (Gulf War I)	49
Chapter 8: 1986 Christmas Day, Bessbrook Camp, County Armagh N.I.	67
Chapter 9: Christmas Day (In the Desert)	72
Chapter 10: The Andy Flower School of Tact and Diplomacy	74
Chapter 11: 17 January 1991	78
Chapter 12: Iraq War, 2003	83
Chapter 13: Gulf War I (Continued)	89
Chapter 14: Let's Get This Show on the Road	110
Chapter 15: They Think It's All Over	130
Chapter 16: Home Time	136
Chapter 17: Poetry Corner Part Two	140
Chapter 18: Bosnia 1992	173
Chapter 19: Vitez	183

Chapter 20: Enniskillen/Armagh Border, 1979	189
Chapter 21: Vitez (Continued)	192
Chapter 22: Kladanj	195
Chapter 23: The Recovery to Vitez	210
Chapter 24: Vitez the Sequel	222
Chapter 25: Kakuni	226
Chapter 26: Tuzla	235
Chapter 27: Tuzla (The Return)	245
Chapter 28: The Move to Split	249
Chapter 29: Home in Time for Tea	252
Chapter 30: Poetry Corner Part Three	253
Chapter 31: Fallingbostel 1993	268
Chapter 32: Batus	269
Chapter 33: Civilian Life	272
Chapter 34: Prologue	278

Chapter 1
Ramblings

The first part of most works of writing is usually called the introduction. The introduction usually sets the scene, introduces the characters, explains the history and justifies the reason for writing the document in the first place.

I have just completed reading through the introduction and have concluded that I have been rambling on for quite a few of the following paragraphs and therefore have decided that this first section should not be called introduction but ramblings.

There are also ramblings at the start of each verse of poetry within this book, this is to set the scene and prepare the reader for what is about to come. At this point, I can now feel your excitement growing with anticipation that you may have finally found a writer who will keep you entertained for future years with the collection of works he has written. Well! This is the book's first disappointment. This is probably the only book I will be writing.

"Oh no," I hear you say.

Actually, I do have quite a few humorous, historical and factual stories included within these works, with me as the main character in Gulf War I 1990, Bosnia 1992 and even Northern Ireland where I was asked several times by the Queen to go and wander through the streets and fields for six months at a time, whilst the IRA sympathisers threw bricks and flaming bottles of petrol and worse at me. Yes, there are worse things.

After my first proofread, I decided that there was a lot of boring stuff only army types or engineers would be bothered with and to be perfectly honest it was stuff that on reading it I found boring myself. Following this disappointment on my part, approximately three thousand words of drivel were deleted. If you still find some bits boring well! I tried my best.

It also turns out that if I want to mention names or include personalities in photos within this book, I am required to gain their permission first. As most of the stories are between 30 to 40 years old that is not possible, so sorry guys, if you wanted your 15 minutes of fame through this medium that cannot now happen.

I do include a few names of the people I am still in touch with or that I am positive would be quite happy playing a role in these infamous historical events.

On all operations, Northern Ireland, Gulf War 1, Bosnia and a hundred other operations and exercises with HM forces I always packed a guitar.

1. Play to the troops and raise the morale in the hardest times.
2. To give the troops an object to throw abuse at, which ties in with item one.
3. To give myself some peace and get away from the bloody troops.
4. There was always someone else who could also play a guitar, so it was a great chance to get away from routine and learn some new songs and styles of playing guitar.

Three sections of this book are based on a selection of verses written as lyrics for songs over a period of 50 some years. I have adapted them to read more like lines of verse rather than song lyrics.

Obviously, some of the works that were intended to be song lyrics do not translate that easily into lines of verse, so please be lenient. The works range from me being a young daft teenager, to joining the army and leaving the forces to start leading a new life working as a trials/project/design engineer for major defence companies, up to the point of me being an old daft pensioner looking back at life and taking every opportunity to jump in the motorhome and find more adventures.

There are snippets of humour and horror, laughter and loving, culminating in a few verses of me just being me.

The verses are in alphabetical order rather than the order they were written, I believe that this allows the reader to jump between periods in my life's
history of ups and downs rather than following the zigzag pattern my emotions usually follow.

I have written this book from the experiences I have gained throughout this time. Although there has been great happiness in my life for the most part, during this period it has never ceased to amaze me all manner of things that we humans are quite content to do to each other.

This can range from petty stealing or damage to property and violence by neighbours and so-called friends, to full-blown war in the case of Gulf War 1 and horrendous war crimes in the case of Bosnia, and the Irish bombers of the 60s, 70s and 80s. The way total strangers are quite happy gaining an advantage at the expense of unknown vulnerable individuals leaves me gobsmacked.

Don't even get me started on the lean sentences the law courts dish out to these individuals when they do get caught, and the unbelievable release of IRA murderers during the Good Friday Agreement.

On the other end of the spectrum, are the nice people who go out of their way to help people. I mean really go out of their way. So far, out of their way that they turn a man who wants to be left alone into a person that is quite content to tell these nosy buggers to leave me alone and go bother someone who cares.

Needless to say, this book will not contain any restraints on my comments and thinking in order to pander to the nice brigade and be seemingly politically correct. When I was a lad, WOKE was something you did in the morning not something you had to concentrate on every time you wanted to speak. You should never judge a man until you have walked a mile in their shoes. You can judge all you want then because they are a mile away and they don't have any shoes, so they cannot chase after you.

There are also other aspects of life gained from family, friends and loved ones. This in itself has been the subject of verse for millennia. Many of the verses are just stories completed using only my imagination. Some are from actual events and some like most writers are just dreams put on paper.

Humour has been and still is one of the most important aspects of my life. Even when the occasions do not warrant it, I find myself trying to put a humorous take on the occasions. Sometimes this is not appreciated by those affected, and I suppose this made me come across as callus and uncaring but that is just the way it is and it was all done with the best intentions.

Inspiration for these verses comes from all manner of friends and acquaintances, there are no credits here. Those that made a big part of my life know who you are. Those that didn't will not be reading this book anyway. I actually started compiling this book initially so I had a record of a small part of my life. I do not really want to end up as an old, faded photograph on somebody's hall wall with future generations of my family not being aware of the life I have had.

I freely admit that some of my verses are very amateur and whilst not really caring so long as I had a record of the words in hard copy. However, reading some of the verses again and concentrating on the words and not on my fingers working like buggery to get a decent tune out of an old guitar, has actually brought meaning and feelings that had been lost years ago back to me, so if nothing else this has been a worthwhile exercise for me.

The fantastic thing about getting older and losing bits of memory as the years sped by is this; As a songster it's always a surprise when playing your own songs, you can find out how the stories develop over the years. A word change here and there can put a completely different reflection on the meaning.

Even a subtle change in accent when singing a line can change the mood. Each verse can open up a memory from a time capsule from when you wrote it. What was happening in the world and who or what I was involved with or in at this time?

Remembering the people who were in my life during this snapshot brings so many long-lost memories flooding back.

The verses are all my own work but there may be the odd phrase, lyric or saying that has crept in. If it has then credit to the original writer as the lyrics obviously stuck in my mind and made an impression on me.

Within this 'Book of Words' are two short stories Gulf War 1 and Bosnia 1992. These are not historical exact references and facts but are stories that I have taken from my diaries written at the time and are historically correct to within a day or two apart from the Gulf War 1 which I broke this three-day war into an hourly true account.

I hope you enjoy reading this book and can reflect on some of the thoughts behind it, although it should not be read when you require some serious or profound reading. Recollections of the subject matter or events other people also witnessed may vary as they always do. After all, it was 30 to 40 years ago. These stories are as I remember them and may have changed slightly as they have been told many times over the years.

It is, perhaps, better read whilst warming a good wine or whisky in the cup of your hand, or after a few chilled beers. Read the verses a few times and something may stick.

When reading the verse section, as they were originally song lyrics, it may help to see if you can imagine a tune or a rhythm in your head to follow.

Chapter 2
Where Shall I Start?

I want this book to reflect the life I had once I had become an independent person and so I shall skip my childhood years and concentrate on my life from the time I was in my late teens. However, just for the record, my childhood was pretty standard with a father, mother and elder brother who lived in our own bought and paid-for house in Rothwell, Leeds, West Yorkshire.

We went on summer holidays each year as a family to the Yorkshire seaside towns. Wales, Norfolk or other normal tourist attractions on the east Yorkshire coast, but never abroad. We owned our own house and always had plenty of food on the table but never had too many luxury items so we learnt to mend, repair and look after the things we did have.

I had a great childhood and was allowed to roam freely out in the fields, disused quarries and dirt tracks. I would climb trees, ride bikes and generally have a good time with the gang of six to eight kids of my age that lived in the streets around my area. Through the summer months, we would meet up as a gang and then one of us would raid the family pantry for a bag of sugar.

We would then encamp in the nearest rhubarb field hiding under the leaves and after stripping the skin off the juiciest rhubarb stalks, munch rhubarb until we were full. I regularly played football on the pitch that was at the end of the lane. The pitch was opposite some erected whale jaw bones that were the main feature of the main road leading to Rothwell.

There were also the remains of an old mansion next to the pitch, where we could play in the cellars or climb the massive trees that surrounded the property. The reader must remember that all the things kids did in the old days were not impeded by health and safety restrictions as this had not been invented then. Not a phone or computer insight nor would there be for another 40 years.

I remember only coming home when it was time for tea, which I would know as there was the big St Georges Hospital clock on a tower which I could see from all my play areas.

The sand quarries were the place where I was happiest. The high, steep sides were perfect for riding our bikes up and down. We could balance on the top of one side and then throw ourselves over the edge reaching breakneck speeds as we dropped the 40 or so feet to the floor of the quarry.

Once at the floor, we would peddle like mad to maintain the supersonic speed we had achieved on our descent, and then climb the opposite side hoping to be able to jump the bike in the air as we came to the top. Our knees and elbows were constantly covered in cuts, bruises and grazes from our attempts to beat our previous world records.

The quarry was also a dumping ground for the nearest housing estate, so we could trawl through the rubbish for hidden treasures. Upon finding two or three broken push bikes, we would take on the challenge of making one good bike out of the three. This is probably where I first found my interest in engineering, playing with brakes, ball bearings and gears. I was very successful at making scramble bikes for use in the quarry.

On a rare occasion, someone would discard an old motorbike or scooter and so we would proceed to get it running and make a scramble course, riding around on the bike for as long as it would continue running, on the petrol we pinched from our parents' garages.

The water quarries were full of wildlife and so we knew the names of all the birds and fishes that lived in them. In the summer, we would go rafting and fishing as well as swimming. The swimming was usually an effect of the raft not working as well as we had hoped it would.

Our gang dens were located in the old air raid shelters left over from World War II. This is where we would base ourselves between our activities and planning our next adventures. In the field at the bottom of my avenue, there was a circular brick structure which was a mine air shaft. This was about 10 feet across and six feet high, with an old pully wheel on a steel bar across the top.

During harvest time whilst making dens and tunnels using the straw bales in the field, we would occasionally pinch a bale of straw from the field and the gang could shin up the side of the structure and hang over the top, looking down into the void. The shaft was perhaps a hundred feet deep.

We would set alight the bale and watch as it fell into the abyss and then explode into a flash of colour as it hit the bottom of the shaft setting light to the old gases that were present down there. What could possibly go wrong?

In those days, every kid had a piece of string, some matches and a pen knife in their pocket. Nobody ever got tied up, stabbed or set on fire.

I was always interested in making money, so I had several paper rounds, delivering morning and evening papers, Sunday papers and even the sports final.

This always allowed me to buy the things I wanted at that age.

My early teen years were spent in Rothwell at the youth club or playing football in the park, so all in all nothing unusual to write home about. I was not an outstanding student although I was in the second highest class in my year. I had a few girlfriends, some of whom came from the local home for wayward girls.

It was not a borstal but more of a home for girls that needed moral guidance. Anyway, they all seemed pretty nice to me even though my mother did not approve. Especially, when the police parked outside our house for the neighbours to see when enquiring if I knew the whereabouts of an absentee when one had gone missing. This happened a few times.

My brother is about three and a half years older than me and when we were young that gulf was quite large, so his group of friends did not mingle with my group of friends. He was very good at sports at school always being in the school football and rugby teams whereas I was always quite mediocre. I did improve once I reached my late teens but was never going to set the world on fire with my skills.

Once I joined the army, I suppose we grew even further apart as we only saw each other a couple of times a year and I never really had a chance to go out socialising with him in the pubs as brothers do. However, we were always on friendly terms and I don't think I have upset him too much over the years even though our lifestyles do differ greatly.

I left school in 1972, after several years of not really being bothered with school lessons or what I was going to do with my life. My parents were always advising me to pay more attention at school but I preferred daydreaming whilst looking out of the window.

My school report always commented, 'Could do better', which was probably true.

This did not help me at home as my brother always had very good reports. I had already secured an apprenticeship at the local copper works before I left school which was part of a company called Imperial Metals Limited, a subsection of I.C.I. This was located in Hunslet, about a mile and a half from where I lived. Just outside the Leeds boundary.

In-between leaving school and starting my apprenticeship, I worked on Leeds market for a while and then on a market garden farm about two miles from home where for six or seven weeks I walked to the farm in the early hours of the morning and then spent eight- or nine-hours driving tractors and picking vegetables and rhubarb until early evening when I came home with a brilliant sun tan but totally knackered. At the time, I was dating a girl from Puerto Rico from the naughty girl's school and I was browner than she was.

Once my apprenticeship started, I would wake up, grab some breakfast and run over the mile and a half down a disused train line and over fields to arrive almost on time at my place of work in the apprentice training building.

The fields I ran over have now got the M1 to A1 link motorway running across them. All the water quarries have been filled in as have the sand quarries. It was quite disappointing to see all my memorable places had disappeared when I visited there a few years ago. At the time, the Skelton Grange power station was next to the copper works.

This was a massive power station with seven cooling towers and three tall stacks as well as the large electrical distribution factory next to it. This was decommissioned in 1994 and flattened and now it is as though this backdrop on the horizon from my house never existed.

After about 18 months of learning how to use laths, millers, shaping machines, drills and grinders, I was moved from the apprentice training building and into the actual copper fittings factory. Here, I was introduced to an old chap who was retiring. He told me I was to have his job when he left. I had to learn the job he had done for the last 45 years.

This job consisted of sitting in the same chair in the same maintenance pen waiting for a fault on a machine to occur within the factory. At that point, he was then called to fix it or reset the problem machine if it went out of tolerance. Once the machine was repaired, he would go back to his pen and sit down again. For about two weeks, I followed him about whilst he showed me all the machines, what they were, what they did and how to maintain them, as I was to be the replacement machine fitter/setter. Within the first few weeks of having my future planned out for me, I was pretty sure this was not the life for me.

When going into the factory, I had to have three union cards and as I walked through the door there were three benches with the three different union representatives that checked I was in their union before they would then allow me to enter the factory and work. This was what was called a closed shop. No union. No work.

If a machinist was working too hard and was producing more fittings than the union man thought he should produce in an hour, the union man would put a board on the machine stopping him from working the machine until his hourly output had dropped. This was so that the weights and measures man would not expect all the brothers to produce the same number of fittings per hour.

I decided that I could not work in these types of conditions and get into a factory way of life that all the people around me had already slipped into. My life was being run by hooters and bells that controlled shift changes, clocking on start times and clocking off finish times. This I did not want.

At this time, the three-day week was just starting and there were strikes all over the country, fuel shortages, electricity and transport cuts and with the loss of half my wages due to restricted working hours, I decided to get out of there and I joined the army. This was something that I had thought about doing for a while.

Chapter 3
You're in the Army Now

As I had almost finished my apprenticeship, I automatically qualified to join the REME (Royal Electrical and Mechanical Engineers), where after my initial six weeks of basic soldier training, I was taught all the necessities of how to live within the army system. How to press kit, shine boots and march in step with other soldiers who were also trying to march in step with me.

I was taught all the basics of how to fight in a war and hopefully, how to survive in a war. This part I paid particular attention to. After the most basic of soldier training, I was moved to Bordon Hampshire for my first 18 months in the army I trained to be a vehicle mechanic at the School of Electrical and Mechanical Engineering.

I served in the REME for 22 years, starting with the rank of craftsman after basic trade training, progressed through the ranks and ended up as a warrant officer class II (Artificer Quarter Master Sergent).

Straight from trade training, I was posted to Detmold in western Germany to a field workshop where we repaired all types of military vehicles within the Detmold area. There was not that much to do around the camp during free time, so most nights were spent in the local bars or doing sports. After six months, I met an English girl called Ursula who was on holiday.

I met her in a local bar and although she was with someone else, as was I, I slipped my address into her handbag and once she had returned to England from her holiday, we started writing to each other. Three months later, she returned on another holiday again to see her parents who lived in Detmold.

10 weeks after that we were married and the rest as they say is history.

Ursula's father was English and was working in Germany at the army camp, however, her mother was German and quite a few of her mother's side of the family were quite wary about whether to accept me into the family, as this was only 30 years since the end of the World War II and German people were still feeling the effects of the sanctions imposed by the victor's policies.

Once her parents had decided that our relationship was serious, they decided they should organise a meal for us. This is when I first met all the German side of Ursula's family. Ursula's auntie owned a restaurant and so we were summoned to arrive for a certain time. As we walked into the room, there was a long table with a vacant seat at either end for Ursula and me and about 10 relatives already seated.

I had not met any of these relatives before and they were all sitting there smiling at me. As there was no room to move around the side of the table to get to my seat, I decided the best plan of attack was to get on my hands and knees and crawl the length of the table until I arrived at my seat at the other end of the table. This was taken a number of ways. Most thought it was hilarious and Ursula's mother looked like she wanted the ground to swallow her up.

This certainly broke the ice. I think the mother-in-law spent the rest of her life never knowing what I was going to do next, but whenever Ursula and I had a discussion, she usually took my side.

The British Army was in Germany to deter, with the help of other NATO countries, the Russian Bear from invading Western Europe. The Iron Curtain extended through Berlin and around the East German border. The reason it was called the Iron Curtain was that the border had a 15-foot steel fence stretching along the country border. Every four hundred meters or so was a 50-meter-high guard tower.

From this tower, East German soldiers could monitor what was occurring around the perimeter fence. In front and behind, the fence was a hundred metres of ploughed ground that was liberally sprinkled with land mines. This was to stop anyone trying to break through the fence from the west but more importantly, to stop East Germans escaping to the west.

Ursula's auntie escaped from East Berlin hidden in a large speaker cabinet. If she had been found, she would have been dragged out and executed on the spot.

Every so often, we had a crash out which was to simulate an Eastern Bloc military invasion into Western Europe, specifically Germany. All the units in BAOR (British Army on the Rhine) had to dash into our respective army camps, mount our vehicles and bugger off to holding areas in preparation for WWIII.

This was really good fun as nobody knew when this was going to happen, although generally, it was usually three in the morning when it was pouring rain.

As a person with the lowest of low ranks, it was great watching all the chiefs running around like headless chickens trying to get everybody accounted for and each vehicle assigned to a qualified driver. We had to get every vehicle out of camp and into the allotted league area in the allotted time frame. As I progressed through the ranks, this eventually led to me years later being the headless chicken having to do this job and all the lower ranks laughing at me.

Every six weeks or so, our unit would go out on exercises to practice being at war. This happened throughout my military career but as the defence budget was cut every year the exercises grew less frequent and the amount of people and vehicles grew less. The area we went to was always towards the East German border.

Towards the end of my career, the defence cuts were so bad that an armoured personnel carrier that should have had eight soldiers in the back only had two soldiers in the back, and when the objective was reached by a company force only 20 soldiers would assault the objective instead of the one hundred soldiers expected. It was all quite sad actually.

One dark night, we lost the battalion we were supporting in our armoured tracked recovery vehicle. We had been left behind to repair a casualty vehicle and the battalion had carried along the convoy route as this was normal practice. It was up to us to catch them up as soon as we could. About two in the morning, we decided that it had been a long day and we were knackered. We pulled off the road and reversed over a field towards a fence.

We had a few beers and then a good night's sleep, as we could find out where to go in the morning. On waking up, we realised that we had actually reversed into the East German no man's land which was mined and the wire fence we had backed up against was actually the East German boundary. 50 yards along the fence was a guard tower with several East German soldiers with binoculars all pointing our way observing us.

At this point, we started the vehicle up, flicked them several V signs and gently extracted ourselves out of the minefield using the same tracks we came into the field the previous night. We then bumbled off in our own merry way to find the battalion and with another funny story to tell.

The work when on exercise always involved long hours as we had to repair vehicles and move along with the convoys, often with a vehicle in tow. It was also quite dangerous as a lot of the work was done at night with minimal lighting. We had to practice working in a war environment and avoid detection by the enemy.

This was known as working in a tactical situation and was a pain in the whatsits as it made the task so much harder, and there was always someone shouting, "Turn off that light."

We also sometimes had to carry out all our tasks wearing a Nuclear, Biological and Chemical protective suit including a respirator which made it hard to breathe and see out of as the eye holes always fogged up. As most of our breakdowns occurred when on the move if it could not be fixed immediately, we had to drag the casualty vehicle to a safe place to work on it which was usually outside. Usually, in the wind and rain. It was also bloody good fun driving along in armoured tracked vehicles playing war with big boys' toys.

On one exercise when we were driving down the road trying to meet up with our unit, we were pulled over by the German police. It was a German bank holiday and we should not have been driving on the road in that period. We conveniently found a guesthouse car park to pull into and then spent the next three days of the holiday parked up waiting for permission to move.

We had no radio signal, so nobody knew where we were, also more to the point, nobody could bother us. If they did find us, we were not allowed to drive the vehicle on the public roads anyway. Even more importantly, I was still of the lowest rank and the vehicle commander a corporal was in charge, so I did not care.

That night, we went into the pub and the landlord welcomed us but told us that we could drink in this room but could not go into the function room next door. No problem.

During the night, I noticed a young lad playing a guitar in an alcove between the rooms. I managed to borrow the guitar from him and we all sat in our room playing various singalong songs. Eventually, a lot of young people came from the function room and began requesting songs and singing them with us.

This went on for a while until a group of older miserable buggers came from the function room and started shouting at them making them go back into the function room. It was only when enquiring why they were so unhappy that I found out it was the local communist meeting. At the time, it was strictly forbidden for British Army personnel to fraternise with communists.

We had a fine time for the rest of the weekend but were in big trouble when we eventually found our missing unit and had to explain why we went missing with a 54-tonne recovery tank for three days near the East German border. I found it prudent, not to mention my new communist friends.

During this posting in Detmold, Ursula gave birth to a daughter, DonnaMarie. We moved out of our private hiring flat and moved into our first married soldier's accommodation. I suppose this was the start of us living a normal family unit life.

Donna was only six weeks old when my father unexpectedly died from a heart attack, and we all had to fly back to the UK for the funeral. It was such a shame; he never had a chance to see his first grandchild. He was only 62. Although we never had a close father/son relationship, he always provided for the family and brought me up knowing the true value of manners and respect for other people.

He very seldom raised a hand to me and when he did I probably deserved it because as they say in Yorkshire, I were a reet bugger, always up to mischief of some kind, like the time our neighbour concreted his drive and I ran down it, touched the garage and ran back again through all the wet cement. Oh, how we laughed. In my defence, I was only about eight years old.

After a year, I was posted to Dortmund a hundred miles south of Detmold where I was introduced for the first time to the armoured track vehicle called a FV432. This was a 16-tonne armoured track vehicle of which there were several variants.

Little did I know that for the next 45 years, I would be involved with this vehicle up to the point where I left the army and worked as a civilian designing, conducting trials and running a production line to update this type of vehicle.

During this posting, I completed many exercises, a six-month upgrader course, a few tours to Canada and a six-month Northern Ireland tour and in the next three years, I would have only been home for about a year; missing Donna's first tooth, first step, and first word.

It was also whilst in Dortmund that Ursula presented me with our son Jon.

Time progressed and the next posting was to Munster, again in Germany where I was asked to complete another Northern Ireland tour this time as a covert operative. This is explained in more detail further in the book. This posting was quite good as we were part of the Air Mobile Force and everywhere we went was in helicopters, so a jolly old time was had by all.

Whilst in Munster, my mother visited us in Germany. When she was in Detmold visiting my in-laws, she suffered a heart attack and until she was well enough to travel home, had to stay in Germany for three months. To this day, we will never know how she managed to call the British Army medical centre and get the ambulance to her. She was on her own in the in-laws' house and did not know the address.

Apparently, she found the Detmold Medical Centre phone number and told the receptionist she was having a heart attack at my mother-in-law Freda Travellers' house which was a German address and not in the army quarters area.

Luckily, Freda worked at the medical centre and the receptionist knew Freda.

They quickly got an ambulance to her address and took her to the local Krankenhaus where she had an emergency triple bypass operation. She stayed with us for a further three months until she was well enough to return to England.

Much to Ursula's delight.

My mother was always quiet, as they say, Prim and Proper.

She was always very well-dressed and was raised in quite a well-to-do family as a child. She very rarely understood how we could live our lives not planning our lives very long in the future and doing most things on the spur of the moment. At one point, when my mother and auntie were staying with us, some friends turned up at midnight and needed a place to sleep. Without even questioning the accommodation arrangements we told them they could.

My mother was beside herself with the logistic problem of where people would sleep. We only had beds for 6 people and there were now nine of us. But as always, we managed. This was just the way we lived our lives, as I never could tell when I would be going away again on some tour or another.

As long as we had some money in our pocket, we would do lots of things on the spur of the moment. We went to southern Germany camping once with no money and lived on fried egg sandwiches for a week, but still had a great time.

Whilst in Detmold we had some friends who were in the Royal Artillery. The nickname for an artilleryman is Plank taken from the old days when the artillery used gun planks to stop the field guns running back when fired. Therefore, Artillerymen were known to be thick as planks. When Ursula and I had been talking about him in front of my mum, we referred to him as Plank and she was led to believe that was his actual name.

On the day he came around to see us, I was introducing him to my mother when she announced, "I have heard everything about you, Plank."

This set the tone for the rest of the evening.

In 1982, I was posted as a Corporal to the 1st Scots Guards Battalion in Pirbright Surrey. The Scots Guards were everything you can imagine them to be. Whenever someone imagines what it is to be a soldier or starts pretending to be a soldier, they start marching around using exaggerated movements and shouting at everyone that is near them. Well, that sort of typifies what being attached to a Scots Guards battalion is like. A camp full of soldiers marching around shouting at each other.

They were the guard battalion for the city of London, and every royal residence within London as well as Windsor Castle. I speak in more detail of this battalion later in the book. To describe the three years I spent with the Scots Guards follows as such: The main thing Scots Guards do is press kit, polish boots, march about and shout at people. This is when I realised that most of the time, I was not one of these types of people. It was not a happy time for me but I did manage to get loaded on some promotional courses and get my HGV1 licence. I also completed yet another Northern Ireland tour which I will embellish in detail later in the book.

During the royal duties period, whilst the Scots Guards were changing the guard and doing all their marching stuff, being REME, we were not allowed to parade wearing bearskins and all the pomp and ceremony of the full-dress uniforms, as this duty was reserved for smart soldiers and not the riffraff we were presumed to be. I did do a few guard duties in the Buckingham Palace guard room though.

Whilst there you have to be aware of all the dignitaries that are staying within the palace. As there are a zillion bedrooms in the palace, the in-residence board looks like a list of the world's most important people. Although the people guarding the palace do not see the residents very often, they have a great responsibility to keep them all safe. When we had the chance to come into contact with the residents, we were treated more like a necessary annoyance than someone who was there to protect them.

When we were in the army, our children attended army schools. Unfortunately, they do not all carry out the same teaching syllabus. As REME, our children were made to change schools every couple of years as and when I was posted. This meant that Donna had to start in the bottom stream and work her way up to the top stream. She would only just settle into a routine and then I would be posted again and as she had not been taught the new school's syllabus, would have to start all over again.

With this in mind, it was decided to send Donna to boarding school. We had friends who had kids in boarding school and they loved it. Donna went first for a year and was very homesick and she and Ursula used to talk on the phone a lot as she was not happy being away. The school was mainly day boarders and at weekends she was basically on her own with no friends to play with.

After a year, there was an opportunity to send Donna and also Jon now he was old enough to the school where our friend's kids went. Although Donna settled in well Jon hated it and so after 18 months, we took Jon away from boarding school. We gave Donna the option to leave also but she wanted to stay as she had many friends there.

There were a lot of children from diplomatic families there and she often bragged about knowing princes and other dignitaries children. She would remain there for another four years before leaving and starting school at a weekly boarding school in Germany once we were based in Fallingbostel. Once there, we saw her each weekend.

Throughout this whole school experience, Ursula missed them terribly. Although Donna did end up with a great education and speaks really nicely, I do not think given the choice we would send them to boarding school again.

The whole time I was in Pirbright were very hard times on the financial side of life, especially with Donna in boarding school. As I had a fully functional workshop with hydraulic ramps and welding gear, every night Monday to Friday when possible, I would work on the camp soldiers' cars. I did general repairs and servicing as well as buying cars from auctions and sprucing them up before selling them. This at least kept the wolf from the door.

In 1987, I was loaded on an artificer training course, again in Bordon, Hampshire at SEME. This is an 18-month course where we complete our HNC, BTech and Senior Military Training (How to be a proper soldier) and leave with the rank of staff sergeant. In the REME, a soldier cannot progress further than a staff sergeant without doing the course. An artificer is known as a Tiffy.

Once the course has been passed, Tiffy is generally the brunt of most jokes around the workshop by all who do not or cannot qualify to rise to the heady heights of artificer staff sergeant. It is, however, the artificer-trained soldiers who ensure all the major decisions within the REME workshop structure are carried out on time, on budget and with the minimum amount of fuss.

It was probably the fact that I had done this course that enabled me to get the job as a trials engineer once I had left the army and moved to Civvy Street.

I found the academic side of this course very hard as I was one of the older students in my course of 12. However, I was the most experienced. I found all the practical things quite easy but the maths, science and physics were hard due to the fact that I am as thick as a whale omelette. I learnt how to work out mathematical problems systematically rather than applying the reason they were worked out that way.

This usually got me a correct answer without having any idea how I did it. In the 30 years, after completing the course there has still not been one moment when someone has asked me to calculate the moments about a beam when designing and building a bridge or work out the area below a curve using calculus. I suppose someone thought it was a subject we needed.

Also, the scoring system to pass each phase was so high that I struggled to attain the pass marks on the amount of weekly tests we had to complete. Our scores were then transferred to the civilian grading system for our HNC qualifications, In the end, I ended up with all Credits and Distinctions on my diploma.

I was teamed up with a guy called Dave Fulford and as both our surnames started with F, we were generally paired up together for most projects. I stayed friends with Dave and his wife for years after this course until the cancer took him a few years ago. Throughout this course, we had to complete a project. Ours was to design a new cooling system for a small reconnaissance-tracked vehicle.

We completed the project and visited a lot of civilian industry places to get our technical information and Linda typed all the project out and put it together in nice smart professional folders. Remember, back in 1988, Dave's computer was the best that money could buy. It was an Omega 500 with a dot matrix printer.

About two weeks before the presentation, Dave and Linda went to Linda's works function and Dave sat next to the chief design engineer for her company. Dave got talking to him about the project and the engineer drew a cooling system on a serviette using all their company parts. Over the next few days, he recommended all the components the system needed, the price it would cost, the flow rates and the power required to drive the system.

This was far better than our effort. With all hands on the pump, we rewrote the 12-month project in two days and gave our presentation to all the officers on the engineering project panel. Needless to say, we got top marks for it and I don't feel a bit guilty about Dave doing all the legwork as I had helped him out on several occasions during the course on other tasks, and that's what teamwork is all about.

After the course was completed, we were all posted to different units. I was posted to Fallingbostel to the 1st Battalion the Staffordshire Regiment who had just taken charge of the new Warrior Infantry Fighting Vehicle which had just come into service with the army. Unbeknown to me, this vehicle would be a major part of my life for the next 30 years.

When posted to another unit, a married couple had to go through a march out procedure. This is where the married quarter has to be cleaned to a very high standard. A married quarter is taken over by the soldier and includes pots, pans, cutlery, carpets, curtains and furniture. In fact, everything else that a poor soldier needs, if he does not own any household items himself.

All these items need to be scrubbed clean prior to march-out. Over the years, a married couple slowly substituted everything in the quarter for their own furniture and things but if there is not a facility to wharf the old stuff this, has to be stored somewhere and then brought out again for march-out.

Once the quarter is cleaned, a senior rank has to come and inspect the accommodation and pass it as clean. All the paperwork has to be signed, prior to allowing the soldier to leave the unit and move to another unit. Needless to say, this involves a lot of hard work and stress as most of the fitments within the quarter are ancient and something like an oven will require hours of scrubbing and still not be up to the inspection standard required.

Obviously, on the day of the march-out tensions are high. The wives are expected to leave the quarter prior to the inspection, in case, the inspector picks up something she has spent hours cleaning and tempers flare. On one occasion, about 10 minutes before the inspection, I noticed some old candle wax drips on the living room carpet.

I asked Ursula to get some brown paper and with an iron, gently go over the brown paper and the wax drops should melt and stick to the paper. Unbeknown to me, Ursula selected some brown wax paper and not the normal brown paper from the cupboard and promptly welded the whole sheet to the carpet. PANIC.

With very little time left, I found a knife and sharpened it as sharp as possible.

I then proceeded to shave the carpet, peeling the wax paper off the carpet as I moved along. Once this was done, we quickly rearranged the furniture to hide the shorter-depth carpet pile. We let out a sigh of relief and then the doorbell rang as the inspector arrived. He completed the inspection and gave us a clean bill of health apart from the customary bill to clean the cooker.

Looking at the house history, every occupant of this quarter had been billed for a dirty cooker for the last five occupants. It is just the army's way of proving they were in charge.

During another quarter march-out, we stayed overnight at our friend's house prior to the march-out inspection. This was to prevent us from messing things up, as everything was laid out in the regulated way for inspection. All the cutlery, pots and pans were laid out in a line on the kitchen table. As we opened the front door, we were greeted with the sight of white dust and glass covering the black ash staircase from the attic to the ground floor.

I had cleaned the fluorescent light tube that was located on a high ceiling in the attic void prior to leaving the previous night. During the night, the fluorescent tube had become detached and shattered all down the wooden stairs. Another mad panic and a very rushed cleanup operation had to be completed prior to the inspection.

Chapter 4
Stand Back, I'm in Charge

On arrival at Fallingbostel, I was thrown into the hectic life of the 1st Battalion the Staffordshire Regiment an armoured infantry battalion, Part of the 7th Armoured Brigade the Desert Rats.

As part of the REME Light Aid Detachment (LAD), I was now a staff sergeant—Tiffy. I was in charge of about 20 armoured vehicles and a C Company fitter section of 10 tradesmen, mechanics, electricians and armourers. Our job was to repair and maintain these 20 vehicles, so they were in a state of readiness at all times.

During the first week of this posting, I was tasked with going into the single soldier's accommodation block and packing up a soldier's belongings, to send back to his parents. He was a tradesman within the LAD and had died in the workshop due to an accident. He had been trapped between two Warrior vehicles and crushed to death whilst the vehicles were manoeuvring within the workshop.

I did not know this soldier and have only seen a photo of him once, but his name sticks in my mind even now. I fitted all his possessions of his life in one cardboard box. Surely his life consisted of more than this. This event also made me aware that I was now back working with armoured tracked vehicles again which was a million miles away from my last 18 months, where I was in a safe environment, and sat behind a desk in a school.

Ironically, when on an exercise, 10 months later I almost crushed myself between two Warriors when the vehicles were parked one behind the other on a steep hill. The Warrior 10 meters in front of us had a hand brake failure and rolled backwards down the hill into the next Warrior behind it. There had been a group of us standing in front of that Warrior and after the initial warning shout everyone bomb burst away from the intended impact area.

I ran sideways and ran straight into a high wire fence trapping myself between the fence wire and the side of the Warrior, which had missed me by inches. The Warrior then came to a stop resting against the second Warrior. One chap had dived under the Warrior and another had simply stepped into the rear doorway of the Warrior that was rolling down the hill.

Several guys were sitting on the front engine decks and witnessed the whole incident. Luckily, nobody was hurt. After this incident, when on a steep hill, we always choked the vehicles under the tracks, so this did not happen again.

Throughout my career, we have had to be aware of just how dangerous the job is even during peacetime. Armoured tracked vehicles weighing up to 70 tonnes are very unforgiving even when moving around camp at 10 miles per hour.

Once on exercise, these brutes can potentially move at 50 miles an hour with the driver and commander battened down and visibility severely reduced due to looking through periscopes and optics. On tactical night moves, all lights are switched off and the driver follows the vehicle in front which has a small light at the rear to guide him.

The newly issued Warrior vehicle is such a radical change to the old, armoured infantry vehicles we have been used to. For a start, it is twice the size and has an armoured turret with a cannon and a machine gun mounted in it. The old vehicles could only attain a maximum speed of 30 miles per hour, whereas Warrior can reach 50 miles an hour.

Also, the suspension is fantastic and a driver does not even have to consider slowing down for a bump or bad terrain as Warrior just takes it in its stride. When commanding such a vehicle, the commander is totally confident that he can go where he intends to go. Previous vehicles required a high concentration and appreciation of the ground conditions or the vehicle would very soon be stuck if the conditions were not favourable.

My last six-month posting in the army was as the maintenance advisor to the battle group in BATUS. (British Army Training Unit Suffield). BATUS is about a quarter the size of Wales and we practice battle group attack formations for three weeks, cumulating in a full-blown battle group advance from the top of the area to the bottom of the area and then back to Camp Crowfoot which is the base.

Whilst I was there, we had seven deaths in the training area in this six-month period. I had to investigate two of them as there was a vehicle involved. It was my responsibility to prove that the vehicle was not the cause of the incident. 90% of all fatalities on British Army exercises all around the world are operator error due to pressure/stress, poor training or failure to carry out correct procedures.

The remaining 10% is down to shit happens and wrong place wrong time. I suppose this can also be said for the same within a civilian environment, be it a workplace or just driving a car.

For the first year in Fallingbostel, we were kept busy. Constantly, on exercises. After each exercise, we would always return with funny, shocking or interesting stories of events that took place during our time away. Although the Warrior vehicles were brand-new, the Warrior recovery vehicle had not been issued yet, so we had to make do with a 1960s Centurian tank recovery vehicle.

On one of the first exercises with my new fitter section, I was commanding this 50-tonne monster through a German village when the engine cooling fan disintegrated and sent the fan blades through the 50-gallon petrol tank. The petrol then leaked into the vehicle hull and out of a hole in the hull, ending up running in a stream down the village high street.

When the village fire captain and his crew with a fire engine turned up and looked at the now one hundred meters of fuel running as a small stream through the village, he started screaming at me about diesel fuel contamination. This was the point, I explained to him that it wasn't diesel, it was benzine. And all the local onlookers should really not have lit cigarettes in their mouths.

At this point, he went into a complete meltdown. A thousand litres of foam later, he was still not a happy man, and although we had stopped any more fuel leaking out of the hull, he wanted to get us out of the village.

The recovery asset turned up and hooked on to us and then dragged our vehicle out of the village and down the road with my crew perched on top of the recovered vehicle. This left the fire captain and his crew to clean the road. Once up to full speed, it was quite a nice ride looking at the local scenery as it flashed past. Well! It was a nice ride until we were dragged around a bend too fast and slipped off the road and into a field of crops.

So now, there are two 50-tonne vehicles bogged down about 50 metres into a field of crops when the nice fire captain turns up again and starts screaming at me. For some reason, he did not care that I was an innocent passenger sitting on my recovered vehicle having a nice ride in the sunshine when the mad driver in the first vehicle lost control.

Anyway, to cut a long story short it took another day to be recovered back to the battalion formation and a lot of report writing for the fire captain's damage compensation claim.

All these exercises were building up to a Canada tour in Alberta, where we went out on the prairies in the BATUS training area. It really is an impressive sight watching Warriors and Challenger battle tanks at full speed charging over the undulating ground and firing at all the dummy targets scattered over the area. I absolutely loved working at BATUS and was fortunate to spend a total of over two years there during my career.

Once on the prairie, I could see for miles over the rolling grassy hills and at night the northern lights are regularly seen. The fantastic electrical storms light up the sky for miles. I often used to lay in a waterproof bag on top of a vehicle and watch the sheet lightning flash across the sky. Once the storm drew closer, the lightning would hit the armoured steel vehicles and bounce from one vehicle to another leaving the stench of ozone in the air.

At that point, I would dash inside the vehicle so I did not get frazzled. Looking over the undulating hills of the prairie it did not take much imagination to envisage the Indian hordes racing over the hills to attack the wagon trains so often depicted in the movies. All in all, I found it a marvellous place. There are even out-of-bounds areas fenced off that are ancient Indian graveyards.

After the three-week manoeuvres on the prairie and when the battle run had finished, all the vehicles were cleaned and the kit stowed away, we usually got three or four days off to visit local towns and relax.

I had been to BATUS several times and had seen most of the local sights already. So, during my six-month stay as maintenance advisor, I would take my Land Rover back onto the area and just stay on the prairie at a place called Cyprus Hills overlooking the Milk River for a few days.

Once the battle group has moved back into camp after the battle run, all the wildlife returns from the north of the area. I regularly had moose deer and elk walk past my little camp and the coyotes used to scavenge any scraps of food I had not cleared away. Just for a few days, I was totally at peace without a care in the world.

On one occasion during a battle run, I was looking for a vehicle that was missing from the area and was believed to have taken the wrong track and passed through the BATUS perimeter boundary. This was very easily done if the vehicle commander did not know exactly where he was as all the grassy prairie scenery looked the same.

I had driven to the far north of the area and was standing on top of my Land Rover scanning the prairie with my binoculars and in the distance I could see what we called a nodding duck. This was an oil pumping station that had a pump that just nods up and down all day, pumping oil.

Around Calgary City, there are thousands of them. Next to the duck, I could see a man working, so I jumped into my Land Rover and drove the three miles or so to speak to him. Although he had not seen the missing vehicle, I was very surprised to see he was an old friend I used to sit next to at school. Small world, isn't it?

Throughout my army career, which was 17 years at this point, the army was all geared up for protecting against the Russian hoards attacking Western Europe and now suddenly without warning, due to the collapse of the Soviet Union, the Berlin Wall came crashing down. Most of us were totally stunned as this had been our main reason for the British Army being in Germany for all these years since World War II.

I was quite disappointed as we had just moved to Fallingbostel and Berlin was only a short drive away. Ursula, the kids and I were going to visit East Germany next year and buy some cheap stuff that everyone was telling us about.

Along with the collapse of the wall came the thousands of Trabants. Two stroke motorcars clog up the roads and motorways and choke up the air with their blue smoke. Thousands of East German people moved from East to West Germany and just about bankrupted the country, as the government had to give them repatriation money and find homes for them all.

They always say that you should not wish for something because you might just get it.

Once the Canada tour was over, we were all sent on leave for a month and then we were to start to train for yet another Northern Ireland tour. Unbeknown to us, whilst we were on leave worldly events were taking place and my future was about to change in a big way.

But first. Some poetry.

Chapter 5
The Poetry Corner Part One

A WHISPER IN HIS EAR

I think everyone at some point has lost a friend or lover who was such a big part of their life. Losing contact for whatever reason with never to be seen again friends, or never again to share a meal or a drink or a laugh seems to bring out the melancholy in me. It also brings out the smiles, once these good times are remembered.

Circumstances and life's priorities get in the way of simple plans. Be it work commitments, families, money problems etc. Many passing acquaintances have come and gone over the years and it's only when a photo or tune appears that we wonder, 'Whatever Happened to Them'. Just writing this has reminded me of the old adage, 'I'll Never Forget Whatshisname'.

All night long he waited on that hill.
Wondering where she was, and if she loved him still.
She would meet him, where they kissed that first night.
She said she would call him when she got there tonight.

When they met, he was sitting on his own.
Staring out to sea and looking all alone.
She asked him for the time, he gave it with a smile.
She asked if she could sit down for a little while.
Then she faded away, like a whisper in his ear.
Like her voice, he used to hear.
And he never saw her smiling face again.

Day after day they met on that hill,
Talking and laughing as all young lovers will.
They spoke of the things they would do before they died.
They promised they would never leave each other's side.

Week after week the summer came and went.
She left in September and said they'd still be friends.
She said they would meet on that seat up on the hill.
And whilst she was away, she would think about him still.
But she faded away, like a whisper in his ear.
Like her voice, he used to hear.
And he never saw her smiling face again.

Month after month, changed to year after year.
He waited for that call; he thought she made it clear.
That she would return to that quiet lonely town.
And climb up that hill when the sun went down.

Then late in November, the call—it finally came.
He heard a stranger's voice; he heard it say his name.
She said she could see him, on that seat up on the hill.
She asked if he forgave her, and did he love her still.
She had faded away like a whisper in his ear.
Like her voice, he used to hear.
And now he hoped to see her smiling face again.

BODRUM BAY

Three years on the trot, we went to Turkey and went aboard a Gullet. A Gullet is a twin-masted boat that is crewed by 3 people and usually has seven couples as guests totally unknown to each other, No! Not that kind of holiday!

On day one, everyone climbs aboard and takes off their shoes and then the boat sets sail. Shoes are not worn again until the following week, apart from the odd time when we would anchor at a dock for supplies. The rest of the holiday is spent eating, drinking, reading, and swimming and more drinking. During the whole holiday, you don't see any other civilisation.

Sleeping on deck under the stars, guaranteed 30 degrees Celsius and no rain. How peaceful is that. Our tranquillity was only spoilt once a day as the ice cream man sailed up in a little boat with the 'Just One Cornetto' theme blaring out of tinny speakers selling all types of ice. One year we had such a tremendous group of people we were planning to all go again the next year. Unfortunately, Covid19 struck and plans have been put on hold for the foreseeable future.

The following verses are the story of just one of these holidays. I was challenged to tell the story of the holiday in a song to be sung at a fancy-dress party the following night. Also, the challenge was to mention everyone on board and something they did whilst on the boat.

Recently my friend went again on the boat and I recorded this song for them to play and sing along to on the boat, as they were going with some of the original crew. After I sent it to her, she said I had changed the tune and the chorus. I was totally unaware of this but she had a recording of me singing it the day I wrote it. She didn't say if it sounded better!

Well, we set off from Bodrum Bay. With 14 souls on a holiday.
Haul away lads, Haul away, sail away.
And the captain sailed the boat away on the deep blue sea.
Haul away on the deep blue sea.

The sea was calm, the boat was steady. With the cook Ercut and the sailor Eddy.
Haul away lads, Haul away, sail away.
We drank some wine and pints of Effies. On the deep blue sea.
Haul away on the deep blue sea.

And Mark showed us some magic tricks, and Nessie called him a flaming witch.
Haul away lads, Haul away, sail away.
I laughed so much I got a stich. On the deep blue sea.
Haul away on the deep blue sea.

When you're tying a line, you've got to think fast.
Ercut jumped and he grabbed the mast.
Haul away lads, Haul away, sail away.

And the dingy it went sailing past, on the deep blue sea.
Haul away on the deep blue sea.
Debora gave us all a prize, then right before my bloody eyes.
Haul away lads, Haul away, sail away.
She took it back and I nearly cried. On the deep blue sea.
Haul away on the deep blue sea.

Oh, Captain lay your anchor down, we don't want to run aground.
Haul away lads, haul away, sail away.
But we swam so far, we nearly drowned, on the deep blue sea.
Haul away on the deep blue sea.

Fiona's story was Eaton's mess. She'd not cook for me I guess.
Haul away lads, haul away, sail away.
And the Shit Head game it was the best. On the deep blue sea.
Haul away on the deep blue sea.

We had a fancy dress one night. And the boy's make-up was very nice.
Haul away lads, haul away, sail away.
But my bra dug in, it was bloody tight. On the deep blue sea.
Haul away on the deep blue sea.

One night we went to steal a boat, with a fishing line and a lot of hope.
Haul away lads, haul away, sail away.
But Allison's plan all came to nowt. On the deep blue sea.
Haul away on the deep blue sea.

Poor Andy prayed for a bite; He caught a shoe that put up a fight.
Haul away lads, haul away, sail away.
And he caught a minnow in the middle of the night. On the deep blue sea.
Haul away on the deep blue sea.

On the last day, we sailed to port. We said farewell and away we walked.
Haul away lads, haul away, sail away.
But we made some friends in the time we spent, On the deep blue sea.
Haul away on the deep blue sea.

DIAMOND RING

I have become a good judge of character over the years and I am a great believer that so long as you know a person's character you can deal quite successfully with them both on a professional and personal level. Of course, every now and then I have been bitten but I would rather have it that way than be untrustworthy of everyone. Needless to say, I only get bitten once and never get bitten twice by the same person or circumstance.

This is a short story about an untrustworthy chap. We all have heard of them or met them. Rough families often get a bad rap about being untrustworthy, but in this case, they meet their match.

And I will buy a diamond ring to make a bride so fine. And I will give you everything and tell everyone you're mine I know you are a gypsy thief, your father fights and swears.

His eyes flash hate as he smiles at me, I pretend I just don't care.

But I will buy a diamond ring to make our lives so fine.
And I will give you everything and love you for all time.
Your mother flashed her thigh at me, your sisters on the game.
You brothers wait in line for dole, to them each day is the same.

And I'll still buy a diamond ring to make a bride so fine.
And I will give pearls and things and tell everyone you're mine.
Your uncle owns a gambling ring, your auntie knows the rules.
She taught her girls to trick the men and treat them all like fools.

Yes, I'll give you a diamond ring and say that you are mine.
I'll smile and grin when I tell you jokes. I'll pretend that you are fine.
Your brothers they are wise to me, their threats are not in vain.
They have told me to leave the town, and not return again.

I was going to give a diamond ring, But the flame has died inside.
As night fell down, I stole your love, Your heart and all your pride.
Now I have told a hundred lies and told them all my life.
I'm leaving with your father's car his wallet and his wife.
Ha Ha.

ECLIPSE

I was on holiday at Hayle in Cornwall on the Towans (big pointy structures of sand topped with grass) overlooking the beach at St Ives Bay, during the 1999 eclipse. It was very eerie in the darkness. Looking around at the other Towans, each of the Towans was topped with a group of people waiting for the eclipse, all staring up at the sky, looking like a group of meerkats.

Each person had filtered lenses to protect their eyes from the sun's corona. Just before the eclipse happened, I noticed people staring at me. They obviously had not seen someone in Speedos and a welder's helmet before.

When visiting Penzance, St Austell or St Ives, I notice all the young people flooding the streets after coming down for a change of scenery for the summer. They do a bit of surfing, take in the beach parties and generally mellow out for the summer's duration. The light is fantastic for the artistic people to sketch, draw and paint. The whole Cornwall scene seems to promote a feeling of ease and contentment.

I love going to Cornwall and if it wasn't for all of us Grockles it would be a beautiful peaceful place to live. Grockle is the Cornish name for a tourist.

As the Cornish say, "Grockles are like piles. They hang around, turn red and they are a pain in the arse."

Lots of single people travel around the country far more now than they did in the past. It is so easy to jump in some form of transport and be at your destination in only a couple of hours. Lots of tourists come to Cornwall as part of a group just looking for a bit of fun and perhaps to meet someone special.

> Darling, did you feel the burning sun?
> Sit on the dunes, till the darkness comes.
> Looking back, was it just a dream?
> What did you feel when you left home?
> Do you wake up scared when you're alone?
> Do you feel safe when you're with me?
>
> Listen can you hear the crashing waves?
> Feel the spray in this misty haze.
> Look! Did you see?
> The sun gets covered, and the moon turns black.

And all the people, they stared right back,
Through the filtered lens. At the diamond ring in the sky.

People, they move from town to town.
So much to do as they dash around.
They never have time, to stop and see.
I sometimes wonder what they'd do.
If this old sky stopped turning blue.
And the darkness didn't go away.

Maybe you could stay with me that night.
Stay till dawn, till it gets light.
All through the night,
Till the sun breaks through.
And the sky turns blue.
And in this world, there's just me and you.
And hold me tight till the darkness goes away.

If you listen, I will say to you.
Anything that you want me to.
What would you want me to say?
Should I be strong and hard as nails?
Or should I be quiet but oh so frail?
Or should I be, just me?

FEELING BLUE

Most of the military operations I took part in involved being away from home and family for prolonged periods of time ranging from three weeks to six months. I have a good laugh when watching 'I'm A Celebrity, Get Me Out of Here'.

They sit around crying their eyes out reading letters from home! They've only been away from home for a week or two for God's sake!

When I go away from home, I take a guitar no matter where the destination may be. If it's in some back of the world place with an adverse climate, then the old, battered guitar comes with me. A prolonged stay in a hotel once I had left the army, allowed me to take a good guitar and also afforded me access to several folk clubs where a stranger could just turn up and have a beer and sing some songs.

There is always somewhere I can steal away and have a bit of me time. I would make up a tune and just sing some words to it. Sometimes a song takes years to develop the lyrics or the fiddley guitar bits. If I listen to a recording, I made 30 years ago, I can hardly notice some songs as the lyrics change and the way I pick the strings change over time.

Some of my best lyrics and tunes were composed late at night and forgotten when morning came. With modern technology, these can now be captured on mobile phones. Some songs take seconds to write and remain simple for years.

This song came along on one of these occasions.

I thought I'd write a little tune,
Just so you know I think of you.
When I am so far away
I think of you every day

So! If you're ever feeling blue
And don't know what to do.
Well then just hum this little tune.
And I will be with you.

The rain may fall and turn to snow.
The fog could roll and the wind could blow.
But there's only one thing you should know.
I love you.

So! If you're feeling kind of low.
And you don't know where to go.
Just lay back and close your mind.
I'll be here all the time.

The rain may fall and turn to snow.
The fog could roll and the wind could blow.
But there's only one thing you should know.
I love you.

Thought I'd write a little tune,
Just so you know I think of you.
When I am so far away

I think of you every day.
Every day

FOR DONNA

I wrote this song the day my daughter Donna was born, and she is now on the wrong side of 40 with two 14-year-old twins.

I remember leaving the German Krankenhaus where she was born and as I walked down the road people were staring at me and laughing. After a while, I realised that I still had the big bright blue plastic shoe covers on my feet. Who said Germans don't have a sense of humour?

It was two days before Christmas and Ursula had to stay in hospital for five days so myself and my father-in-law hit the town for a few days. But I don't remember much of that as I may have had an alcoholic block. We tagged along with ten or so Air Corps chaps from the barracks, which were heading through the town.

Every time one of them got a round at the bar we just held up our hands and got a free beer. This went on for most of the night. I don't think they ever suspected I was freeloading off them. I paid the price though as I had a hell of a hangover the next morning.

The saying time flies is a complete understatement as time also slaps you in the face as it rushes past.

It should really state, "Time flies past you and leaves you completely gobsmacked about how so many things happened so quickly."

I think about this every time this old bugger looks back at me from the mirror.

Where did the time go?

Some people, like me, seem to breeze through life by just doing the best they can all the time. I always deal with life with a conscience of what needs to be done and what is right. Other people seem to struggle on a daily basis just to survive a crisis every day. My children Donna and Jon have battled through life with a father in the forces and the dangers and worries that brings, and moving home every couple of years so not being able to have a stable adolescence.

Donna's last few years have brought on further worries with the twins being born premature and both herself and her husband surviving cancer. She has, however, always got a bright outlook on life and always seems to be looking forward to the positive things in life.

Anyway, as I was saying, I wrote this song the day my daughter Donna was born. Read it to the tune of 'Green Sleeves'.

Sleep now my little child of snow.
I will see you in the morning.
The bitter wind outside does blow.
Stay close stay warm I love you.

Donna, you're the only one.
Donna my heart's desire.
Donna, please don't cry for me.
Because you're my only daughter.

And as the years of time pass by.
And Mum and I are old and grey.
Remember how I sang this song?
When there's no one left to guide you.

Donna, you're the only one.
Donna my heart's desire.
Donna, please don't cry for me.
Because you're my only daughter.

GRAVESTONES

One of life's great past times, when visiting places on holiday, is having a stroll around the local churches and walking through the graveyards reading the short epitaphs on the gravestones and wondering what lives the residents led all those years ago. Every graveyard has a story of some famous person being buried in it.

The church in Rothwell, Yorkshire has Blenkinsop. And as everyone knows he invented the rack railway from Middleton to Stockton. So, if nothing else you can now answer a history question on Mastermind after reading this book.

I spent six months in Bosnia, at the start of the Balkan war working for the United Nations. We were the first British unit into the Goinjy Vakuf-Vitez area and had to set up bases and open up new humanitarian supply routes, as well as help the refugees find safe borders. In this time, we dealt with half a dozen religious factions. When I saw the way they treated each other, I turned my back on religion forever.

Every religion seems to have its only one true God. There must be hundreds of the only one true God. Who's to say which is the real one? I'm not saying there isn't a God. I'm just saying if there is, I don't think he cares anymore.

With this in mind, I do wonder at the majesty of the large churches and cathedrals. It is not just the reasons they were built, but the actual skill of the stone masons all those hundreds of years ago without all the modern equipment of today. Still, after all these years even though not attended as they used to be, they still have the focus in the heart of every town and village. The church gate still remains the common meeting point for friends and lovers to meet.

Words on the stone gave away his years.
Names of the family beside him told of his tears.
A beloved husband, a father, a son.
But where had he been, and what had he done?

As the lichen and moss cover his grave,
Did he know he was dying? Do you think he was brave?
Or did it come suddenly by car or by gun?
Was it his fault? Did he know what he'd done?

Had he found another, since leaving his wife?
Another mother and lover to be at his side.
And did they grieve for him and kneel by his grave?
Or was he alone in pain and afraid?

As I wait for my love by the cemetery wall.
The names that I am reading, I don't know at all.
Did they leave a record of the things that they had done?
Or are they forgotten now that they're gone.

My collar turned up; the cold wind cut in.
There's damp in the air, I shiver again.
I look down the road, there's no one in sight.
The grey of this day is turning to night.

And now through the gloom, there's a woman bent down.
With flowers for the grave, she tidies the ground.
She lays down the flowers, talks with a smile,
To the man in the grave who has slept there a while.

And she tells him of all the things she has done on that day.
Placing a stone on the flowers, so they don't blow away.
And she talks of years ago and the times that they had.
Then with a tear in her eye, she says, "Goodbye Dad."

Then without looking back, she disappears from sight,
Back to the car, she then drives into the night.
I look back to the flowers the grave and the stone.
And say, "So you're really just resting, you're not really alone."

Then a shout through the night. Someone calls out my name.
I return to the present; I have finished my game.
I walk back to the road where my lady awaits.
With a last look around, I close the wrought iron gates.

Chapter 6
Introduction to the Action Bits

My stories from the Gulf War, Bosnia and Northern Ireland are just that. Stories. Just an account of what happened, where and when and by who. It is a story about normal people doing the jobs that they have been trained to do and they do not expect any accolades or extra payment for the deed done.

However, there are times when to complete the task, to save a life, to stop the atrocity, soldiers do have to put themselves in the line of fire as there isn't any other option. To do nothing would have repercussions on their conscience for the rest of their lives.

The media loosely throws around the word Hero every time something outstanding is done for one person by another. Admittedly nurses, doctors and surgeons do a fantastic job saving lives on a daily basis. But I am not sure they can wear the badge of Hero.

The exception being the actions carried out during the pandemic when their lives were at risk and volunteers giving medical aid in war zones and during environmental catastrophes, Firemen and police would qualify in certain circumstances when there was an option to do the job and put themselves at risk for the sake of someone else or just walk away.

99% of heroes are not seen on television or written about in books nor are they always a member of some form of government service. Heroes can come from all types of people who are just carrying out a normal day in their life when suddenly, out of the blue, an extraordinary circumstance can happen and they find that they are in the middle of a nightmare. Everyday heroes are doing things above and beyond normal expectations because it is just the right thing to do.

Being brave is not about being fearless, it is more about being full of fear but doing the thing that frightens you anyway. Sometimes, people are knowingly putting their lives at risk, but usually, they are just doing what is needed without pausing to think of the consequences. It is only afterwards when the fireworks are over and during a time of reflection do they start shaking, crying or just think,

Wow! That was a wild ride.

I have seen many a man shake and cry after a scary event. Perhaps, these are the people who were the bravest of all and full respect should be given for their efforts. For some, the bragging rights of telling the exaggerated story of what happened to their mates afterwards is worth more than gold.

Chapter 7
Operation Granby (Gulf War I)

Introduction

This is not a story of great courage or tactical genius. It is simply a true story of a section of 12 men, striving to maintain a balance of professionalism and sanity, sprinkled with the obvious bursts of hilarity, that a body of men will use to break up the routine when living together in a desert and going through an unforgettable experience for six months of their lives.

It is a story taken from notes I made at the time the events happened, of my thoughts at the time, and of my reaction to certain circumstances.

Although it is now quite a while later, and my views on the situation have changed in certain aspects, this story has been written with no changes to my thoughts at the time, or my outlook on life during Operation Granby, Gulf War I. Throughout the war, there were heroic tasks undertaken and obviously, there were atrocities caused by both sides as there always are in war, this is not intended to be a story of tactics, historical events or battle-winning characters.

It is just a story about what happened to a small Royal Electrical and Mechanical Engineer (REME) fitter section attached to C Company. The 1st Battalion of the Staffordshire Regiment, an infantry Company within the Staffordshire regiment, and the tasks and trials put upon them by the desert, the heat, the sand and the war.

Italy, July 1990

With the chatter and laughter of Jon and Donna in the background and Ursula sleeping on the beach beside me, the Mediterranean sun poured down on our slowly browning bodies and I was thinking that in only a few days I would be leaving Italy and heading back to Fallingbostel West Germany to start work again after a brilliant three-week holiday in Pisa, Italy.

This was the second time we had travelled the one-thousand-mile drive to the American army base in Italy, from Fallingbostel. With a caravan on tow, we would take two days travelling through the Austrian and Italian Alps, and then we would camp under the trees in this recreational base with full American camp facilities, a private beach and lots of American-style food restaurants. All for 250 of our best American dollars for a three-week stay.

The forthcoming year would be nowhere as hectic as the last one. For the last 12 months, we have done nothing but military exercises, building up to a battle group camp in BATUS, Canada. The programme that has been set out for the unit over the next year starts off with the Company training, in preparation for a Northern Ireland tour over Christmas.

For the first time in my career, I am part of the Rear Party. This is the group of people keeping the workshop ticking over whilst everyone is away on the Northern Ireland tour. This makes a pleasant change as I have already done three tours of Northern Ireland. The first name drawn out of the hat when an Op Banner tour (The name for a Northern Ireland tour) comes around is usually mine, but not this time, oh no.

This is going to be such a cushy year, with someone else getting soaking wet and freezing cold, on the mountains of Armagh. As I dozed back off to sleep, the furthest thing from my mind was the spot of trouble that had occurred in Kuwait just before I left for Italy.

July/August 1990—The Build-Up

Back in uniform and back to work in Fallingbostel, Germany. The government are announcing today which British troops will be going to the Gulf. We should be quite safe though, as the Northern Ireland tour training we are doing is in full swing, and there are 40 other infantry units to choose from. I do not think that they will stop our schedule. We are to parade at 1630 hours for a talk by the commanding officer.

At 1400 hours, we listened to the news to find out which units had been told that they had drawn the short straw knowing that it could not be this unit as we would have already been told straight from the horse's mouth and not by hearing it on the radio. Wouldn't we?

Although army communication systems from those who know to those who don't are poor, to say the least. Decency will prevail in the upper echelons, so we'll definitely not be going otherwise we would already know, wouldn't we?

Wrong?

The first short straw out of the hat is the 1st Battalion of the Staffordshire Regiment to which I am attached to. After the initial feeling of disgust towards the hierarchy for keeping us in the dark, the squaddie humour kicked in straight away. As we left the parade ground where we were informed officially of the decision, the storeman stood by the side of the square handing out sandpaper sheets and explaining that these were our maps for the next few months.

We set about organising a work programme to ensure all the vehicles would be 100% effective when we deployed to the Gulf. This included drafting in 30 extra tradesmen to put our manning on a war footing. We also borrowed 50 extra mechanics to help out with the massive workload that we had to put upon ourselves.

Every vehicle had to be inspected and repaired, spares demanded, begged, borrowed or stolen. Whilst this was going on, extra activities had to be worked out. Military training was organised, including first aid, weapon handling and NBC training.

A rigorous fitness programme was set up, this was to improve our stamina and weed out all those who could not make the grade. The reason behind this is that at the moment nobody knew what we were getting into, and nobody could afford to carry dead wood. The term for dead wood in the army is Biffs. Unfortunately, it turned out that this Light Aid Detachment (LAD) had more than its fair share.

A Biff is someone who, whether by injury or bone idleness, could not pass the physical tests put on them. Up to this point, we believed that we had only two or three of these people, but in a few weeks, we found that we had been carrying over a dozen. Obviously, some were using this as an excuse not to go to war.

More replacements were drafted in to take the place of these fat and lazy people who had a Biff chit. A Biff chit was a certificate stating you were excused for fitness training and more importantly active operations. It was amazing to find out just how many people had been harbouring these terrible injuries for so long without telling anyone about them until they realised that this was for real.

There were a few, however, who were carrying injuries collected during their previous military career in such a way that they would become a burden in the months to come if they were deployed and I bear these people no malice at all.

After the initial turmoil, all targets were reached within time and after a six-week period of 14 to 18-hour days, for seven days a week, everything was stowed, packed and ready for operation. Fitness training carried on and it was not unusual to run 10 miles or more and then nip home for a shower and be back at work for 0900 hours and complete a full day's work.

The battle personal fitness test (BFT) is a three-mile run of walking and running for the first one and a half miles followed by a sprint back to camp for one and a half miles, all done in boots. For someone my age, I was allowed 10 minutes 30 seconds, which I could normally do quite comfortably, but now, I was seeing times under nine minutes.

This was incredible as I was still puffing my way through 20-plus cigarettes a day, and the units of alcohol I used to consume regularly in those days would make my doctor throw a hissy fit. If any of my fitter section came in behind me, they would feel my wrath as I was 10 years older than them and I would expect them to be well ahead of me.

After gaining this state of mind and fitness, the enjoyment I felt from plodding along the tracks and paths would stay with me for years in various forms of running, walking and cycling. It's such an easy way to clear the day's problems from the mind.

The actual departure dates kept slipping to the right, which was good because that meant that I could spend quite a lot of time with my wife. However, the downside was we were now in a peak physical and mental condition.

If our departure was delayed any longer, our standards would start slipping as everything was geared so that we arrived in Saudi Arabia just as we hit that peak. Another downside was all the infantry soldiers were being trained to be a lean mean fighting machine and to get into the state of mind to fight a war.

Once the soldiers arrived downtown in the evening and with the beer flowing there were many occasions when they wanted to start the war early with each other.

Ironically, after years of the local German townspeople complaining about the British soldiers drinking too much, fighting and spoiling their town, when the commanding officer put Fallingbostel town out of bounds due to the recent trouble caused, the local Burgermeister travelled to the camp and asked if they would rescind the ban as the pubs were all losing money.

Once all the soldiers left Fallingbostel to embark on the war, the town virtually went bankrupt until we returned. A lot of the remaining army families that were left in Fallingbostel went back to the UK and the local economy only picked up once we and the families returned.

Finally, the vehicles were taken to the docks and started their two-week-long passage to the Gulf, which in itself was a logistic nightmare as it was not just the vehicles that needed transporting but all the spares and equipment required to maintain the vehicles and troops embarking for an indefinite period of time in unknown conditions.

The first panic has just spread throughout the company lines. The Arab states are alcohol-free.

19 October 1990

Well! this is the big one. Tearful farewells to Ursula. She was very brave but I knew that as soon as I drove off, there was a good possibility that she would break down in tears. This did not make it any easier for me to put on a brave face as I walked out of the front door, ready to start the long journey to Saudi Arabia. As we were getting on the coaches to leave, some of the lads had bought their wives and sweethearts and were saying their goodbyes.

I was glad that I had said my goodbyes to Ursula back at the flat instead of prolonging the agony. My main concern was that the children were at boarding school. I hadn't seen them since September, so I never really said goodbye to them properly as I would have liked to.

We were driven by coach to Hannover airport. Whilst on the coach I noticed some of the senior ranks on the back seat were acting strangely. It soon became apparent that on the coach was a sergeant (Name withheld) who had been posted from the battalion a few months before. He had applied to come back to the battalion but had been refused. So here he was now hidden by jackets being smuggled into a war zone from Germany.

Once arriving at the airport, we were immediately loaded into a plane leaving Germany's green land far behind. The stowaway sergeant now hiding under the seats on the plane. Looking out of the aeroplane window I realised that it was to be six months before I saw a tree again.

After four hours of flying, we landed in Cyprus and were all shunted into a reception area whilst the plane refuelled. The bar opened and knowing that it would be our last chance at a beer for months, as the Gulf States are alcohol-free, we carried out a project that included draining Cyprus of anything alcoholic.

We almost made it. If it hadn't been for some spoilsport telling us that our transport was waiting, we would have achieved our aim. We all trooped back onto the aeroplane and I slept through the second stage of the journey. It must have been all the excitement of the day.

20 October 1990

After a long tiring journey, we finally landed at Dhahran airport at 0300 hours to the hot sticky heat of the Saudi night. We were then bundled into buses that looked like they would break down before leaving the airport, never mind taking us all the way up the coast to Al Jubail. On leaving the airport, we drove past row after row of fighter aircraft and helicopters. It was at this point that I realised how big the whole operation had become.

When we observed the might of the American equipment, it made our little British contribution seem a little bit insignificant. It took three hours of driving over the desert before we reached our destination. All the time, we were taking in smells and sights and to this day I do not know why anybody would fight a war over this sand patch. It stunk.

On arrival at Al Jubail, the stowaway sergeant marched up to the commanding officer and admitted what he had done. He was demoted to corporal for being absent without leave from his unit and later promoted again back to sergeant, as he was a brilliant section leader with all the qualities for the job at hand.

He was very strict with his platoon and could often be heard berating one of his soldiers for doing something wrong. Several years later, whilst on a tour of Northern Ireland one of his soldiers snapped, shot and killed him for shouting at him and demeaning him in front of his friends.

21 October 1990

We arrived at Al Jubail Port and were immediately shunted into huge queues to make sure that all the paperwork was in order. I then found a nice cosy spot in an old aircraft hangar we named the pig pens for obvious reasons, and made myself comfy along with two thousand other soldiers.

My main memories of this terrible place are the oppressive heat, the flies, the hard work that we did when the vehicles arrived, the flies, the lack of toilets and showers for so many people and the terrible food that we were forced to eat. The flies. If it was possible to survive without eating, then I would have gladly put up with the hunger pains to get away from the torture the cooks were dishing out.

Oh! And the flies. I know everybody always jokes about the standard of army cooking but this stuff they were dishing out was disgusting. The worst part was that there was nowhere else to go to get something to eat. So, it was a case of eat it or starve. Most of the lads ate the bare minimum and fed the rest to the millions of tropical fish that lived alongside the harbour wall. At one point, we tied some beef fat to a length of lock wire, and then onto a block of polystyrene.

We persuaded one of the locals to take this bundle into the middle of the harbour in his boat, to see if we could catch anything. He laughed at us but did it anyway. We had only given it a few tugs when with a massive splash the beef and polystyrene disappeared out into the ocean, never to be seen again. No fish tonight then. The sooner we moved into the desert and started cooking for ourselves the better.

Before leaving the port, every Warrior power pack had to be lifted for immediate modifications to be carried out. A Warrior is a 25-ton armoured fighting vehicle, it carries a crew of 10 and can travel at 50 miles per hour. Its main armament is a 30-millimetre Raden cannon that can fire a high explosive or armour-piercing shell, this is backed up with a Hughes Chain Gun that can fire six hundred rounds a minute.

A Warrior power pack is a three-ton lump of metal that includes the 17-and-a-half litre engine, gearbox and cooling system. The reason for the modification was to bring them to a higher state of reliability and also to lag the pack compartment with an aluminium foil to reflect the heat away from the hull. Our main concern was the heat that we would encounter once in the desert.

Whilst in the process of doing all the work on the vehicles (whilst all the vehicle crews took it easy) we received newspapers from home. In one article by The Observer, commented on the fat lazy men sunbathing all the time on the quayside. It then stated that these were the men of the REME and the REME always stayed well behind the battle.

"Thank God, these are not front-line troops."

The fat lazy men were in fact tankies from the Queen's royal Irish Hussars. In approximately three seconds, we had found the public relations officer, and after explaining (in the nicest possible way) a certain white-faced journalist from The Observer apologised and promised an apology in the paper to follow. This did in fact happen.

The fact that the accusation was on page two and the apology was at the bottom of page 22 was expected. After this incident, all reporters were treated like the scum they really are. Even later, when the reporters came into the desert, they were ushered quietly away from the area the REME were working in.

As there was a large concentration of REME personnel at the port, several old friends appeared that I had not seen for years and it was nice to spend some time with them talking about the good and bad times we remembered. Dave Fulford was my partner in crime on the 18-month-long artificer course we attended in order to qualify for our staff sergeant promotion.

He heard me laughing in the distance as I do have quite a distinctive and loud laugh. He set a beeline for the noise I was making among the hundreds of armoured vehicles that were parked up. He finally tracked me down by honing in on my voice and surprising me.

I had no idea he was out here sharing the heat, discomfort and flies with 10 thousand other soldiers in this poxy place, so it was good to spend an hour and share a brew with him reminiscing for a while and knowing he was as miserable here as I was.

Fitness continued which proved very hard in the climate, an easy three-mile run would leave us drained for hours. At this point, we were drinking six to eight litres of water a day to prevent dehydration. To have an idea what this is like try drinking two pints of water an hour every hour for a day, we did this for a month until we fully acclimatised.

Most of the time we just sat around waiting for nothing to happen. Often just sitting by the canals or docks watching the tropical fish swim below. It was also fun watching the Arab workers around the dock, and betting if just one of them was going to do any work that day.

All around Al Jubail are freshwater canals. These come from the desalination tanks and spread out into the desert for the locals to grow crops. It just shows that even in the middle of the desert there can be fresh water if someone is willing to pay for it. Why do we keep getting adverts on television to donate to drinking water charities, if the provision of fresh clean water by a country's government is so cheap?

It is standard practice when entering a building with a weapon to quickly check it is unloaded and this is something that is done naturally by soldiers continually used to carrying weapons. However, give a pistol to an officer and they may get over keen.

On one occasion, a major went to clear his weapon too enthusiastically and actually put a round in the chamber and pulled the trigger to check it was clear.

BANG. The pistol went off. Luckily not hitting anyone.

Then to make it worse the major started dancing all over the place waving the pistol around in the air and shouting, "It wasn't loaded. It wasn't loaded."

Well guess what? It was because you just loaded it, you cretin. Eventually, somebody grabbed him, took the pistol off him and led him away. If an ordinary rank and not an officer had done that, he would have been bounced from here to breakfast time and probably demoted. This officer probably just got counselling and was probably told not to do it again. We were just lucky nobody was hurt.

All the vehicles have had the modifications done and are now lined up in Company lines ready for dispersal. Normally, my fitter section of eight has to maintain 17 vehicles but due to the role we were playing this time, both vehicles and tradesmen manning was increased two-fold.

The vehicles that were my responsibility were:

2 Warrior Command Variants
12 Warrior Infantry Variants
3 Warrior Milan Anti-Tank Variants
1 Warrior FOO (Forward Operating Officer, Artillery)
3 Mortar vehicles
2 FV432 Ambulances
432 REME Command (Me)
1.Ferret Armoured Cars
2 Bedford Trucks
2 Land Rovers
2 Tracked Ammo Carriers
1 REME Warrior Repair Variant
1 REME Warrior Repair and Recovery Variant
Total 34 Vehicles

N.B. For the rest of this story, the crews of Warriors and FV432 armoured vehicles may be referred to them as wagons. i.e., "I got back in my wagon."

When in the desert, one tactical bound (10 kilometres) behind the company would be the colour sergeant who brings all the food, water, fuel, ammunition etc. Each front-line vehicle carries enough food, water and ammunition to last about 4 days.

When in attack formation if 7plt call signs 10, 11, 12, 13 (pronounced one zero, one, one two and one three) or 8plt call signs 20, 21, 22 and 23 get engaged by the enemy, then 9plt call signs 30, 31, 32 and 33 move into a backup position fighting a rear-guard action. In the centre of the formation, the company second in command (2i/c)(OC Zero Charlie) will position himself behind the officer commanding who is in callsign OB (Zero Bravo).

Behind them is my contingent three x REME wagons Call signs 24A, 24B and 24C, two x Ambulances Call signs 14A and 14B, and two x Ammo carriers. To the flanks are the Milan and mortar vehicles. All these vehicles behind call sign OC drive on immediate standby to be tasked to any area of the Company formation when needed.

Battle formation: When we are on the move, we stagger our formation 7plt, 8plt, 9plt then Head Quarters (HQ).

HQ is Company Commander (OC)

Company second in command(2i/c)

Sergeant Major

The REME vehicles located in the centre of the group contain my REME fitter section of mechanics, electricians, armourers and recovery mechanics.

Call sign 24A SSgt Artificer (Me), Bones, Ship and Graham

24B Martin, Brummie, Chips, Head (Edwards)

24C Butch, Taff, Mick Mooney and Mick Botha

This was quite a small fitter section, to look after so many vehicles, especially as my main responsibility in the coming months was to ensure that all 34 vehicles could drive and fight effectively. All the vehicles were manned to full strength, which is to say, each Warrior carried 10 men.

If a Warrior breaks down, then the crew stay with the vehicle until either that call sign is repaired, or a replacement can be found. This was not normally a problem. However, if this war did start then a broken-down vehicle would be a stationary target, so I was indirectly responsible for the lives of over 170 men, who were depending on me and my section knowing our job and all the tricks of the trade to keep those vehicles battleworthy.

C Company Formation

```
7 Platoon                                                          8 Platoon
□ □ □ □                                                            □ □ □ □
                              OB
                              □
                              OC
                              □
                              24A
                     24B      □      24C
                     □               □
Milan Anti Tank            9 Platoon                          Mortar Section
□ □ □                     □ □ □ □                             □ □ □
                              FOO
              Ambulance       □           Ambulance
              □                           □
                           Ammunition
                              □
                              □
                         Stores and fuel
                              □
                              □
```

During the cool of the night, I would get the lads together and talk about every different situation and scenario we might come across. Every thought or doubt the fitter section was worried about or had concerns with, was talked about and bought out into the open. I did not want any nagging problems being held in, we would no doubt have enough on our minds in the months to come.

We finally left the port on the second of November and headed deep into the desert. The humidity dropped as soon as we left the city. This was replaced with a clear dry heat. It was so relieving not to be soaked in sweat 24 hours a day.

I had previously served as a mechanic with several different units and was experienced working on Land Rovers and trucks as well as tracked vehicles such as armoured personnel carriers and main battle tanks.

This latest posting was a Warrior Battalion and although I had not physically worked on these vehicles before being posted to this unit 18 months ago, the role of an artificer is to manage the team as well as give mechanical advice and make decisions to ensure the fitter section performs to the best of its ability.

02 November 1990 to 12 December 1990

Once the vastness of the desert was taken as normal, as was the fantastic majesty of the early morning sunrise, the sudden disappearance of the sun after the evening sunset and the sheer vastness of the sky at night, life became one long exercise gearing up for war. At first, the main problem was navigation. On the numerous exercises, I had been part of when on unfamiliar ground I was used to reading a map that had roads, forests, trees, rivers and hills in detail.

Contour lines on the map enabled me to imagine the hills, re-entrants and valleys allowing me to have a rough idea of where I was. The desert maps were just like a blank sheet with grid lines drawn on but no features, or details whatsoever.

Everything had to be done by compass bearings and due to the terrain, after a 20-mile move, we would find ourselves to be a mile out. During the day, this was not a problem, but at night with no lights, it may as well be 50 miles.

Thankfully, the platoon commanders and OC were issued satellite navigation equipment. (Nobody had mobile phones in those days, and if we did where would we charge them?) This meant we could go from bearing to bearing on the move and not have to dismount every mile to get a true direction. This is what we had to do when we were free running, due to the magnetic field around the vehicle hull making a compass useless.

As REME we are constantly being called out to repair or recover Warriors and other vehicles which meant we spent a lot of time free running on our own all without a sat nav. At night, we would drive around until we thought we were near the casualty vehicle, which may be a mile away.

We were limited to a three-second transmission burst on the radio to ensure our position could not be tracked by the enemy. Once near the casualty vehicle, we would call on the radio for those waiting for our assistance to show a light. Immediately the desert will come to life for a second with 20 or 30 pinpricks of light from various vehicles all around our vehicle in the local vicinity of two to three miles.

The lights would then be turned off after a few seconds, leaving us in the pitch dark again. We then have to be more specific by naming the call sign we are looking for. Eventually, we would find the customer and start work on the vehicle, often all through the night, finishing just before the next day's manoeuvres were about to start. Obviously, we would be involved in this day's manoeuvres so we were getting very little rest during this period.

Cat naps were the order of the day. I tried to let the vehicle drivers get some sleep at night if we were not moving. During the day, we were just parked up waiting for something to happen. Following the company formation, the driver would let me cat nap until it was time for us to be involved or if he heard someone call us on the radio.

The sand caused major problems with the Warrior engines and no end-of engine pack lifts had to be carried out to rectify overheating faults or just worn-out engines due to dust inhalation by the engines. The engine air filters were not man enough for the job they were designed for and so after several modifications, a more efficient air filtration system was evolved.

Prior to the modification, the engine oil quickly became saturated by the silica in the sand ingestion and so every hundred kilometres we changed the vehicle's engine oil.

As my fitter section vehicle crews had been formed prior to deployment it took a while to get to know each other's way of working. By now, each crew knew exactly what the other member would be doing and so the time to lift the power pack out of a Warrior had reduced from 40 minutes to 10 or 15 minutes.

However, no matter how many vehicle breakdowns or how small the problems the vehicles suffered from, a set training programme had to be met so work was hard and frustrating at times, but of course, each day brought its lighter moments.

I will take the next few lines to introduce you to one of my crew. 6 feet 2 inches in somebody else's cotton socks. If it can be bumped, he will bump it, drop, drop it, smash it, smash it and so on. The reason behind this is that he's a clumsy gangly youth with no coordination and his sense of direction in life is iffy and, in the desert, can be hilarious.

A quick job at night on a vehicle, one hundred meters away usually ended up with the whole fitter section searching the sand dunes until dawn for this poor orientation-challenged youth. However, he remained one of the team throughout the tour and a member of the ground elite force the Desert Rats. He was also one of the most genuine and conscientious men I have ever met. And has probably done very well in his future career in the REME.

Time and training programmes flew past and every conceivable scenario was practised and then practised again until we finally got it right. We hoped.

During our stay in Al Jubail docks, we visited the 1st Marine Corps in the desert. For some unknown reason, the transport wagons dropped us off two miles from their location so we had to march with full kit weighing 120 pounds, plus weapons in 100-degree heat to meet them. Needless to say, upon arrival we were overheating, sweating profusely and totally fed up.

This amused the Marines who obviously let us know that we would never be fit enough to be a Marine as they were the best fighting soldiers in the world. The fact that nobody in our group had acclimatised yet as we had only been in country two weeks didn't matter to them as they were so full of their own praises.

Having said that, they did look after us well for the day and gave us a good insight into how their army ran, but as far as the best fighting soldiers in the world go, I will explain later how we found out what a slack bunch they really were. OooRa.

12 December 1990

Finally, the Company training is over and after six weeks of solid work, it is time for a long-deserved rest. Unfortunately, those who know best have decided to start battalion training a week early. More work as usual. Never mind I will book myself some leave when I get back home and I can sleep then.

One thing that was taught in depth was camp hygiene as nobody wanted to have diarrhoea or sickness, so therefore, hygiene and cleanliness were paramount. The young lads in the section initially were constantly shouted at by the vehicle commanders for not tidying up or leaving food out. All washing up had to be done immediately after a meal as we were having a major problem with flies. Thank God they were not the biting type.

Toilets (latrines) were dug 50 meters away from the wagons. Each wagon had two or three, two-litre water bottles stuck into each other to form a tube and buried in the sand for people to pee into. This centralised the contaminated area rather than everyone just peeing where they wanted to which was usually up against the wagon.

16 December 1990

During exercises, all situations are practised and there is nothing more exhilarating than being on a battle run at full speed across the desert watching the Warriors fire and manoeuvre. To an outsider, it looks as though everything is in turmoil but during these manoeuvres the aim is to give protection to those vehicles or troops on the ground, moving into position and for them to cover you when you are moving.

By now, we were honed to split-second timing. Every couple of hours, the manoeuvres pause to go over any points that need raising, to give everyone a rest and to find time for a cup of tea and a bite to eat.

The crews in the back of the vehicle get very seasick whilst the vehicles are running over the desert, especially if the terrain is undulating. Some of the guys never did get used to it and would dread getting into the back of the wagons. One of my constant problems was getting hauled over the coals by the sergeant major.

One of my sergeants, constantly allowed the crew in the rear of one of my REME vehicles to stand up with their heads and shoulders above the armoured vehicle hull. As we were now training as though this was a real war situation we had to stay under armour as though there was a possibility of being under fire.

I know it was hot, noisy and nauseous but that was the rules and it really annoyed me after every route march that I was getting a bollocking for this crew being allowed to do whatever they wanted to do. Even though I passed the bollocking down to the sergeant, this did not seem to make any difference as he would not exert his authority over his men.

A standard practice of the infantry sections was when resting outside of the vehicle, to place the rifles on top of the Warrior Road wheels, of which a Warrior has 12. This keeps the weapons off the ground and stops the rifles from getting sand in them.

This is a good practice so long as when the driver decides to move the vehicle, they remove the rifles, otherwise, as the Warrior moves away and eight rifles may just get run over and destroyed. Oops.

After the second time this happened and several rifles took on the shape of a banana, the practice of placing the rifles on the wheels was stopped.

Battalion training had now been completed therefore all the lads had to do was about 12 hours of work, fixing a few minor vehicle problems, and then it was time for a nice long kip.

17 December 1990

We have just been warned off, that tomorrow the Company will be playing enemy for the US Marine Corps. We load up onto the low-loader transport trailers and move one hundred miles north. After unloading, we were briefed that we had to act like Iraqi troops, which is to say, sloppy and unprofessional. This exercise is to give the Americans confidence, but if I know the Stafford's, poor old Soldier Blue is in for a very rude awakening.

0400 hours: The first of our reconnaissance patrols has just arrived back from the American location, loaded with booty and the spoils of war proffered from the American vehicles. Proffed is short for profit. That is to say, borrowed, lent, stolen, taken. This could be any item whatsoever that the soldier decided would be better in his possession than with the rightful owner. American weapons and equipment are littered all over the place, and where did they get it?

From the Marine HQ Company, that was located in the centre of the Marine Corps location. The reconnaissance party apparently waited until 0100 hours and then just walked into the camp area and helped themselves. They left only after chalking the Stafford's Knot emblem on the Yank C. O's vehicle. Best fighting soldiers in the world, they are, honest!

0800 hours: The American Colonel and a contingent of 20 Marines for backup have just arrived at our location and he has asked for all the missing equipment back. We gave him the weapons but unfortunately, nobody could find all the good kit (Sleeping bags, jackets, helmets) that could be sold or bartered for trade later in the day. The pale-faced colonel and his contingent left. He was unhappy Tonto.

Throughout the day we would carry out normal fire and manoeuvre exercises. The Americans had to keep asking us to slow down, this is due to the Warriors being able to go faster in reverse than the Abrams tank can go in a forward gear. On every phase, we out-manoeuvre the Americans. This must be due to the previous training we have undergone plus the fact that one-on-one a Yank will never get the better of a British soldier.

At one point, three Apache helicopters came over a ridge and simulated a hellfire missile attack on my vehicle. By the time, the umpire had driven up to tell us that my vehicle had been completely destroyed, all my crew had put slings on. I explained that we had only been shot in our left arms so could still fight on.

He accused me of not taking this training seriously and that we were all dead. 10 minutes later, he drove up and told me that we had to move out and go fix a broken vehicle. He didn't get any reaction from us as we had covered ourselves with sand and put crosses by our heads. What a pillock trying to motivate a dead crew to do a job. However, once we let him turn his face purple as he berated us, we went and did the job. Some people just cannot take a joke.

At the end of the day's exercises, we would park up and put the boiling vessels on for dinner. Boiling vessels are containers within the wagon that can boil water, stews, etc. In one location, we noticed there were palm trees and an oasis nearby, just like in the movies and also a massive sand dune in the distance.

As we stood down for a few hours; me, Bones, Mick Mooney and Brummie Mead had a walk and climbed the sand dune. Upon reaching the summit of the dune, once we had got our breath back, we just sat down on the summit and took in the quietness of the desert for an hour. After such a noisy high-speed day, it was nice just to sit down in our own company and take in everything. The view over the desert was amazing.

We could see other units driving around and the dust clouds being generated by troop movement in the distance but all in perfect silence.

Once acclimatised to the heat, we really started to appreciate the beauty of the desert. The desert is really amazing with its vastness, especially at night. Due to the flatness of the terrain, the sky goes on forever and there are that many stars, certain patches of the sky appear to be milky. Hence the galaxy we are part of being called the Milky Way.

We grew fairly knowledgeable about the star constellations and could navigate at night; confident we would get somewhere near our intended destination.

At another location, we pulled up next to an old shed and some broken-down fencing. As soon as we unpacked and everything was set up for a short stay in this location, with the daily roster of cooking, latrine and sentry protection tasks sorted out, the fence was broken up and we all sat around the newly acquired wood for a company bonfire. Everyone loves a bonfire. No matter where you are.

In the cold European winter or in the middle of a desert, once the fire is lit it draws crowds around it. Everyone just sits and stares at the flames. It must be a primal human hunter-gatherer reaction. Potatoes are found and wrapped in tin foil and thrown into the red-hot embers to cook for an hour before being dragged out and eaten.

Picture 30 guys sitting around tucking into baked potatoes that are still too hot to eat and all the faces are covered in black ash. It looks like a negative of the black-and-white minstrel show.

Out of the blue, an Arab turned up ranting and raving that we had just burnt down his farm. Well! We may have burnt a few rails, but a farm? He has a point though. I don't think I have seen a tree since I have been in this country. It's probably a hundred-mile trip across the desert to find some more rails. Well, well, deary me, never mind.

23 December 1990

We returned back to the battalion area for Christmas with the lads. Morale is sky-high after the last few days of fun and games. I think the Marines were glad to get rid of us so they could get back to their mutual appreciation way of life, OooRa.

During my army career, I have spent several Christmas away from home (3x Northern Ireland tours, Gulf War 1 and Bosnia). It was also standard practice that the single lads on camp were allowed leave to go back to the UK to see their families and the married men would carry out the Christmas guard duties around the barracks.

This was fair for the single guys but quite an annoyance to the married men who had to spend yet another Christmas Day away from their kids. The Christmas dinner could be slipped a day but the kids would still have to open their presents on Christmas Day.

The following story is an incident that happened during an operational tour of South Armagh.

Chapter 8
1986 Christmas Day, Bessbrook Camp, County Armagh N.I.

The rain hasn't stopped for weeks. Working in the Armagh hills servicing the generators on the border outposts is quite hazardous. To get to the outstations, initially, I have to take a helicopter ride to the top of a mountain and then jump out of the helicopter (with a 25-kilogram toolbox). The helicopter is usually balanced on a rock with just one runner in contact, so this is not the steadiest of platforms.

We then keep our heads down whilst the helicopter takes off again not to return for a few hours. I then have to climb to the observation post in a howling wet wind and try to either service the generator or fix a fault in these conditions. How many people do you know who get a helicopter ride every day as their daily commute? Once the generator fault is rectified, I can get into the warmth of the observation post and wait for my lift back to Bessbrook Camp.

This has been my life for the last three months looking after the generators on three observation posts on the border hills, and in the Crossmaglen and Fork Hill outpost camps all of which are within an area known as Bandit Country.

Finally, it is Christmas Day and I have a day off.

0100 hours and there is a Scots guardsman standing by my bed telling me that the electric generator at G30, one of the observation posts has gone down. G30 is situated on top of a mountain and has several garden sheds sunk into the ground and covered with steel sheets to defend against mortar attacks. Between the sheds are trenches just like in the first World War films.

Within each outpost, there is an observation tower that is best described as a steel pylon with a steel shed perched about 50 feet up it. From this shed, the soldiers can look through naval binoculars over the border hills and look for any suspicious activity taking place around the surrounding roads and farms. The magnification of these binoculars is fantastic and a car number plate can be read from quite a distance away.

This is very good in fine weather but as most observation huts are raised high up on a pylon-type structure, when looking through the binoculars in a strong wind the tower sways backwards and forwards. The view of what the operator is trying to observe moves constantly from left to right making it hard to focus on a given point. This actually induces the operator to feel seasick.

I tell the soldier that I will attend to the electrical breakdown first thing in the morning but he stresses that this is a priority task and I need to go now as there is a helicopter coming from Aldergrove airport one hundred miles away to take me to the location. Cursing, I get all my warm, wet weather kit on and grab my toolbox and run down to the helipad and wait for the soon-to-be-arriving helicopter.

The helicopter arrives and away we go into the pitch-dark rain and wind. As we approach G30 I see all the perimeter lights are on and everything seems to be working as it should be. Although confused, the helicopter lands as instructed and I disembark. Whatever happens, I am stuck here now for the night.

I cower down as the helicopter powers up, disappears into the black night and returns to Aldergrove. I crawled through the rotor down wash and the horizontal wind and rain. When I arrived at the outpost trench system I was freezing cold and soaking wet and I made my way to the operations control shed.

On reaching the shed, a Scots Guard Warrant officer is sitting there grinning at me. I am at this point completely confused about why I was here. When asking him what was wrong with the generator, and why on earth had I been called out on such a shitty night?

He said in his broad Glasgow accent, "Andy lad, I was sitting on radio watch in my shed on a cold wet Christmas morning and everyone else is asleep. The wind is howling around this bloody mountaintop, the rain is bashing against the door and the roof is leaking. I have the electric fire on the maximum three bars and I am still bloody freezing."

"I've read all my books and seen all the videos available and I'm bored stiff. So, I thought I knew! I'll get Andy Flower up here. He always cheers me up with his jokes. So that's what I did. So, tell me a joke."

The more I tell this story, the more it sounds like I'm making it up but it is the honest truth. Who knows how much the great British taxpayer had to pay for that little jaunt in the chopper? After a couple of egg banjo's and a mug of hot tea and whisky, I also saw the funny side and a good time was had by all until the morning came and the helicopter returned.

An egg banjo is actually just a fried egg sandwich. It gets the name banjo as once the person bites into it the yoke usually spurts out and runs down the owner's jumper, forcing the owner to hold the sandwich in his left hand and wipe the yoke away with a rag as though strumming a banjo.

I was attached to the 1st Battalion Scots Guards for four years in the mid to late 80s. They were a very funny mob to be attached to. Their main job in life for six months of each year was to perform royal duties at Buckingham Palace and all the other royal residencies in London. This meant that for six months of the year, they were marching around London royal residences changing the guard in their best kit and bearskins.

For the other six months of the year when they were not on the royal duties, they were practising marching for when they were actually marching around London again in the public eye. They also had to take part in all the royal state ceremonies and foreign royal/presidential visits.

Running in parallel with this was the pipes and drums band that did all the marching practice but also blew into bagpipes and tin whistles or walloped drums all day long. When people tell me how magnificent the marching bands are nowadays, I still cringe at the thought of the noise I had to put up with all day long during the time I spent with them. I love strawberries and cream but not if I have to eat it every day.

As a body of men, the Jocks were okay but the guardsman mentality was just far too military thinking for a poor REME tradesman.

As I was in REME, I was not expected to put a bearskin on my head and perform royal ceremonial duties but I was expected to attend guard duties around the camp, therefore, I had to attend the guard mount where the guard had to form up on the parade square and be inspected by the orderly officer. The inspection was carried out after the actual guard had done several marching manoeuvrers that I never did master.

This would not have been too bad if I was just following what everybody else was doing. Unfortunately, I was at the time a sergeant and actually the chap who had to shout out the orders for the rest of the guard to follow. After four years of guard mounts, I don't think I had the guard facing in the correct direction at the end of the manoeuvre more than half a dozen times.

It always took another additional command to get them to face the correct direction for inspection. Needless to say, I lost count of the extra duties I accumulated which was the standard punishment for cocking up the guard mount.

On one occasion, I got everything right and the officer came onto the parade square to inspect the guard. I took a step forward to salute him and as I saluted, I noticed that there was smoke coming out of one of the officer's mess windows.

Without bothering about the officer who was himself in mid-salute himself, I fell out the guard from the parade and ran with the guard members to the officer's mess where I coordinated the throwing of a tumble dryer that had caught fire out of an upstairs window. The following morning, I was marched into the adjutant who thanked me for my prompt actions and for saving the officer's mess from further fire damage.

I was then promptly marched out of his office and into the RSM's office and given extra duties for not asking permission from the officer before dismissing the guard to fight the fire. I won't even tell you what they said when we bolted two skateboards to the bottom of an old windsurfer and started surfing it over their parade ground at 40 miles an hour. Some people just take life too seriously.

Although I didn't perform the ceremonial duties around the royal residencies (Buckingham Palace, St James Palace and Windsor Castle) when the Scots Guards were on guard duty, I did have to carry out duties at these places as a guard commander, tucked out of sight in the guard room where no one would pay any attention to me.

Whilst on duty, there we had to be aware of who was in residence and there was a board on the wall showing who was in residence in the respective palaces around London. This usually totalled 20 or 30 royal or presidential dignitaries from all over the world. Needless to say, a lowly sergeant guard commander was not allowed anywhere near the grand halls where I may bump into somebody far above my standing.

I did during my career in other locations meet and talk to The Duke of Edinburgh, Prince Andrew and several members of parliament. John Major came out and visited the troops in the desert just prior to Gulf War 1 starting. He came to give us a moral boost and spoke to me in a deep and meaningful conversation.

He said, "Hello."

I replied, "Hello, Sir," and then he was gone.

Later in life, I occasionally as a civilian design engineer of the Bulldog vehicle, had to take the vehicle to military shows and introduce the new vehicle to the top brass and the press to show them what they had spent their millions of great British pounds on. I had to instruct various dignitaries on how to operate it and drive it around a short cross-country course. At one point, I was commanding a Bulldog vehicle around the cross-country course whilst Lord Drayson drove.

We had a set route to drive which took about five minutes. At one point, I told him he couldn't go down a track he was aiming for as it was not part of the agreed course.

At this command, he replied, "I'm the Minister of Defence who's going to stop me?"

30 minutes later, we drove out of the woods and noticed that his entourage was in mad panic because they did not know where he had gone. He thought all this was very amusing. Needless to say, all my bosses blamed me, not that I could have stopped him.

Three months later, the original order for four hundred vehicles was increased to nine hundred because he was so impressed with the vehicle. I don't expect the diversion he took had anything to do with this but it didn't do any harm. He later moved from being the Minister of Defence to running the Aston Martin racing team in Le Mans.

Anyway. Back to the story in the desert.

Chapter 9
Christmas Day (In the Desert)

Happy Tuesday was the cry among the Company, as Christmas Day was just another day in the sand. This day of all days was very depressing for everyone stuck in the desert. I found my thoughts returning to Ursula and the children and I felt myself sinking deeper and deeper into self-pity.

Depression soon faded away as there were masses of packages delivered mid-morning, not just from our families but from many people we did not even know, they just wanted to do something for us. Along with lots and lots of hats, socks, gloves, shower stuff, soap, toothpaste also food parcels, cans, biscuits and there were hundreds of mince pies and miniature Christmas puddings.

When in the desert on Christmas Day, another way of cheering up yourself and the three hundred men in the company location is to get the nearest armoured personnel carrier and turn it into a pirate galleon. Once complete, drive at full speed around the battalion concentration area. With makeshift swords hooks and eye patches shouting Ahrrrr. Why are pirates called pirates? Because they Ahrrrr.

Everybody thought this was a great idea except:

1. RSM
2. OC
3. CO
4. Brigadier

Whoops. SSGT Flower is in the proverbial poo again.

Now, there were only so many miniature Christmas puddings you could eat so when the lads were full of all the Christmas food and sweets, they were still left with several hundred miniature Christmas puddings. It was agreed between us that they should share the excess puddings with a camel that was tethered near our vehicles, not knowing that every other squaddie in the Company had done the same.

This act of kindness backfired when about two o'clock in the morning, all hell broke loose with bellowing and groaning and every other noise that a camel can make when his staple diet has been straw and cactus for the last 15 years. He has now been fed 20 or 30 miniature Christmas puddings. Needless to say, I was sorry for the camel who had just had the best colonic irrigation in the history of camels.

In the morning, his owner turned up and when he saw the state of the said camel, he was not impressed, to say the least, with what we had done to Arabia's best racing camel. I explained that he now had plenty of manure for his garden, but I don't think he knew what a garden was.

I explained that there was an enterprising opportunity here for him to offer other camel farmers, digestive clear out of their camels also, as we had hundreds of Christmas puddings left. Needless to say, he was not impressed and so I did not push other enterprising possibilities, as they all involved reconstituted Christmas puddings.

Chapter 10
The Andy Flower School of Tact and Diplomacy

Tact and diplomacy are learnt with years of experience dealing with the hierarchy. Basically, the best form of defence is attack, so therefore it is a matter of knowing the equipment you work on inside out and back to front. To this end, when an officer or CSM goes to bed at night (usually whilst the REME are still working), they have nothing else better to do than think of ways to mess the lads about.

Any suggestions or hare-brained schemes can be shot down and quashed before they start discussing their brainwaves between themselves. If this does not work, then step two is to listen to everything they say and then go off and do it your way anyway. So long as the job gets done then no one is the wiser.

Rule One: Always look around you before talking about anybody or moaning about someone.

We were supposed to be playing enemy for our company's manoeuvres and were moving out at 1900 hours. At 1700 hours, I was told by a young officer that we were moving at 1800 hours. This meant that everybody involved had to rush around to be ready on time. It was whilst I was having a good old moan about this that I turned round and the officer was standing there. As I was in a slightly bloody mood, I didn't even acknowledge his presence.

This was when he did the very foolish thing that young officers are renowned for doing.

He opened his mouth, "It's alright, staff, I can wait a while until you are ready."

Ha Ha, the fool was on the defensive, this is definitely the wrong tactic to use when dealing with a grisly staff sergeant who hasn't slept properly for the last 50 hours. I, therefore, proceeded to tell him that the REME wagons would be ready to roll on time, not a minute before not a minute after, because after all the REME were only here to be messed about by a gallant young and upcoming subaltern of the glorious Staffordshire Battalion.

This tirade went on for about five minutes with various other sarcastic comments and double-meaning phrases. Just as his face was as red as it was possible to be without blowing up.

I announced, "Sir, your carriage awaits."

With this, he got into the back of the wagon and did not utter a squeak for the rest of the journey.

We drove about 15 miles under his instruction of where we were supposed to be going, set up an enemy location and waited for the troops to arrive for an attack. And waited, and waited and waited. All the time we were waiting I kept commenting to the officer about a huge dust cloud that kept moving about 10 miles south of our position and that it was probably our Company looking for us.

He would confidently point to his map and assure us that we were where we were supposed to be. His smug look slowly turned to despair after about three hours when he finally realised that he had taken us eight miles from where we should have been. I explained to him not to worry as it was only 30 vehicles and 170 men that had been driving for three hours in this stinking heat looking for an enemy that wasn't there and that I was sure that nobody would mind at all. (not).

After the exercise had ended and we returned back to our Company location, the officer was climbing off the top of the wagon to give his excuses to the OC when he slipped and fell onto the ground below. After my initial response of laughing, I asked him if he was alright. He said he was and then disappeared around the side of the wagon. Laughing I told the lads what the clumsy prat had done.

It was only when I walked around the side of the vehicle again that I saw he was still sitting there as he was quite badly winded, but was completely aware of what I had said about him.

He was just about to open his mouth and give me a hard time when I said, "Open your bergen, Sir. I am sure you get issued a manual on how to climb off of big tanks."

I could tell at this point in time that I wasn't his best friend, however, he bade me goodnight and left. The following morning the OC told me to stop having a go at the lieutenant as he was trying.

To which I answered, "Yes, Sir. Very trying."

The OC looked at me with a wry smile and then walked off shaking his head saying to himself, "I know. I know."

I think that the OC and I have a mutual respect for each other due to the fact that my fitter section always has had the best vehicle availability within the battalion. He also has had the best vehicle availability for the past year all through the exercises and the Canada training. I can't put it all down to my man management as all my lads are not only very experienced with Warrior, but they are also proud of what they do and the results achieved.

The lads work hard and play harder, as quite a few Staffords have found out at their own expense over the last few months. Several times the infantry guys attempted to get a little too pushy with my guys, thinking they could bully them into something they did not want to do, purely by being a bit over-physical with their methods of persuasion. As is the infantry way. They usually ended up sitting on their arse in the sand, holding a rapidly swelling part of their anatomy.

Well, the medics need practice as well, don't they?

As nightfall came very suddenly in the desert and the fact that there was at the time very little work that needed doing, most of the crew were in bed for eight or nine o'clock. I myself slept in the back of my vehicle on the crew seats. Cpl Graham Cross slept on the seats opposite. At approximately 0200 hours, I awoke to Graham obviously having a bad nightmare about being trapped in the wagon.

I immediately started shouting at him to wake up, at this he dashed across to my side saying, "It's alright, boss, I'll get you out."

He then proceeded (still fast asleep) to look for a knife with which to cut me out of whatever he thought I was trapped in. As I was in my sleeping bag, with my hands tucked inside and the bag zipped up to my throat, I was helpless to defend myself. It was only after struggling into a sitting position, all the time shouting at the daft prat to wake up, that he actually did.

After a few minutes and lots of apologies later, he finally dropped back to sleep. It was alright for some, as I lay awake for ages wondering if I should go around and unload all the weapons, in case, he decided I was an Iraqi and shot me.

Graham's dreams continued throughout the tour and it was quite normal for me and the crew to just sit and giggle to each other whilst he burbled away quite coherently in his own little land of nod.

Camp 4

Camp 4 was a rest and recuperation centre for all the front-line troops. Every two and a half weeks or so the Company would cram onto four or five Bedford trucks and amid curses, groaning, cramps and general discomfort we would bounce down the tracks and endure a dusty two-hour trip so we could:

1. Shower
2. Sleep in a bed.
3. Phone wives and loved ones.
4. Generally, take it easy.

It was a time to play football and volleyball and soak in the sun. It was a chance to get out of uniform and get a bit brown. After all, we couldn't come home lily-white after six months in the desert. This rest and recuperation lasted two days and then it was back to the desert to eat sand for the next two and a half weeks, then we would repeat it all over again. Whilst we were in Camp 4 my fitter section put on a Christmas play for the troops in our Company.

It was a Nativity play with a difference. It was a mixture of Black Adder, the Young Ones and Monty Python. Each character was made to mimic a leading member of the Company. Each officer and senior rank was systematically ripped to bits during the 40-minute sketch.

Everyone except me because I helped write the script. I was expecting the lads to give me a good slagging off without my knowing but they didn't. They probably thought they gave me enough hassle every day and I could have a day off.

It was whilst we were at Camp 4 that a certain day would stay in my mind forever.

Chapter 11
17 January 1991

Operation Desert Storm

I had just phoned Ursula telling her I was fine and that there was no chance of anything happening for a while. I settled onto my bunk, with a lump in my throat. I allowed myself an hour of nostalgia every two and a half weeks. Gas, Gas, Gas. Flashing lights, sirens and people running about like the proverbial headless chickens.

We all fumbled about and put on our respirators and NBC kit and looked at each other, not with frightened eyes, but eyes that said, "Which stupid bugger has lent on the Scud missile alarm, again."

It was at this point that the OC walked into the room and told us that a desert storm was now underway and that we had had a near miss from a Scud missile that had landed in Israel six hundred miles away. The call then came down to NBC dress state 1 which meant we could take off our respirators, and then gas, gas, gas, then dress state 1, then gas, gas, gas. This went on for two hours until somebody went and punched the pillock working the siren.

At this moment in time, I was sharing a room with two platoon commanders, lieutenants of the Staffordshire Regiment. One of them rummaged in his backpack and brought out a goody parcel he had recently received from home. In it was some Stilton cheese, crackers and a pint jar of honey. It was only after he opened the honey and I smelt a heady aroma that I realised it was not honey but Glenfiddich whiskey that had been smuggled into the country.

We then sat down at 0530 hours in the morning on the eve of war and had the best cheese and whiskey party I will ever have in my lifetime; The other officer lieutenant, like me, was also writing a diary but his will have bigger words than mine because he is an officer with a degree and I am only an artificer with an HNC.

The next day, none of the civilian workers showed up for work. Breakfast was non-existent so everyone was sneaking around the camp looking for some remnants they could eat. As we were visitors here, we only had our emergency rations in our webbing which we could only eat on threat of death.

I walked down to the snack bar and I found not only was it open, but a few of the lads were busy behind the counter frying up eggs, bacon and sausages and giving it to a huge queue of hungry squaddies. They were also dishing up cold drinks and chocolate bars from some vending machines they had found the keys for.

Of course, the soldiers from the other regiments in the camp thought this was amazing, but after being with the Staffords for a couple of years, this was all normal to me. After all, if the Arab had turned up, he would have made a fortune at the prices he was charging but he didn't and now it was all free to us. As you may have guessed, there was no love lost between the British squaddies and the Arabs.

I have had a chronic back problem due to a rugby injury years ago. The continual bashing it was taking during all the vehicle manoeuvres was taking its toll so I wrote to Ursula telling her I would not be going back to Camp 4 as the trip there and back in the rear of a truck was playing havoc with my back. During the few times when there was a chance to get to Camp 4 before the war started, I stayed in the desert and just chilled out.

This was quite relaxing as even when in Camp 4, I was still responsible for the fitter section and every time there was a problem with them, I would be dragged off my bed to sort it out. This could range from someone not turning up for fatigues or any other duty, to trivial soldier disputes about whose turn it was to collect the section laundry. These disputes covered all the normal in-barracks incidents that happen when a group of lads live in close proximity for months.

Tempers fray, someone pushes someone else a bit too far with their banter about wife, girlfriend or family then all hell breaks out for 30 seconds and then in a flash with hands shaken, sometimes apologies given, it is all over until the next powder keg incident.

The downside of my not going to Camp 4 was that I could not call Ursula on the phone and have a chat. However, once a person phoned home, after ending the call, we all felt quite down as it reminded us of what we were missing back home. Also, very selfishly, we did not need to hear about any problems at home as we had enough things on our mind out here.

If there were problems at home, most of the time we could not do a thing about it until we came home, so it just left everyone even more frustrated. This did not help the poor wife left at home with no one to turn to and had to deal with all the family problems, all on their own.

On the upside, every day I wrote and received the free blueys, which were blue airmail envelopes on which we could write on and send as many a day as we wanted. I numbered each one so they could be read in the correct order as Ursula received them in batches of 8 or 10 and not necessarily in the correct order.

When most of the Company personnel were in Camp 4, our Company area was very peaceful, with no engines running or people playing games, training or just generally shouting at each other. The silence of the desert was very tranquil and relaxing.

I could go and have a run and then as there was plenty of water available, I could dig a small trench in the sand, put some CARM (Chemical Agent Resistant Material) in it and fill it with water. Leave it a couple of hours for the sun to heat it up and then have a nice relaxing bath.

The CARM Plastic sheet was special sheeting to protect stores from chemical agents that may be fired at us by Sadam. Somehow, I had managed to find a roll (proffed from the Quartermaster) of this very expensive sheeting. As I had loads of additional spares on top of my vehicle, I covered the spares with this sheet.

During the night, with a couple of strategically placed poles, this produced a fly sheet over the top of the vehicle like a tent to give us an area to live if we did not want to be on the sandy ground. Whilst visiting our A2 echelon about 10 miles away from the Company location, the Quartermaster stopped me and asked why I had all that CARM on my vehicle. I told him it was to protect everything I had stored on top of the vehicle.

I did not want to tell him what I had stored up there, as we were not allowed to carry many emergency vehicle spares on the vehicle due to the fact that if everyone did this there would be no stores in the stores. He told me to take it off as he needed it and I should not have it. After a bit of an argument, he realised he was losing the argument and so pulled rank on me. So now I have to drive around with everything on top of my vehicle getting covered in sand.

I later visited the A2 echelon and found all the officers' mess benches where they have their meals are covered with nice tablecloths made from CARM. And with this information, I concluded that the Quarter Master was a REMF. (Rear Echelon Mother F!£$%).

You may have come to the conclusion by now that I do not have a very high opinion of my peers. Even though I am in the army, I have always had a problem with authority. The reason for this is that I am quite happy living in my own little bubble ensuring that everything I am responsible for is done to the highest standard by my team.

I don't need anyone sticking their nose in and disrupting the apple cart. Especially, when after their two-penny worth of comments they will go away and take all the praise for sorting the problem out when the problem was going to get sorted out anyway.

19 January 1990

The company have now returned to the desert and our beloved vehicles after their stay in Camp 4. Everyone is checking vehicles and equipment. All the vehicles are inspected again, serviced and repaired if required. Everyone has their ears pinned to the ground in the aim of gathering any additional information possible. The rumour mill is in full swing and nobody believes a word that is said as all good news only leads to disappointment.

Letters are being received and sent, but no information is being passed out of the desert, not due to security but because nobody has got a clue what is going on. The only way we find out any information is by listening to the news on our little shortwave radios.

Each evening at six o'clock the whole fitter section gathers around my wagon to catch the news and for a bit of conversation with the other fitters who are on the other two REME vehicles. I expect Ursula has more information regarding what is happening than we do.

Spare time is taken up by playing cards and chess or fitness training. We have set up a volleyball court and a steel bar on the recovery vehicle's spade to do chin-ups. There are also scorpion fights set up but these can be very boring as scorpions only move every two days to stretch their legs. One of the corporals from Workshops HQ REME has a pet beetle called Tyson.

Nothing has beaten him yet and must eat twice his body weight every day. Even the largest scorpion doesn't stand a chance against him, and half an hour after he has dispatched his foe, only the claws, shell and sting are left.

Another tradition in the REME is the time-honoured game of knerdeling. This involves two spades, two cans of food and a lump hammer. To play the game, place the spades in the ground 20 metres apart, and stand the cans on the handles. Then take a 10-pound lump hammer and with equal numbered teams standing at each spade, one person at a time lobs the hammer at the opposite spade.

> 1 point to hit the spade blade and knock the can off
> 2 points to hit the spade shaft and knock the can off
> 3 points to hit just the can

This game has been played by REME since the Second World War. A game can last as long as there are still unbroken spades and hammers around.

Injections

The number of injections we had to have was unbelievable. After the initial six jabs we had before leaving for the Gulf, which were standard before departing for a Middle Eastern country, we had to have all things to combat what Saddam could, would, or might throw at us. With this in mind, we had to start taking NAPS. These were little tablets we took daily to combat any chemical and biological stuff Saddam could bomb us with. Some veterans still think it was these tablets that brought out a lot of the strange medical conditions and PTSD that Gulf War 1 veterans suffer from. We also had anti-Anthrax injection for the same reason. The Anthrax injection knocked me out for three days but I still felt its effects three weeks later. I was only just over that when we had to have phase two of the Anthrax injection. We were supposed to have phase 3 of these injections but events overtook us and I did not have the third.

Chapter 12
Iraq War, 2003

After leaving the army, I went to work for GKN Defence which made the FV430 series tracked vehicles and the Warrior armoured infantry fighting vehicle. GKN Defence was bought out later by Alvis vehicles who made the CVR(T) tracked scout vehicles. Later Alvis amalgamated with Vickers who made the Challenger tanks. The company name then changed to Alvis/Vickers. We now had the monopoly on all the military armoured tracked vehicles the British Army used.

It was in my role as an engineer working on MoD projects for the company, that I ended up volunteering to carry out some modifications to the Challenger tanks. Unfortunately, the Challenger tanks were already in the desert on the Saudi Arabia/Iraq border. All this activity took place just days before the Gulf War II started.

As part of the preparation, we had to have the Anthrax injections all over again. The maintenance crews that were nominated from our factories in Telford and Newcastle had to go out to work on the vehicle modifications and had heard all the bad stories about side effects. Most of the guys said they would not have them as they had heard these side effects.

I said they weren't that bad and if I had the injection, would they? They all agreed and so I was the first in line. Bugger me if everybody else were fine and I had a really bad reaction that knocked the shit out of me again.

We were out there for 30-odd days, so I qualified for yet another medal. Each day was long and hard work but as a civilian, I was on triple pay so Ursula had to work really hard to spend it all before I got back home. There were a few ex-military guys in the crews but generally, it was a lot of civilians that had never been out of Shropshire or Newcastle before. They were completely out of their depth in the hot sandy conditions.

Of course, all the ex-military guys also had to undergo all the training along with the civilians, even though most of the course was teaching us what we already knew, and we actually knew more than a lot of the instructors as they had never worked in the desert before. All the training had to be done at an old army camp in Kent and had to be completed prior to leaving the UK.

The courses covered all the normal safety instructions, living in camp conditions in the desert and on what to do in case of attack by enemy forces. This to us was our day job but the civilians were a bit panicky especially when it came to donning NBC suits and respirators. I won't even go into their reaction to the lesson of how to act when being taken prisoner by the enemy.

Living in the barrack rooms during the training was actually a benefit, as we got to know the personalities of the crews we would be working with prior to deployment.

Once in country, it was actually quite amusing to see the civilians panic when the first few false Scud alarms went off. The air raid warning sirens caused them all to run around like headless chickens diving under benches and vehicles whilst the ex-military just casually walked to the purpose-built bomb shelters and had a brew.

The only food we had to eat was the American MRE rations which came in bags and we added water to start the chemical process which would, if not shaken during the cooking process, cook half of the food and leave the rest cold. We slept in an old bombed-out office block that had electricity but no running water so all our ablutions were outside in a communal area.

All toilet facilities were outside Porta cabins. These had been located by some genius to ensure they were in full sunlight all day long. The reader can imagine what these smelt like in the 40-plus-degree heat.

I had found a bed space that was a lower bunk bed and was off the main thoroughfare that was used to cut through the building. Luckily nobody claimed the upper bunk, so I could throw some blankets under the upper mattress and have them drop down like a curtain. This gave me a dark area as the ceiling lights were constantly being turned on and off.

This area was quite peaceful and was a source of envy to some of the guys who complained about being continually woken up by foot traffic on shift change and the lighting problem. It was so attractive that the day we left I hung some old clothes on coat hangers and made up the bed with some old boots underneath so it would be days before our replacements would realise nobody was using them. How childish. How I laughed.

For four weeks, we worked in two 12-hour shifts completing the modifications. The only day off we had was when a sandstorm blew in and we had to take shelter indoors. It was impossible to breathe in the workshop area as a lot of the sand was like talcum powder and would choke the victim.

If breathed in, the victim would get a lung full of silicone dust and be coughing for hours. The workshop had no doors so there was no way of stopping the wind blowing straight through the hanger.

The day Gulf War II started, all the modifications had been completed and we were kicked out of our beds and in an hour were at an airport. 50 bemused ex-workers were now aimlessly sitting around the airport waiting for something to happen. Eventually, we were shipped out of the country on the first available plane.

After flying for an hour, we landed, we were kicked off the plane and told to go and stand in a compound just off the runway apron. After a major investigation involving several local workers who didn't speak English (how dare they), we found out that we were in Qatar. As long as we didn't go into the airport, Qatar didn't have to admit we were in their country. This was so they did not have to admit they were helping the infidel fight fellow Arabs.

All we had to do was sit tight and a plane would be along to take us back home. So, for three days we sat in the compound in 90-degree heat. Every now and then a plane would land and taxi to the front of the compound and drop off any food and soft drinks they had not used during the flight. We were therefore subject to cold aeroplane food for three days. This was not an improvement to the American MREs which are actually quite tasty.

The only entertainment that the lads had available was a rock to kick back and forth between them or come into the tent and listen to me playing the guitar.

Most people chose the rock.

Eventually, a plane did turn up and we all trooped on board and flew back to dear old Blighty none the worse for wear and a few more stories to tell.

Once we were home, I invited my daughter Donna and her husband Shawn around for Sunday dinner and gave them four bags of MREs and a kettle of hot water and said bon appetite. They were amused but not impressed.

Right then back to the main story.

Figure 1: A Collage of photos taken during the Gulf War. Now on my study wall.

Figure 2: OB Officer Commanding C Company Warrior

Figure 3: Self, Daily tidy up of the back of my wagon 24A where I lived and slept for six months with three other crew members.

Figure 4: Graham and I cooking on a Benghazi.

Figure 5: From one extreme to another. Deep snow trials in Finland

Chapter 13
Gulf War I (Continued)

One worry when we moved out to the desert was being stung or bitten by snakes and scorpions. However, most of the scorpions are small and their sting is only like a bad wasp sting. The first person to be stung by a scorpion in our company made a massive fuss about it and someone dived on him and hit him with a shot of morphine which certainly made his day as he was laughing about it for hours. This practice was stopped immediately and only medics were authorised to give morphine until the war started.

Snakes are a very different matter. But if you leave them alone then generally they leave you alone. Of all the people in the combined forces out here, only one person has died from a snake bite, and that was due to him sharing a sleeping bag with it. I was about to say he was just unlucky, but he was careless. Part of daily life was to always check that nothing has crawled into items of clothing, boots or sleeping bags if they have been left around on the floor.

Before we left Germany, I had to give a health and safety talk to the REME guys within our workshop with reference to dangerous insects, spiders and snakes, etcetera. Throughout the whole briefing, one of the soldiers was messing about and continually disrupted the class with his know-all manner. In the end, I had to chew him out and told him that if anybody in this audience were to get bitten it would be him because he was a pillock who would never listen.

Sure enough, move on three months and my mate Craftsman Pillock is on stage in the middle of the night and comes across a Puff Adder on the frosty ground all curled up. He promptly puts it in a Quality Street toffee tin and takes it to his wagon. He forgot about it until the next day when the sun had warmed the tin and the snake was getting a bit hot and feisty. Once he remembered about the snake, he picked up the tin to show it to his mates.

As he cracked the lid off the tin, the snake flew out of the tin and bit him several times on his hand, all in a split second. Needless to say, the snake slithered away to a nearby sand dune and Craftsman Pillock slithered away on a stretcher. After a week in the field hospital, the doctors managed to save his hand.

So, I was correct. He was a pillock.

Most injuries we have been having are sports-related and so we have been told to play nicely and no contact sports. The only problem is that even tiddlywinks can end up being a contact sport when six squaddies are playing.

Generally, someone always gets accused of cheating and as soon as one person dives on top of another for a wrestle, this is an invitation for the rest of the section to pile on top and have an all-in male bonding session. Usually, there is not much blood just a few bruised egos.

Each vehicle or section has its hard man and it's not so hard men. After a period of living in such confinement, the victims of the hard man usually get together and confront the hardman once he is in his sleeping bag and they explain that things are going to change because even he has to sleep eventually. Things then return to an even keel and everything is good with the world again.

Until the next time. Obviously living in such close proximity continually is going to create tension but providing the weather is good, everyone can find a bit of space for themselves. If we were in Europe in the rainy season, things would be very different.

Devil Dog Dragoon Ranges

With a name like Devil Dog Dragoon Ranges, you have probably gathered it was named by the Americans. This was where our final training was to take place before the main push to the north. This area was a lot firmer and the going was better for the Warriors. However, the flattest and fastest ground was called Sabkha.

Sabkha is quicksand with a very hard crust about 120 millimetres thick on top. If a number of vehicles drive over the same bit of land, the first vehicle usually manages the route, but any vehicles following in his tracks where the crust has been broken get about a hundred meters and break through the crust then sink into the goo.

This is when the REME turn up and then spends all day winching the vehicles onto firm land, but only after the sunk vehicle crew has spent a couple of hours digging with spades to free the vehicle. Over the past 25 years, Saudi Arabia's rainfall has been approximately 20 millimetres per year. For the past three days, I have been sitting in the back of the wagon cold and wet as it has not stopped raining for one minute.

The sand in this area is so fine that when wet it takes on a consistency of wet clay. It gets everywhere and sticks like glue and when dry, it is the same consistency of concrete. The worst problem is the weight of the amount of clay that sticks on our boots.

Due to the tactical situation, the Warriors are parked over a large area perhaps two hundred metres away from each other. This is so if there is an air strike or an artillery barrage on our position not everyone will get hit.

As REME we have to carry out daily checks on the vehicles and as there is minimum vehicle movement allowed this means walking to each vehicle with a 20-kilogram toolbox, all our webbing, weapons and five kilograms of clay on each foot. Once one vehicle is sorted then it's off to the next vehicle two hundred meters away.

By the end of the day, groin muscles are screaming out from the constant pulling feet out of the sucking sand, and arms are numb from carrying the toolbox. We can put up with the wind but please stop the rain!

Eventually, the rain stopped and the sand dried out in half a day, so training could resume. All weapons are check fired and now it's time for another battle run. This time with live ammunition. We have waited until nightfall for the full effect. The sky illumination is coming down in front of my vehicle fired from 20 kilometres away, and slowly falling on parachutes. The mock battle has begun.

There were tracer and main armament rounds flying everywhere. It's all very impressive. C Company are going through a trench clearance routine and I am watching them through my thermal imaging sight which allows me to see in pitch darkness over a mile away in black and white with a green tinge, What an amazing bit of kit. As the last shot fades away we all regroup and get debriefed, praised or berated for all the things we did or didn't do that we should have.

The only minor casualties in our battalion were two safety staff and the RSM who got caught a bit close to a fragmentation grenade and were peppered with some small fragments. A few lads were singed by phosphorous when the wind changed and threw the contents of a phosphorous grenade back at them. Another important lesson learnt for the future days to come.

Over the past few weeks, I have noticed a change in people's personalities. Some of the really nasty characters in the Company seem to have mellowed and are actually treating their subordinates decently. Maybe, they realise that in a few days, they could be in a massive firefight where they may be in front of someone with a grudge and a loaded weapon. It has happened before.

I haven't mentioned religion yet. I don't knock anybody's religion. If that's your thing, you can go and pray to whoever or whatever is your God. As time goes on more and more lads seem to be going to Sunday church services. I don't think they have been converted and knowing them as I do, I think maybe they are just hedging their bets believing if the worst happens and there is a heavenly entity, their God will look after them in the afterlife.

I don't go to the church services. I do sit and watch 50 to 70 happy smiling soldiers walk down to the service at 1100 hours on a Sunday morning. And I do sit and watch 50 to 69 depressed morbid souls trudge back up the hill at 1230 hours.

I said 69 because after any meeting there's always one prat who has to stay behind and ask questions.

I don't need any reason to think about anything but the job in hand so I stay on my wagon. There are enough things going on in this place to make a man miserable. Just thinking about what may happen in a few weeks is enough to bring on the blues. I don't need someone spouting doom and gloom and get us thinking about home. I think about home for one hour a day as I write home.

Then it is switch off home, switch on here. Because here is where we are and this is what we have to do. If we do what's right, then we go home. If we get distracted about other things, then we could end up staying here.

A night move involves following 20 armoured tracked vehicles at full speed wherever they want to lead us. Each vehicle throws up an amazing amount of dust and at the rear of the column, we may as well be blindfolded. With all the trenches and tank scrapes around, it can be quite dangerous.

During one night's move, we were rapidly chasing after some speeding Warriors. I had just shouted to Bones my driver to slow down as I could not see anything in front of us but a blanket of dust.

He replied, "It's alright boss I can see perfectly, the ground's nice and flat."

This gave his statement the kiss of death as with a massive crash we flew into an old vehicle scrape. We flew in one end and we flew out of the other end in a second, then came to an immediate stop. On top of the vehicle were all manner of tools, spares, oil cans, fuel jerry cans and rations.

As I was now hanging on top of the commander's hatch after being thrown out from my position I had been bombarded with nuts and bolts and finally half a hundred weight of potatoes.

After shouting at Bones my driver that he was a stupid, gormless, mother@*&%$£, he whimpered an apology to me and the lads in the back of the vehicle, who were very shaken up but uninjured. We all climbed out of the vehicle and set about straightening everything up and securing all the items back on top of the vehicle.

I suddenly heard a rumble in the distance and realised it was getting rapidly louder. I realised that in a minute there would be a squadron of tanks thundering at high speed through the same area, in hot pursuit of the Warriors. They would not even see us parked up until it was too late. I shouted to everyone to get back into the vehicle as we had to get moving.

As we were mounting the vehicle from the front, we realised we had lost the huge metal engine lifting frame that was usually strapped onto the front of the vehicle. There was no time to find it in the pitch-black dusty conditions so with tears in our eyes we set out again trying to find our Company. This was very rapidly turning into a normal night move for us and would fuel our stories for years.

It was two days later when I managed to get hold of a sat nav and retraced our steps of that eventful night. We found a bent twisted knackered engine lifting frame in the bottom of a six-foot-deep vehicle scrape. The whole area was just a mass of tank tracks. The Challengers had driven through the exact same place we would have been, if we had not moved there was no way we would not have been hit.

21 January 1991

Once the live firing exercise was completed, we were flown by a Hercules transport plane to King Khalid military airport as part of the great movement of troops towards the border. Great. No problem. Apart from the fact that our wheeled transport has gone to King Khalid civilian airport one hundred kilometres away.

Whilst waiting for transport, I bumped into John Sweeney an old friend who was on my artificer course. Our wives were good friends back in Fallingbostel and spent a lot of time together organising wives' club meetings and helping out the young mothers who had been left at home for a long period for the first time.

When the men are away from home, the wives that remained in Germany always get together and have social meetings to help each other out and pass the little news they have. More importantly, they give moral support and advice on a hundred other problems that occur.

John and I passed rumours backwards and forwards and told some stories. He told me that one of the stories he had heard was that the Staffordshire regiment was renowned for stealing other people's kit. Of course, I denied that it was stealing and confirmed it was proffing and therefore allowed in the Stafford Regiment's mindset. As I was making my denial plausible a forklift truck parked up nearby with a pallet of rations.

As the forklift operator offloaded and drove away, the Company as one, stood up walked over and helped themselves to the lovely-looking boxes of food. Once they had taken what they needed, someone went to the Hussar regiment next door and told them to help themselves. Which they did. An hour later, a Syrian army major turned up asking where all the rations had gone.

Amazingly, no one knew? He just turned around and looked where the Company were sitting with half an army's worth of empty ration boxes strewn around them. Speechless he stormed away in short, sharp, jerky movements.

Actually, the rations were only dried biscuits, small tins of meat paste and a sweet jammy-type substance. Inside the cellophane biscuit packets, there were little weevil-type insects running around the biscuits within the wrappers but we were starving, so after knocking the insects out all the biscuits were devoured.

Finally, the transport arrived and after a cheerio to John, we were loaded on the back of the trucks. We spent another uncomfortable two hours complaining about how the driver was managing to hit all the bumps on the tracks and stamping on the brake too hard.

At the end of the journey, we were dumped in the middle of the desert with nothing in sight. It was pitch-black with no moon only starlight. We could not make out any features of the area we were in, so we got into our sleeping bags and waited for the vehicles to turn up in the morning. Which miraculously they did.

During the move, one of our workshop corporals who was tasked with moving the vehicles on and off the low loaders was backing a Warrior off a transport wagon trailer in the pitch dark when he accidentally hit one of the transport movement guys killing him. In the investigation, it turned out that the corporal had not had Warrior special driver training.

He was just about to be charged with a serious crime when it turned out that 50% of the drivers in our battalion had not had the training either. It really was not the driver's fault, but the fault of the guy who died.

The transport operator did not understand how much a Warrior rocked up and down on the vehicle suspension when braking whilst negotiating the trailer rear slope and the rear bin had just come down under braking and dinked him on the head, he just wasn't paying attention in this potentially hazardous situation.

He also was not wearing his helmet.

Rather than make an issue of this, a decision was made quite correctly to make sure all drivers and ground operators had more training as soon as possible. The corporal was allowed to carry on his duties as normal. In today's climate, he would have been sent home and undergone therapy and counselling. Back then you just got back in your wagon and got on with it.

We have now moved 350 kilometres in a roundabout route towards our destination, and are now in the northwest area of Saudi Arabia near the Iraqi border. We are the first to be moved to this location and are currently outnumbered by the Iraqi army 50 kilometres away by ten to one, whilst we wait for reinforcements.

On arriving at our allotted plot of land, our first task is to place the Warriors into a defensive arc, and then dig them in. Thankfully three JCB-type diggers arrive from the Royal Engineers and for the next couple of days, they dig sand scrapes for all the Company vehicles. For the next few weeks, we would be living underground with just our turrets or missile systems above the ground and these would be covered with the sand-coloured netting.

In these vehicle holes, our living standards improved as we each had our own areas to look after and we were out of the wind, out of sight from everyone so we could relax our dress standards and take it easy when around the wagon. We still had to be able to move within a 15-minute warning, so all our kit had to be stowed away each time we used it. Nothing permanent can be set up outside the vehicle and the crew has to remain disciplined in running a tidy vehicle.

Luckily, the sergeant major comes around twice a day to check the areas, to stick his nose into my business, moan about everything that isn't important and bollocks anyone in sight for the most trivial of things. I think he is bored because he does not have a drill square he can march people around on.

In peacetime around camp, a sergeant major is responsible for the overall discipline of his company soldiers. As most offences in Germany are the result of excessive drinking, he now finds himself redundant as everyone has been sobered for months. Nobody else can think of things he can do apart from working out the sentry duties which take about an hour each week.

We are in the role of defence battalion and our job is to stop any Iraqi invasion or tactical probe into our area. The Wadi Al-Batine is only a few kilometres away and that is an obvious way in. If the Iraqis wanted to attack Saudi Arabia, this is the most probable direction from which they would come.

The land is so flat and hills are non-existent and the area is strewn with Wadi's which are valleys cut into the sand over thousands of years by the weather. The Wadi Al-Batine is a massive valley 2.5 kilometres wide and hundreds of kilometres long. This is the major geographical feature in our area.

The further north we have come, the firmer the ground becomes and the easier the Warriors move. This cuts down the strain on the engines which in turn cuts down the work we REME have to do to maintain them. Coupled with the lack of vehicle movement, due to the fact we are keeping a low profile, we are actually for the first time finding ourselves to have time on our hands.

The American news channel is broadcasting in this area. The radio is always on. On the hour, everyone huddles around it to listen to the latest developments and any other news that is available from press conferences and other meetings. This was the only way we could find out what was going on in the big picture, as the only brief we get is what was happening in our brigade area.

27 January 1991

Al Kafji was invaded, but after two days of heavy fighting, the Iraqis were repelled by the Americans. The reason Al Kafji was invaded was that the Iraqis did not know where we were and in what strength. So, Saddam sacrificed two brigades to get some intelligence and to capture some prisoners to interrogate them. Unfortunately for them, they were beaten back and no prisoners were taken.

The bombing campaign is going well with reports of hundreds of enemy vehicles being destroyed every day. One tactic is to bomb a square kilometre then drop leaflets on the next kilometre telling the Iraqis to surrender and then bomb the next kilometre. This must be very demoralising for the Iraqi troops as they cannot run away due to the Iraqi execution battalions who are situated behind the Iraqi front-line.

Their sole job is to keep the drafted troops on the front-line and stop them from deserting. During this period, there were many warnings about Scud missile attacks which nobody took seriously, as we were in the middle of nowhere and we believed correctly that they would not waste a missile that size on a target that was small and mobile. During one Scud warning, the alarm came over the radio and everyone got into the vehicles and put respirators on.

After 10 minutes, it was announced on the radio to check our area was clear. Someone came on the radio that it must be because 24B is still lifting an engine pack out of a Warrior. They had been totally unaware of any warning given out. No doubt that will be another bollocking the sergeant major is saving up for me!

When parked in the desert and looking over the flat terrain as the heat shimmers, visions of buildings and vehicles suddenly appear and disappear. These are the fabled mirages shown in films. They are usually related to a man dying of thirst seeing an oasis but the reality is the heat shimmer can bring objects to look a lot closer than they are.

Several times, over this six-month period, I had visions of driving towards a lake or sea, but it was just the heat shimmer reflecting the sky.

It was during this period of sitting around and waiting, that the programme is to set up a production line and get the Warriors up-armoured. This involved mounting large, armoured plates of Chobham armour on the vehicle's sides and nose. We moved with our vehicles about 20 kilometres away from the front-line so it wouldn't matter what noise we made and could work without being constantly on watch for enemy action.

Early one morning whilst we were having breakfast outside the wagon an Australian major suddenly turned up saying, "I need 10 strong blokes to grab some stuff off the Chinni."

A Chinni was a Chinook helicopter. He disappeared as soon as he had appeared and there certainly was not a Chinook anywhere in our vicinity. With this in mind, we all just carried on having our breakfast.

Suddenly, the demented Aussie turned up again screaming, "Chinny, now. Come on. Now."

With this, we stood up and followed him around to the front of the wagons looking for the obvious Chinook.

He looked at our faces and pointed north, shouting, "There. There."

We looked where he was pointing whilst he continued to shout, "There," in the direction of the horizon.

We couldn't see anything and after about five minutes he had to concede there wasn't a Chinny coming anytime soon, so we went back to our cup of tea and cold breakfast. The Australian major buggered off. The illusive Chinny did turn up 15 minutes later and we did help him unload it.

Following this example of an over-excitable officer, every time something needed lifting or things needed doing with some urgency, there were cries of, "I need 10 strong blokes and a Chinni."

It always got us laughing and in a good mood before another shitty task.

The up-armour programme was hard physical work with my fitter section doing all the drilling and tapping that was required on the vehicles. We had one soldier dedicated to running to the machine wagon with a handful of worn-out drill bits and then returning with them all sharpened just in time to take some more back to the machinist. Each armour section was about a meter square and weighed 100 kilogrammes.

Each Warrior had 10 of these sections fitted down the sides and also a 250kilogram nose cone. Prior to mounting these sections on the sides of the vehicle we needed to put on the backing plates and the nose cone chassis. These were even larger and heavier. All this was done in 30-degree heat. And took six or seven 16-hour days.

Needless to say, the lads were worn-out by the time the last vehicle was done. As we did such a good job converting the C company vehicles the commanding officer also asked my section if we would mind awfully helping with the fitting of all B company and battlegroup HQ Warriors. He asked us so nicely, I couldn't refuse.

The armour packs came in massive wooden crates and as we were some distance from the front-line, every night we had a bonfire. This was very relaxing looking into the flames after a hard day's work but also as soon as the sun goes down the temperature in the desert plummets to just above freezing in an hour.

So, it is nice just sitting there eating evening meals staring into the embers.

It is a little-known fact that some of the SAS soldiers who died working behind the enemy lines during this war actually died of exposure due to the cold.

During the up-armour phase, the soldiers used to play a game where they would put a 20-litre oil can with about two to three litres of oil in it on the hot embers of the remaining fire. They would then stand in a circle and join hands. Then it was a case of waiting until the can started to warm up and smoke started emerging from the cans pouring spout. This was a game of chicken.

The first to break the ring lost and was therefore a chicken. To win, the trick was, to wait until the column of smoke and hot spitting oil suddenly stopped gushing out of the spout and started to get sucked back into the can and then run before the can exploded in a mushroom cloud. Oh, what fun. What could possibly go wrong?

Sitting in the back of my wagon with my notebook was the quiet area where I filled in my reports all of which, when not on radio silence were sent in code, which could take hours to translate when a long message was required. I could also work out the possibilities of what may happen in the near future, and what scenarios we may find ourselves in. What scenarios would require shuffling the vehicle crews around?

This reshuffle would probably have to happen in an instant depending on what the scenario was. I therefore had to take a good hard look at my team and the chain of command under me. I had to consider that when the balloon went up, and if I was taken out of the game, who would be in charge of the fitter section.

As I have previously mentioned, my 2i/c sergeant had no Warrior experience and could not control the crew of his vehicle never mind the whole fitter section. Also, he was supposed to be able to give technical knowledge on the vehicle. He had been with the workshop for eight months and had not made any attempt towards learning about the vehicles or to get to know the vehicle crews.

Being the senior rank in charge is a lot more than running around shouting at people, especially when we find ourselves in this position for prolonged periods. Sometimes it was required that a senior rank should show compassion and readily give advice whilst not constantly taking favour with any one individual. All the qualities I look for in a senior rank and that the lads deserve, were sadly missing with this individual.

Allowing him to remain with the fitter section would not benefit anyone in the long term. With all this in mind, I had to move him back to A2 echelon headquarters company away from the front-line.

Enter stage left. The replacement sergeant. He was one of my corporals who I managed to wrangle a field promotion. He is one of the most obnoxious, argumentative and unsociable men I have ever come across. He is also a perfectionist when it comes to the repair of a Warrior vehicle. If the task has not been done 100%, then after a few friendly punches and kicks the victim knows in future to do the job properly and do not take shortcuts.

We had many heated discussions as it was not often that we saw eye to eye, but the state of the vehicles was second to none so he had my vote. There was also the added fact, that the fitter section respected him and so would do as he instructed, and not mess him about as they did with the previous sergeant.

An example of the way he worked can be explained easily. On one occasion, we were expecting an engine pack to be delivered to replace a worn-out engine in one of our Warriors. If we task a Forward Repair Group for a new engine pack, they have to drive to us, fit the new pack and take the old pack away.

On this occasion, the FRG turned up with a brand-new pack but had not covered it up before bringing it here so when they arrived the pack orifices, filters and turbo was full of sand. If we had started it up, the engine would have seized straight away. He rejected the pack and sent them back to get another. Rightly so. When they arrived back several hours later, they broke a part of the hand brake mechanism when lifting the pack into the Company Warrior hull.

The sergeant told them it wasn't a problem as they could swap the bits off their Warrior. After a heated discussion, this is exactly what happened much to the annoyance of the FRG commander. With tears in their eyes, the FRG drove off into the night without a working hand brake.

Several hours later, I heard a lot of shouting and when I went to see what the commotion was there was a warrant officer from FRG shouting his head off at my Sergent, about the way he had treated his crew. My sergeant was stating all the facts correctly and he was very eloquent in explaining how terrible the FRG crew had been and how they should have been trained correctly on how to do their jobs, He stopped short of saying it was this warrant officer's job to do this.

When the Sergeant saw me strolling across the desert towards them out of the darkness, he just said to the warrant officer, "Well, anyway nice to meet you. Here's the Tiffy," meaning me. (Tiffy short for artificer.)

He did a sharp about-turn and then marched into the desert away from the vehicles and carried on marching for several hundred meters until the dark desert night swallowed him up. I didn't tell the warrant officer there were no vehicles in the direction the sergeant had marched. The warrant officer then started venting his anger at me whilst looking me up and down taking in my comfy jogging trousers, Barber jacket and furry hat.

I lit a cigarette looked at the sky and said in my best George Formby voice, "It's nice here, init?"

He then said, "Give us a fag."

Which I did and we both then sat down in the sand looking up at the sky, just soaking in the vastness of it all. After a while, he stood up walked to his Land Rover and drove away never to be seen again. I looked over my shoulder and shouted into the black wilderness.

"You can come back now," I said to the sergeant and then I went back to bed.

After that, we received a brilliant service from FRG and I won't have a thing said against them.

This move of the sergeant back to the main workshop, now meant that Graham, my corporal, now moved from my wagon to command 24C and I received another corporal from the main workshop to replace Graham.

Mail Drops

One day the mail arrived and as I was sorting it out, I handed one addressed to Ship my armourer, As I did this, I noticed that the return address on the back of the letter was that of my daughter. After doing a double take on the address, I accosted him with this fact and finally dragged it out of him that he wrote to her for a laugh after finding her address on the back of one of my letters in the vehicle.

Of course, the rest of the lads found this hilarious at my expense especially when Ship said, "Calm down, Dad."

This, I quickly rectified by explaining to him in the nicest possible way that if he called me Dad again, I would do something to him that would drastically reduce the chance of anyone calling him Dad in the future.

The mail response we received as we were about to go to war was brilliant. I received good luck cards and letters from everyone including whole classes of kids belonging to friends from my dark distant past and even some from people who did not even know me. Donna my daughter and her friends wrote often to both Ship and Bones as well as myself. Bones and Ship now addressed themselves as a collective known as the Mattress Floopers.

Whatever they were. Whenever a letter came with this name on, we knew it was for either of them. We sent a response to Donna's headmaster thanking the whole school for writing to us. I found out in later correspondence that he read them out much to her embarrassment in morning assembly.

I cannot explain the feeling I felt stuck in the middle of enemy territory and receiving a card from 30 or 40 children who I have never met who tell you they are praying every night for me. It gives a person the feeling that we are doing the right thing and eases the load on heavy shoulders.

All the single lads have pen friends, some have dozens and are already planning that during their leave on their return to Blighty, after this little sortie, they will be visiting them all. Lock up your daughters the boys are on the way. Mind you looking at some of the photos we should be telling the daughters to lock up their mothers as well.

Another good thing about the mail drops was guessing which way the booze would be smuggled in next. As I mentioned previously pots of honey were exchanged for pots of whiskey. Anything that was alcoholic and was reasonably the same colour as liquor was substituted. White vinegar bottle for Vodka, Brown vinegar bottle was brandy.

Some even smuggled drinks in via shampoo bottles or aftershave bottles. Ursula's favourite was a screw-top mustard bottle. A winner every time. No, it wasn't an advocate. It was not a see-through bottle.

The food was, to say the least monotonous. We were issued 10-man ration packs and there were various menus to make it varied but as it was all tinned food and very plain, mealtimes were very boring. There were some old favourites like compo sausages, steak and kidney pudding, chicken supreme and curry. All the lads had eaten this stuff for years previously on exercise and for a short period it was okay, but day in and day out for months was the pits.

We added tabasco sauce and a hundred other flavourings but it was still not good, old, home-cooked food. Particularly, if the cook of the day had not been careful and got sand into it. One of my recovery mechanics was a South African who was a very large muscular chap. One day he took Umbridge with a can of corned beef that he could not open and promptly launched it into space.

I have never seen anything thrown that far. He then went off for half a mile and sat down until he had his head together again. Sometimes, it's the smallest thing that triggers a massive reaction.

We had as much water, tea and coffee as we needed but also small fruit drinks in cardboard cartons. These were 50% sugar and I am surprised anyone had any teeth left after six months of drinking six or more of these a day.

Whilst in Camp 4 the lads had visited some ex-patriates and come back with 48 Barbican non-alcoholic beers, some yeast and sugar and a recipe for home brew beer. With recipe in hand and a few clean water jerry cans, they set to work brewing some beer that they let settle for as long as possible before attempting to drink it.

In this case, about a day. It tasted disgusting but it did get the lads pissed and even though they all felt terrible the next day they said it was well worth it.

However, I noticed they never attempted to make another batch.

We tried to set up various charity donations whilst we were here. All were for us to benefit from. We started off by writing to any celebrity we could think of asking for beef-flavoured crisps. Some people did reply and although we didn't get many crisps, we did get a lot of mail back wishing us the best. One newscaster and TV personality actually went out of her way to say she would not be sending us any crisps as she did not agree with the war.

"What's that got to do with anything? Miserable cow."

One successful charity appeal was Operation Comfybum. This was set up by Dave Shea's parents. He was a mechanic in the main Stafford's REME workshop. Within days of them making this appeal public on northern radio, we were inundated with hundreds of rolls of soft toilet paper. We probably received enough toilet paper to supply the whole battalion. What a great gesture and I cannot tell you how much it was appreciated in the practical sense.

01 February 1991

Obviously, something is going to happen soon as tonnes of spares for the vehicles have arrived. We have been screaming for these for months and they have just turned up. Some are not new parts which means they are stripping the vehicles left behind in the UK and BAOR to get us the bits. Not only have I received all the spares I requested but also loads more due to re-demanding them as they had not turned up previously.

More live firing ranges have been set up and our weapon systems are checked and re-checked as the gunners have to perfect their skills. Even the REME vehicles get a chance to have a blast down the range with our weapons. We are carrying thousands of rounds of ammunition, grenades and anti-tank rockets.

God help us if we end up in a position where we have to use the rockets, as they are only accurate up to 75 metres. If I get within 75 meters of the enemy, then I joined the wrong gang. I won't even mention the grenades which I can throw about 20 meters.

03 February 1991

G day has still to be announced and the lads are getting fidgety, but as long as the Air Force was doing the brilliant job that they were doing, we will sit still. One pastime is lying on our backs watching the tanker planes circling directly above us. All the fighter planes catch them up to refuel and then they shoot off to the front-line again.

We can hear the rumble of the bombs exploding and then they reappear for another top-up from the fuel plane. Our day-to-day life would be so much different if we did not have air superiority, and had to look out for air strikes on our position.

Every day, we get updates on how many tanks, armoured personnel carriers and artillery pieces have been destroyed. Apparently, to be a confirmed kill it needs three witnesses. I think the last count before we went through the breach was:

Tank 1685
APC 960
Artillery 1300

We don't know whether it's true or just a propaganda exercise to boost morale.

04 February 1991

Due to the up armouring of the vehicles and the extending of the nose cone armour, we cannot use the front towing eyes for recovery purposes so we had to start conducting trials to use the rear towing eyes for recovery and towing. As normal everyone and his dog wants a written report on our progress and wants it yesterday if not sooner.

I am sure that there must be a hundred people with bugger all to do but think of things for someone else to do. And they are all in Slipper City with their tea and toast.

We have just heard that when G Day comes, the 7th Armoured Brigade the Desert Rats (us), will be the first through the breach and punch a hole deep into enemy territory, with the Americans securing the breach to ensure the supply lines are kept open. We are holding at G-3 and holding which means that we are on a minimum of three days' notice before the war starts.

But this minimum of 3 days could last for weeks. We are holding on full alert 25 kilometres from the front-line. The daily routine is getting very monotonous. All the vehicles are 100% fit, so there is nowhere to go and nothing for us to do part from get bitchy with each other.

We have practised moving to the breech twice and I am still impressed with the amount of equipment there is considering we are only brigade strength and we have not even seen the vast American might yet. All the special equipment and weapons we have been promised over the last few months have arrived.

The vehicle crews are trying it out so they will be proficient with it when the time comes. A lot of the equipment received are prototypes and have never been used in anger before. I wonder if they trialled them after they had been covered in sand for 24 hours a day?

Bones and Ship have been going through a hardest man in the world competition. This is carried out in a very non-violent way, as only Bones and Ship could. First, they stopped sleeping on top of the wagon that had been warmed by either running the engine or from the sun to sleeping on the ground.

This brought on comments like, "I slept in a draft all night it was the best freezing sleepless night I've ever had. I loved every minute."

Bones would reply, "You, Nancy boy. You slept on a roll matt, I didn't."

Every trapped finger or hit thumb brought cries of, "Ow! Ow! That was brilliant."

Usually, through gritted teeth. Even on morning stand-tos when we had to go outside and lay on the frosty sand, they would get into the trenches with minimum clothing on to stay within regulations. At 0530 hours, the temperature is usually around freezing. They would look at each other saying what a lovely day it is. As soon as stand to was over, they would dash back to the wagon almost blue, telling each other how much they were sweating because the wagon was far too hot.

These escapades would last through the periods when the food was accidentally burnt and they would be fighting over the cremated bits stuck in the bottom of the boiling vessel. At one point, I caught Bones digging a trench to his shell scrap. When asked why?

He said pointing to a cloudless sky, "It may rain and then I can have a lovely wet place to sleep."

This went on for a month until they both mutually agreed they were both the hardest man in the world. However, after this day they both continued to sleep on the ground outside the wagon. Just to convince themselves.

20 February 1991

We still do not know where the breach in the border will be, although we suspect it will be about 50 kilometres west of the tri-border of Saudi, Kuwait and Iraq. This will put us smack into the middle of the Republican guard force stronghold. This is for two reasons.

1. If we take out the Republican guard, the conscripted army will see we mean business and will surrender or run away.

2. The Republican guard force is the only thing stopping the Iraqi army from deserting back into Iraq. Although the Republican Guard is the Iraqi elite (the same as Hitler's SS in the Second World War), we do not believe that their professionalism or equipment is a match for us. However, we will be outnumbered three to one which means to break even we have to be three times better than them to win four times better.

The whole border has massive sand banks built up 50 feet high and one hundred kilometres long. The enemy has built a sand bank one behind the other, two or three times. In front of, and between the lines of sandbanks, aerial photos show minefields and a line of turreted guns pointing towards Saudi Arabia.

The breach that I continually mentioned is a route that will be cut through these defences about one hundred metres wide to allow a mass of armoured vehicles to pass through all at once.

So far, we have been deploying a deception plan. And this seems to be working. For the last six weeks, we have been on radio silence. Meanwhile recorded radio broadcasts of old exercises have been transmitted all the time 150 kilometres east of our position. So convincing is this that five divisions of the Iraqi forces have left a position directly in front of us and moved to this area.

Leaving our breach point with very low protection.

We have also been restricted to minimum movement and have been living in a vehicle scrape for two weeks.

We had an intelligence brief today.

So far there is only 7th Armoured Brigade in this area. Half the size of an Iraqi division. 60 kilometres north of us are:

1. Armoured Divisions
2. Mechanised Division 12 Armoured Brigades.

We are hoping to get some reinforcements here soon because if they find out we are here they may pop over the border and start picking on us. I spoke to the OC and asked him if he would mind awfully if he would wait for these reinforcements before we attacked them. Hopefully, they will all go home for teatime.

We only move at night with no lights. Radio silence at all times, no fires. Nobody moves during the day due to the dust we would create. We don't make any loud noises including shouting in case they have reconnaissance parties out trying to find us. Can you imagine hiding two tank regiments and a battalion of Warriors in terrain with no hills? We just keep on digging deeper with just the turrets popping over the surface covered in sand-coloured netting.

Reinforcements will be arriving soon so we will not be on our own and we can move around the local area to carry out essential maintenance. Every vehicle has to have someone in the turret or cupola 24 hours a day, so we are ready if there is an attack. When night falls, the Warriors have night vision so can see up to two thousand meters away.

One night, the alarm was raised because one gunner in a turret could see 20 or 30 enemies walking across the sand towards our position. All guns were trained on the green images through the sights. The enemy was walking slowly and silently towards us through the night. We were still on radio silence so we had runners passing messages between the vehicles. Everything was silent and everyone was poised for a huge fire fight.

Just before we received the order to open fire someone shouted out breaking the tension, "Camels. They are bleeding camels."

Everyone took the mickey out of the callsign that called us into action but at least he was aware there was something coming towards us and at a distance, a camel walking straight on towards a position does look like a man walking towards you.

21 February 1991

Today we had the penultimate O group. As normal the OC John Rochelle was as calm and mellow as normal. Out of all the OCs I have served with, he was among the best. He was quite content leaving me alone to get on with my job and manage my fitter section as I saw fit. This management technique sometimes clashed with the Company's sergeant major's ideas of how to run discipline within the group.

What the CSM did not understand was his company lads were bored if they were not doing something and so it was the CSM's job to give them something to do even if they were pointless exercises. Keeping them busy would keep them from getting into mischief.

My guys were on call 24 hours a day if it was required and could be called out all through the night, so when we were not working during the day it was a time to catch up on sleep and general personnel administration. Unfortunately, it was the CSM's opinion that we were just taking it easy all the time, as after 1800 hours he never came out of his wagon and never actually saw what unsociable or long hours we worked.

Apart from when he came out of his wagon moaning how much noise we were making at 0200 hours in the morning when we were lifting an engine pack trying to fix it for 0700 hours manoeuvres the next morning.

22 February 1991

The conditions for the Iraq surrender are not acceptable so we are now at G2 but we don't know whether this is holding or if the countdown has started. This morning, we heard on the shortwave radio that the ground war had started and the British forces of the 7th Armoured Brigade had punched a hole deep into Iraq.

We all ran from inside the vehicle and looked around to check that we were still where we parked up last night. We were, so we went and had a cup of tea to get over the shock.

Chapter 14
Let's Get This Show on the Road

G day—24 February 1991

Well, it's started. We have moved to the first staging area where we have now joined up with the two Challenger tank regiments, Scots Dragoon Guards and Queens Royals Irish Hussars. These are our close protection units when we hit the trenches. They will also be hitting every enemy tank that they come across within a four-kilometre zone.

We have been warned that when taking prisoners of war to check they have not booby-trapped themselves as there may be fanatics among the regular army. I cannot imagine many of them doing that so it was probably a rumour spread to make sure prisoner search procedures are carried out correctly.

Everything has been brought forward 18 hours and we are moving off. We are now in a holding area 10 kilometres south of the breach into Iraq. The breach is approximately 50 kilometres from Kuwait and the tri-border area of Saudi, Kuwait and Iraq. We may go in 10 minutes. We are now on an immediate warning order to move.

The day before we set off for the breach, I sat down and thought of everything I had never said to Ursula and should have. It was only after several attempts that the final script was sealed up and sent to my brother John to be given to Ursula in the event of my death. It was the most morbid thing I have ever done. I have never done this before when going on operational tours of Northern Ireland. It just seemed to be the right thing to do.

I found myself thinking that tomorrow was the big move and I could actually end up getting myself killed. All the coming events were suddenly very real. Up to this point, it was just like being on an exercise in a hot country. Thousands of soldiers all across the front-line were doing exactly the same thing.

With that duty done and with the letters all handed into the colour sergeant, it was time to get our heads back in the correct mindset and not to be distracted with thoughts of home.

Our advantage in a ground war is that the Challenger tank can engage the enemy tanks accurately on the move using its stabilised gun. It can outshoot everything the Iraq army has. Their tanks have a range of two thousand meters and have to stop to fire.

They also do not have thermal imaging which allows our Challenger to shoot and hit on a pitch-black night or through smoke during the day if it can see a heat source it can hit it at four thousand meters. I keep telling myself this to give me confidence.

We also have massive air support if we really get stuck as the A10 Warthogs and the Apache helicopters have already flown overhead and are giving close support in a tactic we call grouse beating. This is to fly around and see if they can flush anything out of cover or cause someone to open fire at them. As soon as they see movement, they let fly the missiles or chain guns. The 30-millimetre chain gun mounted on an A10 Warthog weighs more than a car.

We have been told to mount up on the vehicles as we are moving in 10 minutes. The last few cups of tea were finished and everything was stowed away in its correct place. Drivers and Commanders have mounted their vehicles and our weapons are made ready. Grenades are primed and the anti-tank weapons are close at hand.

All the Warrior crews are throwing the last of their kit into the back of the vehicles. Everyone is running around making sure everyone's personal kit is secure and checking each other out so that nothing has been forgotten. All water bottles are full and first aid kits were secured on webbing. It was during this activity that a rifle shot rang out.

An unfortunate incident has just occurred just outside the vehicle in front of ours. Shawn (Nobby) Taylor one of the Warrior drivers has just been shot by accident. All his section from around the vehicle ran to help him and the ambulance was parked only a few metres away, So the medics were straight on the scene.

He was stable for a while and my crew had the grandstand view from the top of our vehicle watching the medics trying to save him by stopping the bleeding and giving him mouth-to-mouth resuscitation for what seemed like ages. The medivac helicopter took 50 minutes to arrive as they had been tasked to cover the battle at the breach. Sgt Robbo the medic was giving CPR for the whole 50 minutes. Not a very good omen for the next few days.

We heard three days later that Nobby died in the helicopter.

Although we have been waiting again for hours, everybody finds they have something they have forgotten to do. Everybody needs another pee. Yet again we are told that there has been a delay. The breach is secure but we are waiting for aerial recognisance.

They will let us know what resistance we can expect when we finally get into Iraq. More cups of tea are handed out. We stay in our positions as we are on immediate notice to move. A message is passed along the lines of vehicles to make our weapons safe as we do not want another accident.

1230 hours, evening, 25 February 1991

The order to move has just been given and we are off again. Welcome to Iraq courtesy of The Big Red One read the sign by the entrance of the channel in the breach. It had been erected by the 1st American Marine Division. So, this is what Iraq looks like. More bloody sand.

The Americans have secured the breach point and now it's our task to go out on a limb and punch a hole through the Iraqi defences. We have been told to go as far and as fast as possible to hit the objectives with maximum violence and then move on to the next objective. Do not worry about prisoners of war as they will be collected by the main body following us.

We have entered the breach area and apart from a few fortifications and a few trench systems and minefields, it's a romp in the park. Burning vehicles are scattered around with several groups of prisoners of war sitting around in groups under white flags. A lot of the mines shown in the aerial photographs are just hundreds of old car tyres strewn about to look like mines.

The line of armoured turreted guns we were told about are huge steel boxes with four-inch-wide pipes stuck in them. I wonder how many millions of pounds/dollars have been spent by having the Air Force destroy these decoys? Each one is peppered with hundreds of shell holes or lying on its side, the result of a bomb strike. We now know that we are part of the war, but we expected more of a fight.

The drive is at a fast and furious pace, then we stop whilst the Challengers clear the next five kilometres. Everything has gone as practised, which seems strange as no one believed it was going to be so easy. I think everyone believed the intelligence reports were toned down to help our morale and to give us confidence but this is ridiculous. Our main problem is to keep vigilant as a firefight may break out at any moment. Be alert. Your country needs lerts.

Two lines of vehicles move through no man's land. The wheeled vehicles on the right have stopped as they have noticed a firefight going on ahead. We break up from running in a single line and form a Company attack formation and move forward onto our first objective, Objective Copper. It is not expected to be a hard task as the enemy is only supposed to be battalion strength.

When we arrive at the objective, we can see that the Challengers have taken out anything that moves and have moved on to secure the next objective. Zink. At first, there is no sign of life but then slowly one by one Iraqis stand up with white flags and slowly make their way towards us. We just move past them and carry on as there is no time to stop as there are agencies behind us to collect and help prisoners of war.

All these objectives are just areas we have drawn on a map. They are not towns or villages and are spaced a few miles apart. Generally, they are just known concentrations of enemy forces and trench systems.

As we drive towards Objective Zink our tracks make cracking noises as we drive over vast amounts of anti-personnel mines. These do not harm a vehicle apart from damaging the rubber track pads. The lead vehicles shout out when they see anti-tank mines and we stay in the tracks of a vehicle in front of us.

Although we have put sandbags under the vehicle floor plates. The amount of ammunition we were carrying would be curtains for us as these mines are designed to take out main battle tanks twice the weight of a Warrior.

Meanwhile, Call Sign 11 had driven into a tank ditch 20 feet deep, cracking several of the driver's ribs and bashing his head. Luckily, there was not any significant local enemy fire so 24C was able to recover the vehicle relatively quickly and, with a replacement driver thrown into the driver's seat. The Warrior was recovered back in position and was able to carry on with his task with the crew shaken, but not stirred.

The last page and half covered the first day of the war, and although we saw very little aggressive enemy action, the vehicles were constantly stopping and starting and confirming each area was clear before moving forward a few hundred metres and doing it all again.

The troops in the rear of the Warriors were constantly debussing and then mounting up again and every time they did this they did not know if they would be entering a firestorm so it was all very stressful and energy draining. All troops are wearing full body protection and helmets and carrying their personal weapon and a full load of ammunition in their webbing which now weighs about 25 kilograms.

Normally when we stop, we fan out to give all-round protection defensive position and then walk to the OCs vehicle for an O group. As we now have a problem with thousands of anti-tank and anti-personnel mines strewn across the ground, we park nose-to-tail in a long line of vehicles.

This means that now, as I am at the rear of the Company column I now have to climb in full kit and weapon over the roofs of 16 Warriors to reach OB for an O group as nobody is allowed on the ground. By the time, I get to the O group with the 25 kilograms of equipment, ammunition and weapon I have to carry, I am covered in sweat and breathing heavily, much to the amusement of the other platoon commanders.

This was followed by many derogatory comments intended to wind me up. Forming up the vehicles in this formation would be a different story if the Iraqis had decent artillery or their Air Force still existed. If this was the case, we would be forming up two hundred meters apart again.

Even in the safe areas, anti-personnel mines turned up days after the war was over. At one stop, I jumped off my vehicle only to find some hidden mine spikes sticking up between my feet. Quite a chilling moment and I broke a record by climbing back on my vehicle and warning all call signs in this area of the threat.

There were also thousands of cluster bombs we had to be aware of. These mines were designed to explode when sensing a nearby vehicle by the ground vibrations they produced. Luckily, these didn't react. However, what will be will be. There is no other way of looking at it. If we started worrying about mine at this stage, what would we be like when the fireworks really started?

Maybe, I should have said a prayer or two. NATO forces mines are designed to become inert for a set period of time after deploying. This is to avoid maiming innocent civilians after the wars are over and the mines are not required.

26 February 1991

Objective Zink

This is the main objective for today. It all looks easy on paper but man per man we are outnumbered three to one against so we have to make sure we get it right. I am not sure if we have been lulled into a false sense of security or if the confidence in the vehicle commanders is growing.

The radio traffic has calmed down to the level that there is no anxiousness in the voices and it is quite calming that everyone on the radio sounds quite confident in the job they have to do. This is where the hours and hours of training paid off, as everyone is acting out of instinct as we have all been through these scenarios many times before.

0100 hours

We have been told that we do not have any satellite coverage and the next attack will require all call signs to know exactly the location of friendly fire platforms so there are no blue-on-blue accidents. We will attack at first light so the company moves the vehicles into an all-round protection formation. This was my opportunity for me to take a much-needed nap. I fell asleep in seconds.

0200 hours

With loud crashes and bangs, a firework display I will never forget begins; the Multi-Launch Rocket Systems (MLRS) have opened up from 10 kilometres away. The missiles are landing eight hundred meters away but it seems a lot closer. The noise is horrendous. Each MLRS has 12 rockets and we are watching them launch far away on the horizon and following their flight until it seems they will land on top of us.

The canisters are opening directly above us and throwing their munitions forward. There are six batteries firing. Five are firing normal warheads and one is firing bomblets. A smart bomblet is a missile programmed to destroy things located within four hundred square meters of ground. The canister explodes at about a thousand feet and then scatters 280 small bomblets over the area.

Each bomblet carries two thousand bits of shrapnel. As the bomblets explode the noise is terrific. It's like material ripping magnified a thousand times. Each smart bomb takes out a different square area so in the end a three-kilometre by one-kilometre strip has been totally destroyed. The crews have come out of the vehicles to watch this spectacular display. Whilst all this was going on, I could tell by the look on my section's faces that we all thought the same.

They may be the enemy, but this was not going to be a very fair war. Only one day into the conflict and I was feeling sorry for the people that were probably going to try and kill me.

0330 hours

Cautiously edging forward into the smoke, we have been assured by the Challenger squadron that no vehicle inside the kill area is mobile. As we approach the separate objectives, we can see a row of Challengers on the brow of a hill. Over the brow of the hill is a valley littered with burning tanks, armoured personnel carriers and trucks. Already Iraqi prisoners are being escorted away from the firefight.

Our Milan missile crews are called up and start engaging enemy tanks and trucks. In normal peacetime training, an infantryman in the Milan platoon may only fire one missile a year. This usually misses the target due to the operator being so nervous.

Today, the operators have had so much practice and so many missiles to fire over the last month that every missile launch is a first-time hit. Hugging the ground contours all the way to the target to avoid being shot down by enemy fire, the missiles strike the enemy targets again and again.

The company's Warriors have been slowly approaching the brow in battle formation, and now at the given command the pace suddenly increases and then at full speed we drive over the rim and hurtle down the valley side, passing the burning vehicles and leaving them behind whilst we concentrate on the bunker and trench system at the far edge of the valley. The Iraqis who had not surrendered did so after a volley of shots from the Warrior chain guns.

14 Warrior firing six hundred rounds a minute was quite impressive and our main armament the 30-millimetre Raden cannon had not been used yet. The reason for these brief but furious firefights is that the Iraqis were spread so thin

over the whole of the Kuwait border, due to their intelligence being so limited, not knowing where we would be attacking them from.

10 Iraqi divisions had been located guarding the coast in case of a waterborne assault that never happened. This in effect relates to 150 thousand troops that cannot be used in the immediate future. The defensive positions are so thin that once breached they have no depth for defensive covering fire whilst they reorganise themselves.

This is due partly to the Air Force destroying a great number of enemy tanks, artillery and defence positions, leaving the infantry to stand and fight with no armoured protection or transport to retreat. Some of the tanks had been dug into a defensive hole for months and the engines were dead and only the turrets worked by being hand cranked.

They were destroyed by the Challengers from three thousand meters away before they even realised the Challengers were in the vicinity.

All Iraqi rear echelon ammunition stores, fuel dumps and radio stations had been destroyed, so the ground troops were left on their own with very little options for a brighter future. However, after seeing the destruction left by MLRS, where would they run to when everything as far as the eye can see is exploding? They just had to dig deeper protective holes and bunkers, but the bomblets bounce around and find all the hidden places.

By the time the dust cleared, the Challengers had arrived firing at their tanks and the Warriors were in front of them driving at them at 50 miles per hour then halting one hundred meters away waiting for them to make a move. The first reaction from the trenches was to empty their weapons at us but once we returned fire, they realised they had no effect on us at all and all they could do was surrender.

0700 hours

The Challengers and Warriors have set up a defensive position in case any Iraqi forces try and retake the ground for which we have just fought for. At this point, my vehicle had collected 13 Iraqi prisoners of war in the lull of the battle. I had searched them all for weapons and loaded them on the roof of my vehicle.

I had been tasked to move these prisoners rearwards and we were heading to the prisoners of war holding pens a few miles to the rear of the battlefront to drop them off. The system was overrun with so many prisoners of war that the planned collection parties were swamped with the number of prisoners. It was not just a case of collecting them in compounds, as many of them were injured and needed medical assistance.

We had driven about two kilometres when my vehicle engine spluttered and died. This was me at my diplomatic best. With a look over my shoulder and in my best sign language, I nodded at the engine and then drew my figure slowly across my throat to explain the engine was Kaput. I then pointed to the ground to get the prisoners to dismount the vehicle. When I looked back, I saw the look of defeat and dejection had turned to a look of complete horror on their faces.

Yes, the Flower book of tact and diplomacy was at work again and it took me a couple of minutes to explain that I was not going to execute them.

It was only when some other vehicles turned up to cross-load them that their cries of, "No, Sir," turned into cries of, "thank you, Sir" and "God bless you, Sir."

As they left, I gave them a packet of cigarettes and some water. Quite a few were in tears, I don't know if was the knowledge that for them the war was over, or the relief of getting away from a lunatic who didn't know whether to execute them or give them water and cigarettes.

During the fight for Objective Zink one of our callsigns (23) dismounted and as the guy was clearing trenches, they ran straight into a booby trap system. These are designed to make it easy to get into the trench, but once in, everything you touch can explode with the munitions they had wired into the trench tripwire system.

After pondering just how much shit the corporal section leader had got himself into and how deep it was, he pulled out a trusty pair of pliers and cut a new exit through some barbed wire and extracted his team. Nobody knows why the system never blew up around them. He has a good laugh when telling the story, as do the lads who were with him.

Everyone exaggerates the story to be better and more exciting. But I heard their stressed voices on the radio when it happened and know what they will be thinking in the months and years to come when the crowds are not around them and they realise how lucky they were.

All this time, I was clicking away on my camera. Ursula had sent me this through the post. I had noticed that she had also sent a spare film with it which I tucked in my pocket. The film state on the camera displayed a film of 24 exposures already loaded and so I did not get any sand in it I immediately wrapped it in a plastic bag. When the opportunity arose and it was safe to do so, I frequently took photographs as we progressed over the battleground.

Once the film indicator displayed empty, I handed the camera into the back of the wagon along with the spare film, shouting above the noise of the vehicle for someone to change the film for the new one. Almost immediately, there was a response over the internal radio that there was no film in the camera.

I responded with a response, "Don't be so stupid. Of course there was a bloody film in it."

"Oh no, there's not," came the response as though in a pantomime.

"Oh yes, there bloody well is," I shouted with doubt now in my voice.

To cut a long story short. There was no bloody film in the camera and so almost every photo in this book up to this point, I have had to beg borrow or steal.

To rub it in even worse, for the next few weeks, everywhere I turned there was a Kilroy character drawn in the dust on every surface asking, "What! No film in the camera boss!"

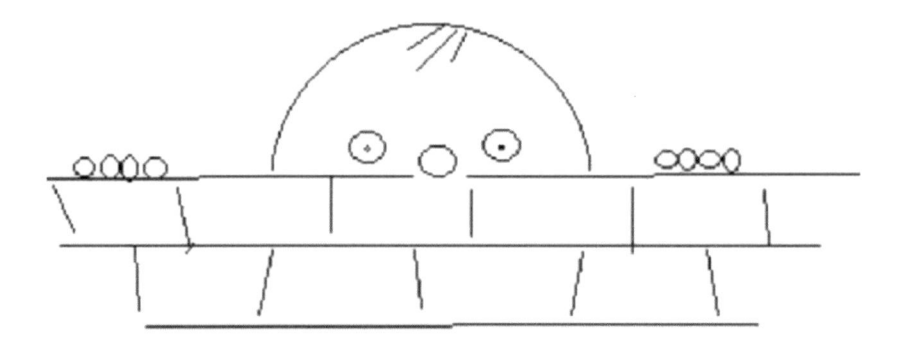

Figure 6: What! No film in the camera boss!

As normal, when everything is happening at once, time flies by so quickly. My REME crews had been dashing about fixing vehicles with failed accelerators and jamming weapons as well as dragging more Warriors out of ditches.

All of the time the bullets were flying around and much to my surprise nobody was injured. We did not have any major problems that could not be fixed quickly. In fact, everything had gone smoothly considering the circumstances.

Everyone was on an adrenaline rush and the morale was very high.

We could see in the distance that parallel to our company, about 10 kilometres away, four Armoured brigades were progressing through their objectives at the same pace as that we were.

1400 hours

Objective Zink was secure and we were now moving 30 kilometres to a reorganisation area, however, there were still small pockets of the enemy around which we had to check and clear of weapons, before sending them rearwards marching under a white flag.

Any group of 5 or more we disarm and make them form a line and tell them to walk back the way we came under the protection of a white flag. Any smaller groups we just drive past and providing they were not hostile we left them to be collected by the main ground force behind us.

Line after line of prisoners of war line the route we had taken from Saudi Arabia. Objective Platinum has been secured with very little resistance and no casualties from our side. We are now moving towards Objective Lead which hopefully is our last objective in this phase of the war.

1800 hours

The last area is cleared and there are burning tanks and armoured personnel carriers, abandoned vehicles and military equipment strewn everywhere. The Iraqis are on the run to the North and West to the safety of central Iraq. Is that going to be our next objective?

At this point, I should mention that throughout my career in the REME, we normally stay two tactical bounds behind the front fighting line which is usually one to five kilometres away from the fighting, depending on the terrain. This has been the normal way things panned out for a battlefront in Europe since the Second World War. These tactics are fine when only expecting to advance 10 kilometres a day.

Moving as fast as we have been the last few days, we have been moving within the Company formation due to the possibility of the Iraqis moving across our rear, and cutting us off from the main brigade battlegroup, which is now some eight hours behind us. As it is, we are all moving as a spearhead of Challenger tanks and Warriors forcing our way through the enemy lines.

If we lagged behind as we had been previously trained to do, we would be subject to possible enemy stragglers looping behind our main fighting force and attacking the lesser-armed rear party.

2200 hours

We have now travelled two hundred kilometres in two days. It's been quite hectic considering the pauses for recognisance and the fighting through objectives. There is now only about five kilometres to the rest area.

Throughout this mad dash, only two Warriors have broken down and these were repaired within an hour, the lads must know that this is due to the long hours and hard work they have put in over the last few months ensuring the vehicles were so well maintained. The term rest area only applies to the crew of the vehicles and the ground troops.

For the REME, it does not mean sleep, it means time to check over the vehicles and armaments, fixing all the little problems before they turn into big ones. Three days without sleep and my mind is getting a bit fuzzy. Much more of this without proper rest and decisions will be wrong and someone could get hurt.

I have made the OC aware of this before, but needs must be. As we are at the three-day point now, I am finding it hard to concentrate between objectives. Once on an objective the adrenaline kicks in but that leaves you more drained afterwards. Let's just hope, we can park up for more than a couple of hours.

2230 hours

In the dead of night, we move through the desert. Although there is moonlight to see the silhouettes of objects we are passing. Burnt-out tanks, vehicles and scorched trench systems now abandoned and litter the area. Fires still lick around the vehicles as the spilt fuel and oil has soaked into the sand that is now acting as a wick. These small fires will burn for hours.

My visibility is only about 50 metres and that is obscured by the dust of the 20 vehicles driving in front of me. Generally, the route we are taking is virgin ground that no tracked vehicles have driven on in the previous weeks, so I am able to follow the fresh track marks that the vehicles in front of me have recently left.

This does tend to concentrate the mind to focus just on this small section of land directly in front of me and leaves me oblivious to what could be happening around me in the surrounding areas.

Out of the blackness tracer round fire streaks towards our vehicles. 7 platoon have come under attack from some buildings about eight hundred metres in front of me. We had already moved into battle formation so were fully prepared. All around the two houses are trench systems and all call signs are under attack from small arms fire. The OC gives his orders and as practised so many times over the last few months, the attack starts.

Each Warrior takes a section of trench 50 metres wide and lays down two hundred rounds of chain gun fire followed by a couple of rounds of main armament and then stop.

The silence is deafening. Reports are now coming in; white flags are reported in several areas but incoming enemy fire is starting up again in many other locations. We open fire again and then silence. More white flags and soldiers start climbing out of the trench systems. Ten, twenty, thirty, fifty, one hundred, two hundred, three hundred?

The mortar vehicles have deployed but instead of obliterating the area with high explosive mortar bombs they have covered the new objective with illumination rounds and the night has turned to day in seconds with flares slowly coming down on parachutes and just before one flare hits the ground another flare illuminates a couple of hundred feet above the target area.

We have stumbled onto two infantry battalions. Prisoners of the war are still flooding in. The troops have dismounted and are clearing the trench systems and dealing with the prisoners of the war.

Suddenly grenades are thrown out of a building's window and our troops hit the ground as the grenades explode but nobody is hurt. One call sign is riding protection in a Warrior just in case enemy tanks come into the area. It is loaded with armoured piercing rounds in the Raden. He hits automatic fire and destroys the building in seconds. Out of the rubble runs an Iraqi still throwing grenades.

Our troops on the ground open fire and he is hit in the legs and chest and is quickly pounced upon by one of our sections on the ground. A medic told me later that he was still alive when he reached the first aid station. I was glad as he was very brave and was still fighting his enemy when everyone else was surrendering around him. He was also very stupid and scared.

All of this was happening on the left flank. Meanwhile, 9 platoons were taking prisoners on the right flank. Suddenly from behind the Iraqis who were walking towards us with white flags flying and surrendering, an RPG rocket came screeching in through the Iraqi soldiers hitting call sign 32 in a multicoloured explosion.

The front of the vehicle burst into flames but the armour we put on only a month ago deflected the missile. The chain guns started up again for 20 seconds and then stopped.

OC 32 sent a casualty report
32 One man down otherwise okay.
OC Clarify man down. How serious?
32 He's dead

Carl Moult had taken the full blast of the RPG7 rocket. It had passed straight through him on the way to hitting the Warrior. The two chaps on either side of him were untouched. Carl himself was carrying an anti-tank rocket but luckily this did not explode injuring his mates. The war was now real and with us. In all, this objective tally was allegedly 150 dead Iraqi soldiers and 286 prisoners of the war.

All taken by 120 men of C Company. The prisoners of war included 18 officers two colonels and two majors. Two captains were left in the trenches, shot by their own men because they would not let them surrender. From the information the prisoners gave us, we found out that this road, where the Iraqis were located, was the main road that all the Iraqis were running down to get out of Kuwait.

As we were collecting the prisoners, out of the smoke to my right I could see tracked vehicles rapidly approaching I didn't know if they were enemies or not but after a quick double take, I could confirm that it was one of the Battalions other companies arriving to reinforce us by covering our flank.

The Challenges also arrived at our location within 30 minutes and headed east down the road towards Kuwait hitting any vehicle that did not stop and surrender. To the west the MLRS had started up again, carpet bombing the road with cluster bombs and hitting anything that was on that road.

The Forward Observation Officer (FOO) Warrior that was attached to us was now doing his job and directing the artillery onto concentrations of Iraqi vehicles that were on the move. The AS90 Artillery guns were firing from 15 kilometres away and the FOO was fine-tuning the aim by moving the barrage one hundred meters here, and three hundred meters there until the shells were accurately on the target.

We sat down around our fitter section vehicles whilst the infantry guys were getting sorted out, patching up minor injuries and refilling ammo pouches and the turret weapons with fresh ammunition after their latest escapade. This gave us a brief rest for a few minutes watching the massive firework show that the Challengers, Artillery and MLRS were laying on for us. This would go on for the next few hours. Nothing will leave Kuwait tonight.

Most of the single lads in the fitter section knew Nobby and Carl. They shared an accommodation block for single men and went to the local bars with them when they were stationed in Fallingbostel. This pause in the battle allowed them a few minutes of reflection before we mounted up again. After a few hours of rest and a brew, we put the vehicles in gear and move off following the Company vehicles in one extended line.

We arrive in the rest area. As we pull into any location, the task lists are handed out to the fitter section and they crack on repairing any faults the vehicles or weapon systems have. The Warriors are looking good but my vehicle's engine has had it.

I have been trying to get a new engine pack for it but our second-line repair line facility is still one hundred kilometres behind us. It's just a case of repair and make and hope it will last a bit longer. Only 50 kilometres to go and then we can grab some proper sleep. The lads are all getting a bit ratty with each other but that is expected as everyone is tired.

White phosphorus is still burning on the nose plate of callsign 32. The crew are just sitting on the ground watching it. The 9-platoon commander casually walks up and wets it before removing it and burying it. Phosphorous burns in the air. All the companies stay away from call sign 32 as they know they have only a couple of hours to mourn Carl and then they will be called to do their bit again.

I still cannot believe that our casualties have been so light. As well as tools and replacement assemblies, our vehicle carries loads of first aid kits assuming that during a firefight any vehicle that needs REME assistance or is damaged could also have casualties within it.

When we started out on day one, we were told to remove the large Union flags we were flying from the tops of our vehicles. On one of our objectives, we saw a massive explosion about 10 kilometres away and assumed it was an ammunition dump being destroyed. It turned out later that nine Welsh Fusiliers had been killed by an American A10 Warthog plane that sent missiles into two Warrior vehicles thinking they were the enemy.

Hearing this the flags went back on. Any identification is a help when fighting next door to the Americans. There was also an incident with a Challenger opening fire on a Warrior. The up-armour we fitted to the Warriors a few weeks earlier saved the lives of that crew. Unfortunately, a captain standing next to the Warrior had both his legs broken.

27 February 1991

0400 hours

We are moving again but this time with news of an unofficial ceasefire. We are ordered not to fire at anyone unless they shoot at us or do not stop. No one is to leave Kuwait.

We found out just before moving off that the prisoners we captured the night before were the elite Republican Guard Execution Battalions. These are the ones that Sadam posted behind their troops to stop them from running away. They are also the ones who killed most of the Kuwaitis. Also, they killed or shot in the legs their own soldiers if they ran away.

Other companies have reported coming across whole platoons that had been shot in the foot so they could not leave their defensive positions. The Arab nation's value of life seems so different to ours. Finding out that they were Republican Guards made our spirits lift a bit as we had apparently left 150 dead in their trenches.

As it happens, today's objective is to stop the Republican Guard Battalions from leaving the Kuwait area. Tank after enemy tank as far as the eye can see was parked up with the barrels pointed at the sky. Some are still smoking from the air attacks but most have just been left by the crews as they think it is safer running for the border than driving a tank.

0630 hours

I had to stop my small packet of vehicles to check the compass against the map, this ensured that we were going in the right direction and did not stray off the corridor we were supposed to be travelling down. When on a steel-tracked vehicle, the compass is not very accurate as a compass works on magnetism to find north and we are riding in a big steel box that makes the compass useless.

A vehicle commander therefore has to get out of the vehicle walk about 20 meters to get clear of the vehicle's influence on the compass, then take a compass bearing and find a spot on the horizon that is in the direction you want to travel. Once mounted back on the vehicle you can drive to the point you had noted then repeat the procedure again.

It is easier at night as we could pick a star and head for it allowing for the arc the sky moved in an hour we could tell how much to aim off for. Whilst stopped I took out my camera to take a photo shoot of the carnage. We were already five kilometres behind the Company due to having to stop to fix one of our Warriors and a few more seconds would not matter. As soon as the Warrior was fixed and drove away, my vehicle engine finally gave up the ghost.

I was, therefore, in the situation that after motoring for one thousand and two hundred miles in the last few months and most of it at the maximum throttle to keep up with the Warriors, my vehicle was finally a casualty of the abuse it had been given. Warriors were much faster than my FV432 armoured personnel carrier (Tiffy Wagon), so when the company Warriors were just cruising, I was at full throttle.

Also, their suspension is brilliant whereas mine is 1950s design and I feel every bump and grind that passes into the hull. We are only five kilometres from the Kuwait border and I have had to request that I be towed by my corporal in his Warrior repair vehicle, much to the glee of the recovery crew, who finds the whole thing very amusing.

Along the main road leading into Kuwait City are hundreds of vehicles burning after being strafed by the Air Force or hit by tank shells. Suddenly, through the camera lens, a figure loomed up at me. It is an Iraqi soldier just sitting by the side of the road. He has seen me and is shuffling along the ground towards me with his foot off the ground.

I ordered him to stop and deployed two of the recovery mechanics to go and investigate and check he was not wired to any booby traps. Just as they reached him three vehicles appeared about eight hundred metres away setting the adrenalin running through my body. The recovery vehicle and I trained our machine guns on them and started shouting for the two crew to get back in the vehicle.

As they ran back to the vehicle, we recognised the vehicles as some of our battalion's ambulance vehicles that were sweeping the route for Iraqi casualties.

As the medics treated the Iraqi soldier, we found out he was 15 years old and had had a broken ankle for two weeks.

As my heart rate returned to normal, I found myself thinking, *What if they had been Iraqi tanks?*

The Warrior recovery vehicle with my vehicle in tow is a very slow target and our armament is no match for main battle tanks. With no fire support, the situation could have been very dodgy indeed.

I put all that to the back of my mind and off we trundled. I found out later that this fate had happened to a REME chap Sergeant Dowling when he had been separated whilst driving an ammunition carrier. He was caught by an Iraqi T65 tank and along with another vehicle had been attacked and killed by the tank.

1000 hours

We have now caught up with the Company who are situated on the main Basra to Kuwait highway. The highway is a duel carriageway and the northern carriageway is littered with burnt-out vehicles where the Air Force has been cluster bombing all the Iraqis running for the Iraq border. It is not a very pretty sight. The Iraqis grabbed anything they could get hold of and drove as fast as possible out of Kuwait City.

The cars are full of televisions, clothes, radios and all manner of things that have been looted from shops and homes in Kuwait. The bodies of the owners of the vehicles that have been hijacked are all at the side of the road leading from Kuwait after being shot including women and children. The bodies of the hijackers are still inside the vehicles after being caught by the RAF.

I never counted the bodies but there must have been hundreds. Some were mutilated and some with no signs of injury at all, as it was the air overpressure of the bombs that killed them.

Several buses full of escaping Iraqi soldiers are burnt out on the road, with their charred remains still inside. Some people jumped out of their vehicles to take photos but I didn't. That memory will stay with me forever. Luckily, we are still on standby in case of a retaliation attack so we did not get roped into the burial parties.

Nearer Kuwait City, there are reports of the Kuwaiti resistance finding Iraqis and Palestinians, torturing and hanging them. The roads have bodies jammed onto spikes and hung from lampposts lining the route. As I said before, in my opinion, Arabs are all as bad as each other when it comes to atrocities against mankind.

When a civilised world fighting force gains the upper hand and the enemy surrenders, as a rule, this means that the game is over and the defeated are treated with respect. I was going to say kindness but that would be wrong. Let's say compassion.

Whilst all this was happening, my callsign 24B commanded by my sergeant still had not arrived back into the Company lines. He had been towing a broken-down Warrior for the last 30 kilometres.

When I called him up on the radio to ask his location, the only reply I got back was, "In a Fu£$%^Ag hole, over."

At this, my whole fitter section broke down into fits of laughter.

On asking his location, he replied, "F$%k knows." More laughter around the section.

I then asked if he needed any assistance to which the reply was, "F£$k off."

So, at least, I now knew that he was as happy as a pig in shit and would have his normal expression of a bulldog sucking a wasp, and we would see him in a few hours.

His repair Warrior 24B with a Warrior in tow had, in the pitch dark, driven over the lip of a quarry and slid uncontrollably down the virtually shear side all the way to the bottom of the quarry. After driving around the bottom of the quarry for an hour, he could not find an easy way out. To attempt to drive out of the quarry the way he came into it he had to re-connect up all the bits of the towed Warrior that he had disconnected to enable him to tow it in the first place.

Then fired up the broken-down Warrior, which was lacking power still from the initial vehicle fault, and in tandem had slowly driven back up the side of the quarry to extract themselves. He then had to prepare the Warrior to be towed again. All a lengthy process and something that he could have done without. Needless to say, he was looking and feeling his best when I met up with him a few hours later.

The OC called the Company together for a briefing and told us our job was done and not to get involved with the tit-for-tat shooting that was still going on between various waring Arab parties.

1300 hours

4 days, 100 hours, 353 Kilometres
                 The war is over. Time for bed and see what tomorrow brings.

Chapter 15
They Think It's All Over

1700 hours

I have been speaking to a medic sergeant who has just been passing a lorry when he saw an old Iraqi with his foot blown off. He has been walking for two days on his stump. All he wants is a bottle of water and be allowed to carry on. Its 40 kilometres from Basra.

The medical officer turned up and re-amputated the infected stump, dressed it, then he was taken to the field hospital.

Over the past few days, I have seen numerous Iraqis with various bits blown off them or bullet and shrapnel holes in them and all they wanted was a bottle of water and some food. Smiling saying the war is over. Indeed, it was over for Iraq, for not only does a country need a large army, but you also need good training and modern equipment.

Most of the vehicles we were up against were 60 years old or more. Also, Iraq wanted to play trench warfare. They actually thought they could play World War I tactics when they were up against World War III technology.

The Iraqi Generals must have known that we would not wait to use the age-old tactics of waiting for the desert to kill the infidel. We had to get the job done whilst it was still their winter. If we waited until the summer and 50-degree heat, although the result would have been the same, it would have been much harder on vehicle and personnel attrition due to the heat.

The Iraqi Generals were probably just doing as they were told by Saddam Husain who ruled with fisted gloves and executed anyone who disobeyed him. This was the whole purpose of the Revolutionary Guard. Their job was to make sure the conscripted army did as they were ordered or else. I have just found out that the old man with the missing foot was only 32 years old.

28 February 1991

0830 hours

186 of the best Iraqi T72 main battle tanks Iraq owns have tried to break out of Basra. We have been rushed to the Iraq/Kuwait border to stop them coming towards our battalion lines. We are sitting on a hill overlooking the valley where the battle is taking place. The Americans are hitting them with everything they have, Abraham's tanks, MLRS and air power. The noise is deafening and only flashes can be seen through the smoke on the horizon.

We cannot proceed further into the valley as the Americans want the final coup-de-grace. The British mandate was to remove all Iraqi forces from Kuwait and that is what we have done. We will not proceed any further, nor will we be proceeding on to Basra, so we will just sit and watch the final throws of the Iraqi army guns go silent.

0930 hours

It's all gone quiet now. No more Republican guard, No more Iraq army in our vicinity. The last tank division has just been wiped out. We can now go back down the road and carry on clearing the main road of the debris.

02 March 1991

My vehicle had been temporarily fixed again for the tenth time, so we could now join in the clearance activities. Whilst we were on a task that involved driving or dragging all the Iraqi vehicles that could still move to a holding area, Bones reported that the engine was running hot again, followed rapidly by the engine fire alarm going off. There was no smoke or flames so I climbed out of my cupola and stood on the engine louvres looking for signs of a fire.

I could not see any signs of an engine fire but the soles of my boots suddenly started bubbling and smoking. At this point, I had to admit the engine had finally and terminally given up the ghost. Bones turned off the engine and pulled the internal fire extinguishers whilst the crew in the back of the wagon debussed. I called up 24B and we were recovered back to 7th Armoured Workshop, a 2nd line repair unit that had now finally caught up with the main spearhead battalions.

We now had spares and second-line repair facilities where I had a new engine pack fitted to the vehicle. Whilst at the workshop location I had a walk around and met up with a few old friends that I knew from my dark distant past. Some I had not seen for years so it was good to catch up.

I found it amazing that even though we were still on a war footing, the regimental staff at the workshop, in the middle of the flaming desert, were still treating the workshop area as a training establishment and were pacing around telling people to march about the place, not just walk, and to smarten themselves up.

The little Hitlers obviously did not have anything better to do with themselves. Little did I know that I would get posted to this unit in three years' time. The unit had not got any better over the years as far as the military mentality was concerned. Once posted there I often wondered why I had accepted the posting.

After a few hours, the vehicle was fixed and off we went to join C Company again.

On the way back, we came across half a dozen old Iraqi anti-aircraft guns all in a line. We got out of the vehicle and walked over to them. They obviously had been strafed by an air attack as there were quite a few craters around the gun positions. The guns were all fully loaded and we sat in the gun seats looking through the sights just to experience the feeling.

With four 30-millimetre cannon barrels surrounding you, it was easy to imagine what the Iraqis thought as they would be able to see the planes streaking towards them and then they would be opening fire at each other, each opponent praying to their own gods. I got out of the gun seat and had a more detailed look around the site. How many Iraqis would have been killed and injured here?

There were broken pieces of equipment and ripped-up uniform material, personal belongings and bloodied bandages everywhere, the whole place had been subject to a severe bombardment of firepower and had been evacuated in a hurry. This scene was replicated all along this Iraqi defensive line all the way to the coast 20 kilometres away.

On arriving back in the Company area, I was told that as far as we were concerned, everything was now cleared up in our sector. Bodies were buried, and cars and lorries were pushed off the road. We had collected all the movable military vehicles within about a 10-kilometre area and parked them in a massive car park away from our troop concentration area. At some point, these hundreds of Iraqi vehicles would be destroyed so they could not fall back into the enemy's hands again.

We were officially stood down with only a few administration tasks to be done. We were free to roam the local vicinity and help out other units if we wanted to.

Everything worth anything has been proffed for mementos. Kuwaiti and Saudi soldiers were walking around the area with bundles of weapons trying to persuade the squaddies to buy rifles and pistols for keepsakes. I know some did and then hid them away in the wagons to try and smuggle them back to Germany in the vehicles.

Years later, if we had a fuel starvation problem on a Warrior, we would find weapons in the fuel tanks that had been hidden away and the tape sealing the plastic bags had degraded and blocked the pipework. Obviously, the owner did not have the nerve to retrieve it once back in Germany as this would be a court-martial offence and would cost him his job.

As I explained previously, proffing is a term used when an attractive piece of equipment has been acquired. On one occasion whilst driving between locations, we came across a bunker system that had been left in a hurry by the retreating Iraqis. Several Company members were taking tourist photos around the area and generally having a look around.

Eventually as happens when young men get bored we started getting up to mischief. The bunker system was full of ammunition, but nothing very attractive to proff.

After clearing it for booby traps, we decided to destroy all the ammunition in this small bunker. A few enemy grenades were primed and thrown in the tunnel and then we turned and ran. We had done this a few times before and usually after a massive bang we had a laugh and then went and found something else to amuse ourselves.

This time, after a loud bang there was a massive explosion and the whole bunker system went up with RPG rockets and all sorts of other munitions flying into the air. Don't the Iraqis know that it's not safe to mix ammunition in one store? Things like that can get people hurt. I think I'll report it to the Health and Safety Committee.

On the way back, down the hill, three Land Rovers full of officers came around a bend and slewed to a stop. (Probably, also on a proffing mission). They asked us what the explosion was. I told them the Royal Engineers were doing some bunker clearing due to all the booby traps.

Also, they should turn around as nobody was allowed into the area whilst demolition was taking place. They gave us a disappointed look and turned around. They went one way and we rapidly went the other. Oh, the stories we could tell our grandkids!

Everyone now had collected an Iraqi AK47 rifle, pistol, Helmet, Jacket, Bayonet etc. Unfortunately, as I have mentioned all firearms had to be handed in prior to leaving Kuwait which disappointed lots of trophy hunters. If we were Americans, we could have taken back what we wanted and then in our hour of need we could have gone into our garden shed, lifted the floorboards and there would have been a complete arsenal to go and fight the baddies with.

Once back in Fallingbostel, it was rumoured that some people had still smuggled armaments across from the war zone and so an amnesty was put in place. Everyone had to hand in their ill-gotten gains and leave them by the single men's accommodation block. After several hours, the senior ranks returned to the single men's accommodation block and only expected to collect a few minor weapons.

Piled up outside the block was a heap of guns, grenades, shells and ammunition that had found its way across the sea. This was far more than we had expected as the vehicles had been searched for weapons at the port and had a certificate to say they were clear of arms and munitions. These items must have been secreted away by removing panels and hiding them securely before replacing the panels.

Anyone who still wanted a gun had to send it away to get it decommissioned but very few were ever returned to the unit by the decommissioning department including a couple of anti-aircraft gun barrels that we wanted for our REME LAD bar.

Before leaving Kuwait, the retreating Iraqis set fire to hundreds of oil wells. The smoke from the oil fires was getting worse and there was a solid cloud above us. If anyone has dived in the sea and looked up at the waves above it looked just like that, but the sea of smoke is moving very slowly and the waves are miles across.

They are predicting that this could take months to put all the fires out. Along with the smoke comes a cold wind and torrential oily rain, which paints a pretty miserable picture of Kuwait.

Well, we did our little bit. It was all over sooner than expected and with only a fraction of the casualties expected.

43 British Servicemen killed. Among the dead:

| 9 were killed by American Aircraft fire |
| 3 killed by American tank fire |
| 3 killed by personal accident |

Chapter 16
Home Time

Ursula wrote to me every day that I was out here. As I did her. All we can do now is wait to go home, still, nobody has said when that will be. More letters are written to say that it is all over and we are okay and we will be home soon. Everyone is jumping on the bandwagon and coming to visit us and give us a congratulatory talk, but nobody can tell us when we are going home.

For now, we have to stay in Kuwait and bide our time and try to keep busy or at least keep out of trouble. This is not too bad for me as I have report after report to write on tactics, vehicle defects` and a hundred other topics. In fact, I'll be up to my ears in paperwork for months.

About two miles away there is the holding pen for all the enemy equipment we dragged into place. Part of my daily routine is to run there and back just to break the boredom and get back into the habit of trying to stay fit and healthy. It's also nice just to get away from things for an hour. If anyone wants to pester me, they can come and find me.

The newspaper reporters came in droves and talked to the Company soldiers and took some photos for the tabloids, but when they came towards the REME wagons they were pelted with leftover miniature Christmas puddings due to what they said about us back in port six months ago. (We still had the puddings in case we came across another camel).

We are finally on our way. A quick helicopter ride back to Al Jubail and then a short stay in Camp 4 to get cleaned up. Now, it's just a case of waiting for the goesehomeybird (Goes Home Bird (Aeroplane)) to take me back to Ursula and the kids, so we can start our life together again. I would not have wanted to miss out on this war as it is something I have trained for years to do.

I have proved to myself a great many things that would not have been possible in other scenarios. Unfortunately, there will be nothing in the rest of my life that will give me the buzz of excitement or the massive dose of adrenaline I have had in the past few weeks. However, where would I find that buzz and still remain safe from injury or worse? I think Ursula would air her views if I came up with a scheme to give myself a similar buzz.

When the day came to move the vehicles back to the holding area in Saudi Arabia, I asked the OC to tell the vehicle commanders that I would appreciate it if they did not race the one hundred miles back to the holding area as this would cause me a lot of extra work. He promised me that this would not happen. His orders, if any, fell on deaf ears as once we were on our way it was a free-for-all for all the British Army vehicles to get to the final destination first.

We flew down the main road at top speed only slowing down as we passed the two-mile straight where there were still hundreds of wrecked vehicles remains that had been the victims of countless air strikes. The remains of the victims still hung in the air.

When we reached the holding area, we were parked up in a massive square formation. I think it was the first time I had seen all the British Army contingent to the war in one place. Everyone was walking about the vehicles collecting their kit and meeting up with old friends. All laughing and joking and generally having a good time.

For once we did not mind sitting around for hours waiting for the transport as everyone was just so relieved that all the work had been done and there was nothing else to get stressed about until after we came back from leave in about four weeks' time. That seemed a lifetime away.

Once the transport arrived, we were taken to Camp 4 and had a shower, put on clean uniforms, grabbed a meal and then headed to the airport. We left Kuwait and Saudi Arabia behind and flew home to Germany. The plane's captain had allotted us a couple of beers to drink on the plane which is enough for most. After nine months without any alcohol apart from the odd smuggled bottle, it went straight to my head.

I also sneaked a couple of large whiskeys and then slept the rest of the flight home. We arrived back in Fallingbostel with the band playing and all the flags flying. Ursula and the kids were there to meet me as were all the Company's wives and girlfriends. There were a few celebratory beers to be sampled and then we went home, only to be savaged by my dog who did not recognise me in my desert combats.

After a long hot bath, I sat in my living room and couldn't think of one important thing to say. I didn't want to talk about the war as that was all I had talked about for the last six months. I also felt I had to go and do something as I had been working 16 hours per day for the last six months and now with nothing to do. Everything is an anti-climax as is everything you wish for when it finally happens.

Anyway, after the four weeks leave I am due, I might feel normal again and slot into life's routine again. I am glad that I'm staying home for leave and not rushing around England trying to see everyone and repeating my war stories constantly when I meet people.

The main point of this latest adventure was that we went out there; to do our job and we did it and just maybe someone will appreciate just how good a job we did. Admittedly, people can comment that it was such a poor job the Iraqi army did, that made the war such an easy victory. But that's what it is all about, winners and losers. This time we won, next time we may not be so lucky, and my story would not be so long.

This is a short story about a short war. How it was in my eyes and how I felt during it. I've reported things as I saw them with my eyes and have stated my opinion on the circumstances I found myself in. Other people may tell totally different stories from where they were standing and the information they had received at the time.

Now, with all that behind me, I can only hope that I am a better man for it in all ways possible. Maybe I should just keep it in my memories, but I know I will never forget that 100 hours.

Footnote.

A few months later, I was told to report to the adjutant's office in the morning. I didn't have a clue what I had done wrong this time. I usually only went up to the headquarters building if I was summoned by someone important. When I walked in to see the adjutant, he told me, "Stand here."

He then walked into the commanding officer's room. I heard muffled voices and then he came back out and told me to march in, which I did still not knowing why and wondering which of my many misdemeanours I was being accused of, or if had someone snitched on me.

One of the medals I have is the Long Service Good Conduct medal which is awarded to me for never being charged for a crime in 18 years of service. In the trade, this medal is called the medal for 18 years of undetected crime.

As I marched into the CO's office the CO sat there with a big grin on his face and presented me with a telegram from the Queen telling me that I had been named on the Queen's honours list, and had been awarded the British Empire Medal (BEM) for outstanding service.

I suppose I would have to get the beers in again for the fitter section as it was all their hard work that had put me in the running for this award.

When I spoke to my OC Major Rochelle afterwards, he said that the officers had a sweepstake, for which company would have the best vehicle reliability during Operation Granby and as his company had won, when the opportunity arose to nominate someone on the engineering side of the Brigade, he put my name forward. As simple as that.

I now wear my medals with pride and pull up a sandbag, swing the light and tell loads of exaggerated stories about—During the war.

Chapter 17
Poetry Corner
Part Two

I DREAMT LAST NIGHT, YOU'RE LEAVING

Leaving is a sin they say, loneliness is the price to pay.

Who would think when you are still a child at school, that the people that you see every day at school will probably move three or four times in their lifetime? Some may stay locally but the majority will move quite a distance away and cut all ties with the life they had previously. Some people will move out of the area due to the necessity of the work of their employment, and others leave to start new families with a partner they may have found outside their local area.

Others may just want a change. I left Rothwell, Yorkshire just before my 18th birthday as I could not visualise myself spending the rest of my working life locked into the factory system where I was working. Whilst I was in trade training after joining the army I was generally free at weekends. For the next 18 months, I came back to visit friends and family at least every three or four weeks. In 1975, I was posted to Detmold in Germany.

After that, I don't suppose I visited for more than two weeks a year. Once my mother had left Rothwell, I probably didn't visit Rothwell more than one day every few years just to reminisce if I happened to be passing. Of all the people I grew up with, I am only in contact with one person from school who is my best man's widow.

After leaving the army over 25 years ago, I settled in Shropshire and still tour the local folk clubs and open mic nights in the area having a sing-song, or more accurately a strum and a yell. For five years, I sang and played around the local area with a young girl called Diana. We spent a lot of time together working out our next set on stage and recording CDs on my computer recording programme.

We also took part in a few Pantomimes in the village hall. Everything was purely platonic and she is a really good friend. She is the same generation as my children and so it was nice to talk in-depth about the subjects I could not talk to my kids about.

Unfortunately for me, love got in the way of our galivanting and she moved down to Bath, Summerset, to set up a home and have two children. It was very selfish of her as Ursula now has to put up with me all the time. I still see her occasionally on family occasions as my son married her sister.

I dreamt last night you're leaving, And I won't see you again.
I never told you, that you were my best friend. I should have told you, But I never ever told you, That you were my best friend.

I know we only messed about, Playing with our songs.
And I don't know the reason how well we got along,
But we got along, I don't know the reason how well we got along.

The last thing I remember we were singing at a gig.
And we were hitting every note of every song we did. It was like falling off a log, it was like falling off a log,
How those notes came flowing through?

But if you have to leave me, I know I will be sad.
But you can call and you can phone, and things won't be that bad.
They cannot be that bad, but you can call and you can phone,
And things won't be that bad.

So, there you go you're leaving, I've a pain inside so bad.
But I know I should be grateful for all the time we've had.
It feels like I've fallen on a rock; It feels like I've fallen on a rock.
But I know I should be grateful for all the time we've had.

I hope you will be happy,
And your voice always be strong.
And I hope you sometimes think of me if you ever sing our songs,
If you sing our songs,

And I hope you think of me if you ever sing our songs.

I'LL TEACH YOU, SON

What must a newborn child think as it emerges into the world? Are they capable of remembering their time in the womb even for a brief period, or does memory re-boot as soon as they are born? There is a bond between father and son just as strong as mother and daughter. Unfortunately, in the Yorkshire genes, it is not natural to show affection.

My son and I are very much alike, the only difference being that my son Jon is very stubborn and will only do what he wants to do, whereas I generally go along with the majority providing there are good intentions. However, once I decide to do something and how to do it I generally stick to the plan.

We both have the determination to see any task we start completed to the best of our ability. Sometimes I stand back to admire one of my masterpieces or a project I have been working on, only to see my wife giving me a look as if to say, I'm not having that in my house. We all know who has the last word. That's why I have a failed project shed.

Thankfully, my son lives nearby, so we often see each other and his two daughters. I wrote this song when my son Jon was born.

> They dragged you from your silent world,
> With beams of light that seared through the dark.
> And from the darkness of your womb
> To noises that were far away before.
> Painful tubes and fingers in your mouth,
> Slapping on your back to make you shout. Don't cry. Don't cry.
>
> Don't you cry and try to hide?
> Just be happy to be alive.
> Don't be sad. It's not that bad.
> Now you're here.
> On through life you'll grow and grow.
> Learning the laws of right and wrong.
> Your skin and muscles so soft now will start to harden slowly.
> They'll grow strong.

The laws of this life will bring you pain,
And teach you what not to do again. Don't cry. Don't cry.

Don't you cry and try to hide?
Just be happy to be alive.
Don't be sad. It's not that bad.
Now you're here.

Love your family every day.
They'll help you keep your fears away at night.
And through the day I will teach you, son.
Although your life has just begun to fight.
The troubles that will pass through your life.
To try and try again until you're right.
But don't cry. Don't cry.

Don't you cry and try to hide?
Just be happy to be alive.
Don't be sad. It's not that bad.
Now you're here.

I'M DOING ALRIGHT

One of the highlights of army life is the company smoker. This is when we have been out on manoeuvres and there is a lull in the activities. Everything stops and a Bar-B-Que for one hundred men gets fired up. After a few days of playing soldiers and running around in the exercise area without proper sleep, everyone is shattered and also very smelly and filthy as washing facilities are very basic, that's if you have time for a wash and shave.

As soon as everyone is gathered together in a Leigue area, out comes the packs of beer and the humour only a squaddie would understand. These smokers last many hours and are great at bringing everyone together. 'We band of brothers'; nothing can match that in Civvy Street.

In Canada, we had a Fijian staff sergeant who was part of the Royal Artillery who I was serving with at the time. He turned up one day with a live full-grown pig. A few hours later the said pig was slaughtered, gutted and prepared. A huge bonfire was then built and lit. This immediately drew a crowd of squaddies from all around the area to form into small groups and stare into the flames.

Large rocks were thrown on the embers of the fire and a few hours later a trench was dug, lined with grass and the hot boulders were thrown in. In went the pig. In went more red-hot rocks and the whole trench was then covered with vegetation, dirt and the bonfire ashes were shovelled over the site.

Six hours later, the company smoker was officially opened the trench was uncovered, and the beautifully cooked pig was consumed along with a large amount of beer. What a night.

All my life, I have loved sitting outdoors staring into a roaring fire, with a whisky in my hand, thinking of nothing, making plans or making lyrics up for my guitar whilst slightly inebriated and knowing that when the morning comes, many of my dreams would not materialise or my lyrics and tunes be remembered.

I was drinking whiskey late last night.
I think my life has turned out alright.
I've looked deep inside and my conscience is clear.
I've listened to my soul, but no screams could I here.
So, I'm doing alright.

It's Saturday night. It's colder than I planned.
The winds getting up, the seas are smashing the land.
But I'm so warm sitting by the fire.
With a blanket on my back, that's all I desire.
I'm doing alright.

The dawn's coming up there are trains on the track.
I'm going to jump me a ride, and I'm not coming back.
She told me, get out and I started to pack.
All the things I own are sitting on my back.

It's starting to rain and the sands getting wet.
The bottle in my hand ain't quite empty yet.
The rain has brought the wind rushing from the south.
Finish my bottle, feel the burn in my mouth.
So, I'm doing alright. I think I'm doing alright.

When I hit town, I'll get me a job.
I won't be a bum. I won't be a slob.
I'll show her things that she could have had.
I show her things wouldn't have been that bad.
That we're doing alright.

We're doing alright.

I'M LEAVING NOW

Thinking about this song title, that's exactly what I did when I was 17. I was part of an apprentice program at a huge copper works factory just outside Leeds. After learning how to machine, mill, grind, file, drill and saw, we were qualified to move on the factory floor. To get into the closed shop factory, I had to parade with three separate union cards and walk past three union member tables to prove I was a member, just so I could work.

I was part of a team who set up the machines. A very old ancient 64-year-old chap in the team was retiring and I was his replacement, although it meant I had a job when there were three million unemployed, I couldn't see myself working in this mind-numbing factory for the next 46 years.

Around this time, I was playing in a band two nights a week and making more money doing this, than the 11 pounds a week I was getting from 5 days working in the factory, I was, however, knackered with all the hours I was working. I did not get back from the band until midnight and had to run three miles to be at work for 0700 hours to set up the machines for the day's work.

One day my father sat me down and explained that I should pack in the group and concentrate on the work until I had passed out of my apprenticeship as they could never take a trade away from me. This was sound advice and so I did this straight away. The following week the three-day week came into effect with strikes and electricity cuts all over England. My pay went from about 20 quid a week for both jobs to five quid a week. Thanks, Dad.

I know I'll join the army. There were no wars at the moment and only Northern Ireland was hostile. I probably would not get sent there anyway. Three Northern Ireland tours later even Northern Ireland was boring apart from the odd hilarious or frightening moments. This was one of the first songs I remember writing.

At some point in everyone's life, they would like to pack their bags, go somewhere else, and change their lives.

I think I nicked the tune from my brother, but as you are only reading this it's pointless telling you that.

Maybe we can go away.
To somewhere where the sky is blue.
Start again, my special friend.
Try and start our life anew.
I can play a song for you. Anytime you want me to.
I can sing a love song for you.
Anywhere and anytime.
I can play a melodrama.
With these withered hands of mine.
I can play the bogey blues, any time you want me to.
Don't you sigh, I'll pass you by,
I'm leaving now, and won't you come too.

What I want is some dream lover,
Stay with me when the day is through.
What I want, and what I get,
Is something I could get from you?
Have I ever let you down?
Even when you're not around?
Have I ever cheated on you?
Even when you're feeling blue?
Do you ever look at me?
The way I always look at you?
The moon shines so bright, to light our way tonight.
Don't you sigh, I'll pass you by,
I'm leaving now, and won't you come too.

I'M NOT GETTING OLDER. I'M JUST SLOWING DOWN.

Age comes to us all. Whilst our heads want to run up and down mountains, our legs just want to walk around the garden. Looking in the mirror I don't see the young strapping lad I used to be looking back at me, I see a face strained in the university of life, wondering who I can pester next.

However, I now walk up mountains rather than run, and I still push out the miles on my bike or swim a mile a couple of times a week. I will probably continue doing so until something breaks, wears out or falls off.

I do seem to spend more time rubbing aches and pains as each year passes. I don't know at what point I am supposed to stop doing energetic things. Years ago, my friend and I would find a pub 10 or more miles away on a map. We would grab our two dogs and walk and run to it as the crow flies. Up and down hills, over farmers' fields and through rivers and streams. Once at the pub, the wives to come meet us at a specific time and join us for a drink.

My sister-in-law is a couple of years older than me and walks 16 miles over the Yorkshire moors several times a week. I let her drag me up Pen-y-gent last year and she broke me. I still have a dodgy knee from that adventure and if I try and tackle any steep hill it likes to remind me. Going up is no problem apart from a bit of clutch slip in the lung department, if I push too hard, but coming back down, I'm looking for a toboggan.

Conversations with friends these days seem to be mostly about aching joints and the number of pills we take. Funerals come around more often and more and more of our friends don't join us for outdoor activities like camping or trips outside as the weather is too cold this time of year.

I'm not getting older; I'm just slowing down.
That's what I told you when I pulled into town.
I know I look different, but inside I still smile.
And maybe you'd like me to hang around for a while.
I'm not getting older; It just feels like I'm slowing down.
We could rent a room or two, and I could hang around.
We could climb a mountain, lay back and look at the sky.
Amazed at the shapes those clouds, make as they pass by.
Just laying back and looking at the clouds.

I'm not getting older; In fact, I think I'm still the same.
You once held my face, and you once called out my name.
When I left town, you were no more than a girl.
And I wanted to find my way and try and change the world.

And now that we're older, does that flame still burn inside?
The days seem colder, without you by my side.
We could buy a house, looking over the sea.
Spend our time, every day just making memories.
Spend our time, every day just making memories.

I'm not getting older; I sometimes, I like to play the fool.
I can make you laugh or cry, I sometimes, I sing a song or two.
Shall l just turn around and drive out of this town?
But I'm not getting older, I'm just slowing down.
But I'm not getting older, I'm just slowing down.
I sometimes feel like my motor has just run down and stopped.

I'M WALKING

I consider myself very lucky as Ursula and I have now been together for 47 years and hand on heart, I can say there have only been a handful of times in that 47 years where we have had a real good barney. All were resolved by nightfall. I don't know if she can say the same. (I probably agreed she was right so I would survive the night as even us, superheroes have to close their eyes when we sleep).

I spent most of my working life working away from home. Apart from the fact that this was a necessity for the job I had chosen, there was more money to be made this way. Now retired, it is strange to be with Ursula all the time and so I have the conservatory to watch all my television programs and Ursula has the living room to watch all of hers.

I also go out a couple of evenings a week to meet up with friends and have a sing at an open mic. Ursula has the ladies that do lunch brigade and all in all, we do not tend to cramp each other's space too much.

Very few couples seem to manage with just one partner throughout their lives. Several people I know are on 2nd and 3rd marriages and speak of this as though this is normal. It always amuses me how all families get on so well with in-laws and then as soon as a divorce threatens then the opposite party is forever known as that Bastard or that Bitch.

This is a humorous story of a husband and wife who are obviously having marriage problems. Although any marriage break-up is bad, I always wonder how people who obviously loved each other so much at some point, can be so hateful to each other after in some cases, such a short time.

(Male)

If there's one thing worse than hoping, it's living your life with no hope. If there's one thing worse than staying, it's just not daring to go.

Everyone moves so fast.
When I just want to go slow.
Everybody they want to stop.
When I just want to go.
And so, I'm walking, I'm walking right out on you.
And I'm talking. And you're not telling me not to do it.

(Female)

If there's one thing worse than dreaming, it's waking up in the night.
If there's one thing worse than loving,
It's hating with all your might.

If there's one thing worse than talking.
It's keeping quiet at the wrong time.
If there's one thing worse than saying it's yours.
When all the time it's mine.
And so, you're walking. You say you're walking out on me.
You've promised me this so many times. This I just got to see.

(Male)

You can keep your mother.
That winging whining cow.
Your father left five years ago.
I'm doing that right now.

I'm going to find me some sunshine, and leave you in the rain.
I'm going to pack up all my clothes.
You won't see me again.
And so, I'm walking, I'm walking right out on you.
And I'm talking. And you're not telling me not to do.

(Female)

I knew you never liked her.
Even though you said you did.
Because when she came around to see me.
You always run away and hide.

But you always take her money.
Even though you said it was cursed.
You took 20 pieces of silver.
When she opens up her purse
And so, you're walking. You say you're walking out on me.
You've promised me this so many times. This I just got to see. (Male)

You can buy your own car.
Drive that one in the ditch.
I should never have given you the car keys.
You never could drive you bitch.

You're not going to get my money, because I've hid it underground.
And if you come looking for it.
That's where you'll be found.
And so, I'm walking, I'm walking right out on you.
And I'm talking. And you're not telling me not to do.

(Female)

Well yes! I scratched your bumper.
And yes! I dented the boot a bit.
And that little gash upon the dash.
Where your fluffy dice did sit.

And I'm sorry about your money.
That you hid in the bank.
But I invested it in the stock market.
Just before it sank.
And so, you're walking. You say, you're walking out on me.
You've promised me this so many times. This I just got to see.

(Male)

So, I'm pulling out of the drive.
You're screaming at the front door.
You've got that twisted mouth stuck on your face.
I won't see that no more.

(Female)

Well yes, I'm glad to see you go.
And I suppose you think you've won.
But I've cancelled all your credit cards.
You won't be gone for long.

(Male)

And so, I'm not walking, I'm not walking right out on you.
And I'm not talking. And again, you're telling me what to do.

IN THAT LAND HE'S NEVER KNOWN

Throughout my life I have visited numerous countries. Certainly, too many to describe what I was doing there and what the country was like in this book. Some countries visited were during military operations and some as leisure breaks with the family. We complain every day about the state of Great Britain but it is only when visiting foreign lands that you realise just how completely messed up other countries are.

When travelling past Austria and Italy heading east or below the mid-United States heading south, it is really a matter of chance if you survive to make the return journey, unless you stick to the secure holiday complex or major cities and towns where you are staying. The world is really divided into the haves and the have-nots. Once away from the populated areas civilisation seems to get thrown back a few hundred years in time.

The have-nots in Great Britain suddenly turn into the haves once they move out of the comfort zone of a law-abiding country and into the poverty of the third world which is only a short plane flight away.

It really is worth getting government advice on whether it is safe to travel to countries abroad. Even the hotel in the supposedly safe haven of the Dominican Republic entertained us by supplying armed guards when we left the holiday compound.

Dominica was the first place where I drove down a six-lane road and everyone drove in the direction they wanted. He with the loudest horn or biggest truck wins. Also, I never realised it was normal for four people and six chickens to take a ride on a moped.

I have visited the hot sandy lands of Saudi Arabia, Kuwait and Iraq on operations on two occasions and by whichever god's grace returned safely home.

Throughout the Iraq and Afghanistan conflicts, Wootton Basset became the main Air Base where the fatalities and severely injured soldiers were returned to their loved ones. Every few weeks there was a procession from the base and through the streets with a funeral cortege for people to show their respect. On each occasion, the local villages and grieving families lined the route and bowed their heads. It is people like these villages that make me proud to be British.

The statement: Thank you for your service, seems so inadequate.

Everything I have ever done; I have only ever done for myself.
And everyone I have ever loved has only ever loved someone else. If the sky were blue and the sea were green, and everything that I have ever seen.
Can only be the in-between, of the now and then of life.

With your blood-red lips and your pitch-black eyes, you stared into my soul.
With my frantic grip on the slippery earth, I have slipped into that hole,
With my tender grasp on what might have been, and what has come to pass,
I've fought and clawed and kicked and screamed and I've always saved my ass.

But now I've found another place that lives 'tween here and there.
I've laughed and cried and spat and lied. To a God who wasn't there.
So as the steel bird lands and the families wait for their loved ones boxed in pine.
I tip my head and thank God, that this son, he was not mine.

My wife she cries every day when she sees the boys come home.
And the crowds they line Wootton Bassett streets, to show she's not alone.
The papers hold the faces of those boys lost in attacks.
And the surgeons piece together the remains of who came back.

The parade, it is over now and the marching men are gone.
They might only be a number, but we loved them everyone.
Was it freedom they were fighting for? Or just their daily pay?
Whilst the parents line that village street and wipe their tears away

But I'll tell you this. If one sweet kiss would stop that boy of mine.
From lying in that bloody sand, so all alone and scared and dying.
I would hold him tight, with all my might, and stop him leaving home.
So, he could not go, and fight a war. In that land, he's never known.

My wife she cries every day when she sees the boys come home.
And the crowds they line Wootton Bassett Streets, to show she's not alone.
The papers hold the faces of those boys lost in attacks.
And the surgeons piece together the remains of who came back.

JOHN AND SUE

Towards the end of my school days, I was the best of friends with a boy called Billy Collins. I think he was probably the best friend I ever had. For perhaps two years Billy, I and a couple of other lads used to hang around permanently and we could not be separated, be it playing football in the park, spending time in each other's houses or chatting up girls at the Windmill youth club.

Later, when we got jobs, we all went our amicable different ways and did not see each other again due to moving in different circles. I was in my first year in Germany when I heard Billy had been killed in a car accident along with David Thompson a chap I also knew quite well. One of my other friends who was in our small group was at the time a policeman and was first on the scene. I don't know who threw the dice that night.

I am with a couple of Facebook groups relating to Rothwell but it is very seldom I come across names that I remember or if I remember them, they don't remember me. However, I live in the hope that someone crops up so that we can both reminisce about the good old bad old times.

This is an early humorous ditty about some fictional characters living in Rothwell, Yorkshire. Abraham's hill was the steepest hill in Rothwell and Billy lived at the top of that hill.

As a kid, it was a challenge to take a run up on my bike try and get up the hill in third gear without stopping. This was the highest gear most push bikes had unless you had an expensive racer which had a derailer and they had five gears. Nowadays even the cheapest of bikes come with at least 15 gears.

John and Sue were some friends I had lost touch with from my teenage years in Rothwell. They were part of a group I would visit the pubs with. Actually, it was two groups, one of girls and one of lads. With this group, we went to Batley Variety Club which was probably the best entertainment club in the Leeds area. I saw The Drifters and The Hollies there as well as Freddie Star.

We also went into Leeds but that never ended well as a group of 17-year-old lads, loads of beer and groups of other lads were never going to be a peaceful ending when the testosterone was running high. I think these experiences put me off going out in a group on the town forever, not that I was afraid of a bundle, I just got fed up with the mither of the actions afterwards. As far as the police are concerned the world over, "If you have been drinking, you're guilty."

I still go out every now and then but only have a couple of beers and leave early.

Ursula often looks up when I get in from a special celebration and says, "You back already? It's only 10 O' clock."

Anyway, this group would meet up a couple of nights a week and have a good laugh. We were best of friends forever for about 12 months and then we all went our separate ways.

There is no truth to this story. It's just a fun song. It has to be read in a Yorkshire accent. Obviously, written around the same time as Irish Nympho.

Sue was waiting in the shadow of the pier.
You could see through her see-through dress and smell the smell of beer.
Flasher John came walking, till he got where had got.
He said I'm going to get me some grub, are you coming with me or not.

John treated his girlfriend Sue to a romantic meal for two.
Three portions of Pilau rice and two of vindaloo.
After they had finished, and the waiter turned his back.
They left at speed because indeed, they had no money for the snack.

After running half a mile, they opened up the door.
To a flat they shared with various friends, numbering three or four.
The room was cold, the gas had gone. Cut off weeks ago.
Looking out of the window, John said, "It looks like snow."

This cold wind that was blowing. It went right in Sue's left ear.
John was pacing around the room; he could feel big danger near.
"Shut that booming door," she said. I do wish you'd remember.
"There's a terrible draft in here, it feels just like December."

"Don't you be so cheeky," Sue looked at him and glared.
She hung his coat up on a hook and ran halfway up the stairs.
"Is there anyone else in here? Or are we on your own?"
John said, "I'll just make some tea," and Sue began to moan.

"What's up with you," John snarled, he snarled again and stared.
He did a rather fast about-turn and ran right back down the stairs.
You've gone a funny shade of Lincoln green, tinged with lilac blue.
John was looking very worried now, not knowing what to do.

As John knelt down just by her side, the front door exploded in.
McPaddy (A policeman) stood there in his prime, He was looking rather dim.
There is a suspicion, he said to them, that thieves and thugs are near.
And I'm going to sniff them out, then you're going to jail, I fear.

McPaddy being a constable, He was trained by boys in blue.
He had kicked the door down before he knocked, as he was trained to do.
I've heard a rumour about some booty. That may not be true entirely.
But I will continue smashing up your house whilst I pursue my enquiries.

Constable McPaddy thought things were not going as he had planned.
I'm going to do you for possession lad. I can see it in your hand.
Anything you say will be taken down by me.
Sue said, "Underpants," and John said, "Feel free."

The moral of this story is the moral of this tale.
Is pay for all the food you eat if you don't want to go to jail?
And if you suffer from stomach cramps, you should know just what to do.
And don't try running home too fast, after a meal of Vindaloo.

LOOK WHAT THEY DONE TO ME

I have smoked from the age of 16 and was a full-blown smoker at 17 finishing a pack a day. At my height of the habit if we had to stay awake for a couple of days when on military operations, this would go up to two or three packs a day. In Germany, cigarettes were so cheap that it was normal to continually pass the cigarettes around during one of the constant smoke breaks.

Luckily, I was also constantly playing sports and running quite a few miles a week, so the smoke did not affect my lungs too much. Over the years, I tried to stop many times and even had acupuncture once to no avail. Finally, once leaving the army on my fortieth birthday I managed to stop and have never picked up a cigarette since. It took Ursula a further 10 years to kick the habit.

My only vice now, if you ask my doctor, is I drink too many units of alcohol. I try and keep it below 20 units a week, and this is still frowned upon by my doctor. I think that is very good with my history of over one hundred units of alcohol plus a week, coupled with a minimum of two hundred fags a week, which was my stable diet for 20-odd years.

As a young teenager, I had a couple of joints but since then have always steered clear of drugs. I do not understand why people become slaves to drugs, discounting social amounts of nicotine and alcohol. What makes them look at other drug users and think, I want to be just like them.

There are always ramifications of people's actions. This is one subject that I have treated with disgust all my life. I cannot comprehend why any person no matter how poor, rich, clever or stupid can ever think that taking hard drugs is going to give them a better life. Once on the slippery slope, there is usually only one outcome.

I do touch on this subject in this song but purely from an ignorant point of view on the subject. I do not tend to have a great feeling of sympathy for anyone involved in drugs or the trouble people get into when trying to gather the funds to pay for them at the expense of the victims.

My iPod plays in the afternoon.
I wrote a text and told my feelings to you.
I told you I loved you and I'd smashed the car.
I said you were my honey, but I didn't have a penny in my savings jar.

And now I'm stranded, strung out and wasted.
Been on a booze binge, I'm so frustrated.
I've lost all my old friends.
Now we're looking like book ends.
It was the drugs in the end.
Oh, look what they've done to me.

But I know where I can get a fix.
Down an alley because I'm full of tricks.
I just have to get one hit.
Then I won't have to use it again.
If I only have one shot.
If I only have a small shot.
Then I can face the world again.
Oh, look what they've done to me.
Oh, look what they've done to me.
They caught me in the wrong house.
They hit me and they knocked me out.
They threw me in a jail cell.
And they threw away the key.
Third strike and you're out.
They threw me in a cell without.

Any shoelaces or any doubts?
Oh, look what they've done to me.

The Judge said 10 years, my dad tried to hold his tears.
My mum she broke down, and my sister had to cry.
My friends said they'd see me.
Every weekend they would visit me.
But these were good intentions, and it's six months since they lied.

But I've only got five years. (Good behaviour).
If I'm a good boy five years.
I'll get myself an ology.
Then I'll get myself a job.
Then I'll call up my girlfriend.
I will call up all my old friends.
If I can just make it through this weekend.
Oh, look what they've done to me. Oh, look what they've done to me.

MAKE THAT CHANGE

Sometimes, people just have to get away from the life they are leading to look for a brighter future. Although they leave the bad things, they also leave many good things and good friends and families. Those remaining have to get on with their lives and fill the hole that is left once the person has left.

Initially, the daily routine seems disorganised but a new routine soon will establish itself, with new activities to fill the missing holes in our lives. Perhaps, the new activities bring in a new circle of friends with things that you have in common.

I know this has happened to me on several occasions. Though we may maybe considered an outsider to the group who have been friends for many years, there is no reason why a new group cannot also be good for a laugh.

As they say, "Life goes on."

Some things will never be the same again, but you should never look back and regret it too much, as there is always some good in future things.

When you left so silently.
Closed the door so quietly.
They didn't know where you'd go.
They didn't know where you'd gone.
They didn't know what they'd done to make you go.

And now I'm living silently.
Living my life so quietly.
Starting to build again, A new life, start again.
And I know what it was that made you go.

People say that in a while,
Things will be different, in a while.
Things will make me smile.
Be happy for a while.
And I'll know what it was that made you go.

Don't you know you can make that change?
Start your life again and make that change.
Don't you know you can make that change?
So, it's time to turn your life around.
To face the world and stand up proud.
The change is taking place,
You've got a brand-new place.
You've got to start again. Don't look back.

I know you left so silently,
Closed the door so quietly.
I know you had to go,
To follow your heart, I know.
You had to leave this town. To make that change.

But don't forget when you go, I'll think of you when you go.
And all the time we had.
We were happy and we were sad.
And all those times we had. Will still remain.

But don't forget when you go, I'll think of you when you go.
And all the time we had,
We were happy. We were sad.
And all those times we had,
I would not change it.

MOUNTAIN AND RIVER BLUES

It's true that the blues are a great leveller, as every guitar player can play blues to some standard. No matter what the mood, there are always some lyrics that can be written to record events, actions and feelings that are current at that point in time. Sometimes funny, sometimes profound, sometimes just factual. I don't know which category this song would fit into. Try and read it to a blues beat and format.

My mama told me when I was a young man, My Papa said it too.
He said, Son when you're an old man,
And you've nothing left to do.
Climb up on a mountain,
Breathe in all you can breathe.
Follow the journey of the river.
From this mountain to the sea.

And your hand starts to tremble.
As that whisky bottle pours.
And that old guitar you've played for years,
It just doesn't get applause.
Follow that river one last time.
Your mama would approve.
And write down your life's rhymes and times.
With the blues.

The river tried to move the mountain,
But this mountain held it down.
And it couldn't go right through it.
It had to go around.

And just when I thought,
All its power had been used.
That's when I felt.
The power of the blues.

So, if you're looking for Jesus.
But you think you found Old Nick.
And you can't find anyone's loving arms,
You can't seem to make love stick.
And if somebody tells you.
There's no direction left to choose.
Just show them the way,
Show them the way with the blues.

So, I followed that river.
And I listened to its song.
How its ripples moved the rocks
And how the rainfall made it strong.
And when I'd done all these things And I had nothing left to lose.
I sat right down,
And wrote my story of the blues.

Now if you're in the wilderness,
And there's nowhere you need to be. Just take some time and look around you, From the mountain to the sea.
And if your life meanders,
Like all slow rivers do.
You'd better tighten up your boot strings,
There's lots more walking for you to do,

NO, YOU IN MY BED

I love sitting on the sand dunes watching the sea rushing in. Generally, if it's in Great Britain there is always a chill to the wind unless it's mid-summer. After the initial thrill of seeing the waves and the power, the sea can exert on the cliffs or on the stonework of sea walls and piers, and once the majesty of the sea birds free flying at breakneck speed over the waves is appreciated, this is the time to admit it's bloody freezing out here.

"Let's go for a nice cup of tea."

Certain perverts in the folk club called this the frustrated farmer's song (Changing the word you for ewe. Making the title No Ewe in My Bed).

Personally, I think that's a load of Baaalocks.

I spoke to you this morning.
You said you would soon hit town. It's now late in the evening, and you've still not been around.
The way you left; I'm not going to look for you.
There's no one here beside me.
There's nothing left to do.

I walked down to the shoreline,
The sun was on my back.
The breeze went right through me.
So, I slowly wandered back.
I can't say if those rays warmed up my soul.
I'm just sitting here this evening.
There's no one here at all.

Is there anybody listening?
Can you tell me what to do?
Wondering if you're out there.
And where you're going to.
There's only one thing I would like to see.
And that's you sitting here smiling.
Talking quietly with me.

A cold cup of coffee is sitting in my hand.
You said you had to see me.
I met all your demands.
There's not even enough time for me to go anywhere.
I'm all alone this evening.
And no one really cares.

There's a big wind blowing.

And it's getting out of hand. Big storm a coming, travelling across this land.

Big reason for leaving going around in my head.

No reason for staying.

There's no you in my bed.

ON THE BREEZE

Another story about losing friends along the way, In the army we moved home every couple of years and it really makes me wonder how many good friends we lose contact with as soon as we move location. Perhaps, these are just passing acquaintances and not true friends. The good thing is, we can meet up after 20 years apart and continue conversations as though we were never away.

I suppose it's best not to dwell on things that we have no control over.

I feel the rain, wash away the pain inside

I know one day, you'll leave to go and live your life, I just hope you'll say goodbye.

I tried to call you; I was a heartbreak away.

I tried to call you. On that day

The wind came in and blew away my only friend.

I'm here again waiting for my text to send.

But you don't reply again.

I tried to call you; I was a heartbreak away.

I tried to call you. On that day

It's now and then, I think of you, or so they say.

It's black and white, the reasons that you went away.

Now, you're just on the breeze.

On the breeze.

ON THE RUN

This story contains lots of exciting components.

1. Love
2. Guns
3. Murder 4 Police chases
4. Hunting dogs.
5. Escaping murderers.
6. Freezing to death.
7. Starvation
8. Broken promises.

It could be a fantastic Hollywood blockbuster. If it had the right producer, director, actors (and lyrics)

Honey, you've been gone since you walked out that door.
I don't miss you anymore; I don't miss you anymore.
I sure am missing you.

Honey, they said you were seeing him at night,
Well, I saw him through my sight, I squeezed that trigger tight.
Now I don't know what to do.

The sheriff's men came for me and tried to hold me tight.
I fought with all my might. I left them in the night.
Now, I'm running back to you.

You told me that you'd love me all of my life.
You said you'd be my wife, as we held each other tight.
I sure am missing you.
My mind is a reeling and my legs can't feel to stand.
I don't know where I am as I'm running through this land.
Now I'm running back to you.
Now I'm cold and I'm hungry, I'm frozen halfway through.
I've outrun the men in blue, I've outrun all my thoughts too.
I don't know what to do.

I jumped me a freight train halfway through the night.
The police lights were in sight. The dogs gave me a fright.
Nearly had me too. I thought they nearly had me too.

My wet clothes are stiffening and freezing where I lie.
I think I'm going to cry; I fear I'm going to die.
I sure am missing you.

The wind, it keeps blowing, through this carriage that I ride.
I'm as cold as death inside, I know I'll close my eyes.
The rhythm of this train, it gets to you.
The rhythm of this train, it gets to you.
The rhythm of this train, it gets to you.

PARENTS SENSES

I suppose all kids want their parents to be proud of them. My father died when I was only 19, so he never had a chance to see me progress through life, with my wife and family. We were living abroad and my daughter was only five weeks old when he died, so he never saw his granddaughter, his first grandchild.

My mother still continued telling me to comb my hair and speak nicely on the occasions that I visited. Also to dress nicely if I was going outside the house.

I used to argue, "I was 40 years old, a warrant officer in the armed forces and a holder of the British Empire Medal which is a Queens Honours award," but this did not stop her from mithering.

I constantly have to bite my tongue when talking to my son and daughter about how I would deal with the issues they go through in life. I am a totally different character to them and they have a much more philosophical way of dealing with things.

They consider the consequences of their actions, whereas I was more likely to barge in, upset everyone and then go away leaving whoever to pick up the pieces. I hope I am a bit wiser now and I also know that your children are always your children no matter how old they are.

If they could see me now.
What would they make of me?
If they could see me now.
How I turned out to be
Would they feel so proud of what I had become?
Would they be so proud if I lived in a slum?
If they could just see me now.

If they could sense me now.
What would they sense in me?
If they could sense me now.
Do you think they would agree?
That I had become all that they wished of me.
That I had become what they wanted me to be.
 If they could just sense me now.

If they could hear me now.
Would they listen to me?
If they could hear me now.
Do you think they would agree?
Would they hear all the words that I said?
Or would they make up their reasons just to be misled?
If they could hear me now.

If they could touch me now.
Would they feel the warmth in my heart?
If they could touch me now.
Would they know that we were not that far apart?
In everything I know.
And everything I sang.
And everything I've tried.
And all I have done.
And everyone I've taught.
And prayed to above.
And everyone I've held,
And everyone I've loved,

If they could just touch me now,
If they could just touch me now.

RETURN OF THE PANAMA HAT

Working away from home for 18 months in Dorchester, Dorset, I made many friends some of which were in the local Folk Music Club. One of the songs that was often requested of me was to play 'Panama Hat' by Eric Bibb. Bibbs's song is about visiting Cuba and staying in the same hotel as Hemmingway when he wrote 'Old Man and the Sea'.

This verse is an account of when one of the friends I worked with started giving me some banter when I was singing it and the folk club regulars took Umbridge with him, asking him politely to leave. A similar thing happened with the same chap a few months later in a different folk club. I was singing a song about what I kept in my pockets.

In the very short break between verse and chorus, I heard, "How many pockets has he got."

At this, I burst out laughing and struggled to finish the song. He got some very disapproving looks from the residents and I don't think he volunteered to come out to folk nights with me again.

I was sitting in a bar, just like that.
Singing a song about a Panama hat.
The crowd, they had heard this song before.
They sang along and cried for more.

I played all night in an alternate pitch.
My feet they tapped and my fingers twitched.
Until the guy with the haircut shouted, "Stop."
The bar fell silent. The pin did drop.

They pushed him right out of that door.
It was the funniest thing you ever saw.
The barman laughed.
The beer was poured.

And the Panama hat was sung once more.
The violin did a solo run.
The accordion played and the Kazoo hummed.
The eggs they rattled and the mandolin strummed,
With four-part harmony when the chorus comes

And then we came to the history bit.
The one where it says where Hemmingway sits.
It describes the taste of that special drink.
It goes down smooth and the ice cubes chink.
It's about walking on the sand and missing the kids.
And about wearing cool shades to cover my lids.
About working on the brim because I like it real flat.
So, let's sing another verse of the Panama hat.

The haircut man now felt left out.
He began to moan; he began to shout.
He banged on the window to be let in.
We all stood inside and began to grin.

He leant on the window and began to sigh.
I thought I saw a tear shine in his eye.
So, we let him in, just like that.
And the song he sang was the Panama hat.

The moral of the story, the morel of the song.
Is you don't have to stay where you don't belong?
And you don't have to curse and you don't have to moan.
Because wherever you leave your hat. It's your home.
Wherever you leave your hat. It's your home.

SEASONS

Don't the seasons seem to rush past these days? We only just get past Christmas, then it's summer holidays and back to the shop to buy crackers and nuts. Well maybe not that fast. We are very lucky to live in England. Each of our four seasons changes the whole scenery that we see throughout the year.

I know we all go on holiday and return home saying how marvellous the things we saw are, but can you imagine living in Alberta looking at the prairie grass all year round or in Lanzarote looking at the lava fields? When we drove to Italy from Innsbruck to the Tuscany Valley, initially the sight of the Alps mountains was breathtaking but after driving through them for six hours they seemed a bit monotonous as we wanted to see the sky.

No, I think I will stick with our green and pleasant land even when it's raining stair rods and freezing cold for four months of the year. There's nothing wrong with the weather, you have just put on the wrong clothing.

> Summer, now it is going.
> Autumn, it draws in so soon.
> Coolness the wind is blowing.
> Not sure where we are going.
> Sorry, for me not knowing.
> How will we ever pull through?

> Autumn, the leaves are turning.
> Nighttime draws in so soon.
> And all the plants stop growing.
> Not sure where we are going.
> Sorry, for me not knowing.
> And for playing the same old tune.

> Seasons they bring their changes. Each one's a different tune.
> The winds of change are blowing. Not knowing which way we're going.
> Sorry, for me not knowing. I hope I will get there soon.

> Winter. The frosts are biting.
> Songbirds have lost their chimes.
> Snowing. Snow drifts are growing.
> Knowing which way, we're going.
> Hoping your love is growing.
> There are clear skies all through the night.

Springtime the mornings brightening.
The sun warms the morning dew.
Chorus. The dawning chorus.
Birds flying all around us.
The morning mist surrounds us,
And then, well then,
The sun breaks through.

Seasons they bring their changes. Each one a different tune.
Knowing which way, we're going. Wherever the wind is blowing.
And whichever way we are going. I will be with you.

Summer is here to cheer us.
Browning our paled skin.
The Blooming world astounds me.
You're loving arms around me.
And I'm so glad you've found me.
And the baby? Oh, the baby!

She arrives in spring.

SOLID AIR

When you sit on the couch after a good meal or a hard day's work, the couch sucks you in and heavy eyelids snap shut and it's power nap time. In the seconds before you awake fully, your body feels heavy but so comfortable. Maybe, I should just lay here for another five minutes.

Feels like I'm breathing solid air.
It's been so long since I've seen you there.
Feels like I'm breathing, breathing solid air.

I remember I was a lot like you.
I didn't care what I had to do.
Feels like I'm breathing, breathing solid air.

Now, the time has come or so it seems.
To throw away all of my dreams.
Feels like I'm walking, walking through solid air.

There's a cloud high in the sky.
I watch it as it passes by, its floating high, high above solid air.

And the sun is so far away.
Saying goodbye to yesterday.
Tomorrow I'll be breathing, breathing, solid air.

SO LONG AGO

It's inevitable that some partnerships/marriages fail, and some people have and some have not. People have different backgrounds and ethics, and I accept that a couple's separation is a natural reaction to a failed marriage. What I don't understand is the planned paths partners take to hurt each other.

What makes them hate each other with a vengeance if neither party has not done anything wrong, and they have just grown apart? I suppose people grow apart but stay together until one of the party gets fed up and does something wrong and this action lights the blue touch paper.

Make up your own story about the couple below. What happened to them? Why did they separate? What had she done? Why did she come back? It's all very intriguing.

He opened the door, to answer the knock,
Which entered his life a moment ago?
The wind it blew in and cooled down the house.
It was already cold. From so long ago.

They said our hellos,
He let her come in,
She took off her coat.
He sat by the fire.
They spoke of a time, it was so long ago,
When they were still friends.
"So why are you here?"

She turned her head and looked at his life.
He had captured that life and hung it in frames.
Were those his kids?
Had that been his wife?
She said he looked tired.
She asked what he did.

And the wind it kept blowing, through the cracks in his door.
And the rain came in, through the holes in the panes.
He asked if she still had that house in the town.
She said that she did,
She said he looked drained.

He walked to the kitchen.
He lit the stove.
She stood herself up. She followed him in.
She put her hand on his face, looked into his eyes.
Then she saw the hate, still burning inside.
She jumped back and turned, as though she were shot.
She grabbed her coat and walked out of the door.

I suppose there was something that he didn't say,
But he was so cold, she was so far away.
She drove down the track, in her shiny new car.
It was worth more than five years of his wage.
Turning the corner, she did not look back,
Some things are the same, some things never change.
Her bag still hangs from the back of the chair.
Inside is a phone. She never did call.
Inside is a box, with their old wedding rings,
From when they were still friends. It was so long ago.
From when they were still friends. Was it really 10 years?

Chapter 18
Bosnia 1992

October 1992

18 months have passed since I returned from Gulf War I and things have slowly returned back to normal, or at least as normal as can be expected in the current climate of troop reductions throughout the army. We still have as many commitments as before but now we have to carry them out with only two-thirds of the manpower and two-thirds of the budget.

As normal, we moan about everything that changes our daily routine and the proven systems we have had in place for ages, but at the end of the day, we accomplish all the tasks given to us. As far as the top brass is concerned we are coping. In reality, we are completely over-stretched.

The answer seems to be that we are paid to supply a service 24 hours a day, so working a 60-hour week even when not on operations or exercise is acceptable.

The downside to being part of the REME organisation is that when there is nothing happening in camp, the unit we are attached to can have time off, play sports all day or just have a normal day where everything can be done in slow time. Dinner breaks can be two hours and coffee breaks can last an hour. Back in the workshop, vehicles still need maintenance.

All vehicles have an inspection and servicing routine which normally highlights faults that require spares demanding and fitting when they arrive. An armoured vehicle is a very high-maintenance vehicle that needs constant attention. This is all completed alongside our fitness training and any trade upgrade training we all have to complete. Whilst in camp we never have any time to just chill out and do anything at a leisurely pace.

To think that, for years we have been situated in Germany to defend Europe against any Russian aggression. When it came to fighting Iraq, we had to remove items (cannibalise) from most of the vehicles left behind in BAOR to enable us to have enough spares to do the job. All the defence cuts have really had an impact on the stores we are allowed to hold in reserve, just in case, we had a major conflict occur without any warning. Just like the Iraq invasion.

On returning from the Gulf, we had to strip the Warriors of the additional armour we had put on in the desert and repaint all vehicles from a desert sand colour to black and green again. All cannibalised vehicles had to be rebuilt to their former glory which involved hundreds of hours of work.

At the present moment, we are awaiting the outcome of a meeting of NATO headquarters to decide if we are going to be sent on a peacekeeping mission into the former Yugoslavia, A civil war has started between the Serbian Bosnians and the Croatian Bosnians. If we do get involved, at least this time we will only be taking food aid to the enclaves that have been cut off, we will not be subject to the pressures of an all-out war as we were in Iraq.

I thought I was lucky when I managed to extend my tour in Fallingbostel, Germany, as I presumed that if another operational tour came up, we would be left out of it. Our recent commitments over the past three years have after all been quite hectic. As it happened the Staffordshire regiment was replaced by the Cheshire regiment.

Although all the logistic support which included the REME personnel stayed in location, as far as politics are concerned the Cheshires are due for the next operational tour and so the REME LAD (Light Aid Detachment) have been politely invited to go with them.

It has finally been confirmed that the 1st Cheshire Battalion are to go to Bosnia along with engineers from Hohne, Celle and 7th Armoured Workshop REME from Fallingbostel. I was due to be posted to 7th Armoured Workshop REME within Fallingbostel in a few months and had been told that I would be moved into the families office whilst the workshop was in Bosnia.

With this in mind, I walked into my Commanding Officer Colonel Bob Stewart's office and explained that I had been with his Warriors since they arrived in Germany from new and that I was the most Warrior-experienced REME staff sergeant that he had. Also, I was going to be in the family's office if I stayed, which was a total waste of my expertise and experience.

Also, as that required someone who could sympathise with the young wives, I was more likely to tell them to sort themselves out and get on with it, as I am not known for my sympathetic manner. I told him my wife had been left to her own devices many times when I was away and that I had not made myself socially aware that the army has changed and now everyone needs to be mollycoddled over the slightest problem. I think this statement made sure that he did not think I was the correct man for the job.

A day later, he informed me that he had actually fallen for my outburst as there was some logic to it and that my tour with the Cheshires had been extended six months until after the operation. I was over the moon but I still had to face Ursula and tell her I was going away for another six-month tour.

Once again, all the Warriors had to be re-fitted with the Chobham armour we removed 18 months ago and brought up to A1 condition in regard to maintenance and servicing as soon as possible. The Chobham armour we removed after Gulf War 1 was returned to us and we proceeded to fit it all again.

Originally, we thought that this would be a simple job as all the original mounting holes were still there in the Warrior hulls, but as it transpired the mounting plates had been damaged whilst in storage and hardly any of the holes lined up. It was only after about three days that the one-day-long task was then complete, with the normal complement of cut, crushed and bruised fingers.

The Warrior vehicles that had been returned to their original green and black after the sand colour painted for the Gulf now had to be painted white for U.N. duty and if anybody has tried to paint white on top of black will realise this takes about three coats.

However, the powers that be assured us that only one coat would be needed and so after the first coat and a lot of I told you so's the programme had to slip yet again as the vehicles did need another coat or two (or three).

Spares were arriving from all over the world and again vehicles that were not involved in Operation Grapple (as this tour was now called) were again cannibalised. Again, replacements had to be found to replace all the sick, lame and lazy personnel we had on our effective strength.

In fact, nearly all the major problem points we had reported post-Gulf War still had not been addressed and we were again having to implement them all over again. Why do people ask for a report upon report if nobody takes any action with the facts we are giving them?

Since the Gulf War, my fitter section has changed drastically with most of the old crew leaving and being replaced by new people posted in.

The fitter section is now as follows.

Mechanics	
SSGT	ME
SGT	Ian Kite
Cpl	Dave Mc Bride
LCP	Ian Butcher
LCPL	Tosh Ainley
Cfn	Tony Clark
Cfn	Phil Grimwood
Armourer	Ed Burns
Electrician	Jim Nicols
Recovery	Tid's Tidbury

Although new to the fitter section most of the lads are experienced with Warrior and we should have no problem maintaining the fleet.

Once the armoured vehicles had been loaded onto the boats, we had a week off with our families. During this waiting period, I decided that Ursula's 2.3-litre V6 Ford Sierra could do with a facelift. I booked the spray bay in the workshop and proceeded to strip down Ursula's car in preparation.

Each panel and plastic bits were properly masked off and the car rubbed down to accept the facelift. I bought some Ford RS red acrylic paint and proceeded to spray the previously dull gold panels with a fantastic bright racing car RS red.

Everything went smoothly and I stood back to admire my work. Brilliant. It was only when I came out of the spray bay that I noticed that someone had been into the main hangar and left a door at the back of the workshop open. The open door had created a flow of air from the spray bay across the workshop to exit out of this open door. The air had moved slowly over a dozen Land Rovers that had just been painted white ready for deployment.

Along with the air millions of tiny airborne Ford RS red paint particles had also moved through the workshop and had deposited themselves on the shiny newly painted white Land Rovers giving them all a pinkish tinge. Oh My God!

The next four hours were spent very gently, going over the vehicles with a diluted thinner and rolls and rolls of soft paper to remove the red tinge, without damaging the shiny white finish previously on the Land Rovers.

Once finished, I then cleaned up the spray booth and disappeared from the workshop leaving the heaters on to cure the Sierra paint. I returned the following day just to pick up the beautiful shiny RS red Sierra knowing that no one would be any the wiser and saying nothing to no one.

A week later, when we returned from leave, I was coming out of the orderly room on the workshop's second floor and the Artificer Sergeant Major Martin Craig. was leaning over the balcony with a puzzled look on his face.

As I walked past, he collared me and said, "Have you seen the Rovers? They have a pinkish hue?"

I stood next to him and looked down over the vehicles. Well! I'll be blown, he was correct. I explained to him that as the guys had had to repaint so many vehicles, they were running out of time and probably didn't mix the two-pack paint together properly, or maybe it was the wrong temperature or the spray gun pressure was wrong. Deciding that I had given him enough food for thought I walked away.

Martin Craig had joined the army at the same time as me and had also served with me in a few other units as well as being my ASM in the Gulf War with the Staffordshire regiment.

Just as I thought I was in the clear and was smiling to myself as I walked down the stairs, his voice rang out, "I know you had something to do with this, Flower. I just don't know how yet."

Note to self. "Don't let Ursula drive past him in her lovely RS red car for the next few weeks!"

Whilst my feelings on this deployment were very similar to the feelings I felt before departing to the Gulf, at least this time we were the goodies and not somebody's enemy. This would make a pleasant change as we were the aggressors in Gulf War I.

The British Army was seen as the bad guys by the Catholics in Northern Ireland, although we were supposed to be the peacekeepers there also. Helping the police patrol the provinces. The Royal Ulster Constabulary (Northern Ireland police force) were mainly Protestants. I can see how we could be seen as leaning towards the Protestant majority populations although certainly not backing the Ulster Freedom Fighters and Ulster Volunteer Force in any shape or form.

The children were living with us now unlike the last time I went on an operational tour, when they were at boarding school, so at least I could say a proper goodbye this time. Last time, it really got to me not giving them a proper goodbye just in case something did happen to me. Little things like that always play on one's mind in the darkest hours of the day.

Nevertheless, things were quite mellow as I was not going to war but departing as a peacekeeper. Little did I know that I would be shot at with bullet, shell and catapult to a much greater extent than I ever was when I was in the Gulf.

When I arrived at the airport, I was informed that I was the chalk commander. The best description of this job is that I was the one who had been dicked with the job of ensuring all baggage and people from the Cheshire regiment actually got on the plane.

All my comrades thought this was hilarious as I had to run around making sure everything and everyone got on the plane whilst they were more interested in where the nearest bar was. The term Herding Cats comes to mind.

After an hour, we all embarked onto the plane and as I got to the door, I was told that the chalk commander could ride in the first-class compartment with the officers that will teach them not to mock me. Not only did I get first-class service all the trip but also just before we set off down the runway, I was asked if I wanted to sit in the pilot's cockpit for take-off, which I did.

This was brilliant up to the point when the nose lifts because then all I could see was the sky as there were no side windows where I was sitting. I did, however, milk every moment with a smug face when telling the guys of my experience.

On arrival at Split, which is a coastal port in Croatia, we stayed overnight in the hangers within the docks complex. This is where our vehicles had been unloaded and the vehicle crews settled down to a good night's sleep as we had a long drive ahead of us the next day.

Unfortunately, we were also bedding down with what seemed like hundreds of stray, hungry and noisy cats so our nice restful sleep was interrupted every five minutes with cats meowing, fighting and searching for food.

I also had to tell my vehicle crews, "No you cannot take a bloody cat with us in your wagon."

The following morning, we were transported to Tomislavgrad (TSG) which is the nearest place the low-loader vehicle transporter could go to the border due to the poor conditions of the tracks and the present war zone borders.

Tomislavgrad was situated in the foothills of the mountains and remained the main staging post for us throughout the tour. The journey was quite spectacular as most of the time we were driving parallel with the coast and the elevation gave a view of 20 to 30 miles over the coastline, so it was just like a free coach tour.

Being over 150 miles from Vitez, which was our final destination, Tomislavgrad was regarded as a safe area. However, shortly after leaving that location, it was subject to an artillery bombardment of 150 artillery shells. From that, we can presume that it was not that safe if you compare it to going for a McDonald's in Leeds. (But the food was obviously better in TSG).

After unloading the vehicles from the low loaders, we loaded all our personal kit that we would be wearing and using for the next six months, into the storage bins on the vehicles and said goodbye to civilisation. We climbed into the vehicles fired them up, checked the radios were working, our weapons were loaded and formed up at the foot of the mountains ready for the long journey to Vitez.

We then perfected the art of hurrying up and waiting as the army is prone to do after years of practice of moving troops. Finally, at nightfall, we started moving forward up the mountain not knowing what reception we were going to receive once we arrived in our operational area or indeed if an operational base was actually ready for us, as the daily changes in the front-line position were moving constantly.

At first, the tracks were manageable but as we climbed the steep gradient the temperature plunged into minus figures, the snow and ice got deeper and the tracks got narrower.

In a short while, we found ourselves having to dismount on many occasions to guide the vehicles by hand signals as the tracks in places were only six inches wider than the vehicles and very slippery. A tracked vehicle steers by braking one track and driving the other. This, in fact, induces a skid to allow the vehicle to change direction. The Warriors had the ability to turn very quickly into 30tonne sledges.

There was also the very minor problem of the fact that to the right of the vehicle was a shear rock face and to the left a drop of at times four hundred feet, not that we could see it as it was pitch-black and a drop of only 10 feet was just a black void. We therefore had to assume that every black void was a killer drop, as every now and then we saw the twinkle of a house light far below us. After returning on this route during daylight hours, we were not far wrong.

The design of tracked vehicles is to ensure that as little ground pressure as possible is necessary to allow it to pass over wet boggy ground or sand without sinking in. This was a definite negative asset as we continued along the passes and I found myself in a permanent position of getting ready to jump for my life every time the vehicle started to slide.

My location in the vehicle commander's hatch is about 10 feet high so just jumping from this position is no mean feat. Jumping into pitch darkness from a moving vehicle increases the risk of injury tenfold.

Before starting this journey, I had taken part in mountaineering and I have also experience in abseiling and parachuting. After this little jaunt in the country, I now hate heights and although I did not have an option as the job has to be done, I will never again volunteer for anything above sea level again.

For months after Bosnia, every dream I had involved heights and climbing or falling. I suppose I had some form of PTSD. (Don't tell anyone or they will all want some). 30 years later, I still don't like working when I have to climb past the sixth or seventh rung on a ladder.

After eight hours, we finally arrived at the first checkpoint overlooking Prozor Lake. Although we had no concept of how far above the lake we were (It was still dark and the reflected lights of the town on the lake seemed miles below). At a rough guess, I would estimate at least a thousand feet.

It was at this point, that we were told that the reason we moved at night was so that the vehicle commanders and the drivers, would not be able to see how far down we would fall if we came off the road, and thus not scare us. Wrong! During daylight, this checkpoint had a marvellous view overlooking the picturesque town. The lake was a shimmering blue and the reflections were just like looking into a mirror.

On numerous occasions afterwards, when travelling to Split or Tomislavgrad we used this parking place to have a coffee, take some photographs (I had made sure I had a film in the camera this time), and generally mellow out.

As we were the first British battalion to enter Bosnia in force, nobody actually knew what to expect and how we would be received by the locals once we were on the ground.

Throughout the journey, we came across hundreds of refugees either walking, in cars or more than often on a horse and cart carrying all their belongings with them. Some looked like they were just out for a Sunday drive, others looked starving and completely shocked by the whole experience. I have no doubt that as we are nearing the front-line these sights will become more and more common and we will have to get used to it as much as possible.

This journey is taking us hours to complete. The speed we are travelling is just above walking pace, unlike before when any military operation I have been involved with, the area had already been navigated and marked as a route. Here we are in the pitch dark as there are no streetlights and only a few road markings.

In this case, we are following the vehicle in front and now we have negotiated the mountain tracks, have to stick to the main roads not knowing if we are passing through a hostile area or not. As we approached Prozor the town took on a very sinister look. What appeared to be a quiet peaceful town now, up close, was scarred with bullet holes and shell fire damage, with some buildings still smouldering.

Continuing through we followed the valley floor driving down a small icy windy track that follows a small river. We were heading for Vitez via Gornji Vakuf where B Company were going to be located. (At the time Gornjy was relatively untouched, but soon was to be the scene of a major battle that left it completely destroyed.)

My favourite sergeant who was with me in the Gulf and still had an expression of a bulldog sucking a wasp even when he was happy, was now with B Company and we regularly bumped into each other on the road and swapped pleasantries, as soldiers tend to do. And sergeant, if you are reading this now, I meant every abusive word.

(As a footnote this same sergeant came looking for a job at the place I worked once I left the army. As he was an excellent tradesman, I recommended him for the job of service engineer on the Warrior due to him being an expert on Warrior. All he had to do was go to the interview and talk nicely. I put him up at my house and wished him good luck in the morning. He didn't get the job, nor did he ever thank me for getting him the interview or putting him up for the night. Why am I not surprised?)

All the villages we passed through had planks of wood propped up outside the windows, this was to limit shrapnel damage and more importantly to avoid snipers in nearby woods taking a potshot. Snipers were soon to be a problem for us also. It is nearly impossible to find where just one shot comes from when looking at a whole mountain covered in trees.

The strange thing that struck me was a solitary house could be burnt out but the houses next to it were untouched and then another would be burnt out. Neighbour shooting neighbour. I found out later that this was ethnic cleansing, which at first started off with the villages kicking out the victims and burning down their houses but now at this present time, the victims were being systematically killed.

In some villages, it was Muslims being murdered, in others it was Croatians (Croats), and the villages may be only a mile apart. Also, when the Serbians were attacking, both the Bosnian Muslims and the Croats fought together but when there was no threat from the Serbians, they would start killing each other again. It's a bit like a defendant pleading self-protection in a grievous bodily harm case.

When the judge asked him, why he punched the plaintive, the defendant replied, "I thought he was going to hit me and so I hit him back first."

It was not just a rage killing they were torturing each other and burning their next-door neighbour's kids as well. There is also a group called the HOS, these wear black uniforms and are a cross between the SS and the KBG who generally interrogate torture and kill anybody they come across who is not a member of their party. 30 years after this tour, when I see an old newsreel sometimes my memories come out of my eyes and run down my face.

The rest of the journey went well with just one minor vehicle breakdown of my vehicle. The accelerator linkage had fallen off my engine and could not be found within the engine compartment. I managed to thread some thin electrical wire around the fuel pump lever and route it over the engine panels into my hand. For the rest of the journey, I was in control of the throttle and guided by my driver.

All the passerby would hear as we drove past them would be my driver shouting, "On hold off…on hold off," for the next 50 miles as I yanked on the wire and held at various positions until ordered to release when he wanted the vehicle to slow down.

After following a single dirt track that followed the path of a scenic riverbed for several hours, we arrived in Vitez without any further problems. Only a few vehicles need coaxing to complete the journey. The locals seemed pleased to see us and it was obvious by the way they were treating us, like a liberating army, they thought we were there to fight for them. Whole families were in the streets bowing, cheering and waving.

Only too soon would they find out that that was not what we were here for. We were not on their side to fight their enemies but to try and keep the peace without shooting either of the warring factions. This would create further tension in an already volatile situation. Our mandate was to remain neutral to all the conflicting parties.

Chapter 19
Vitez

Our location in Vitez was split into two locations. The main battalion was situated in a large school location with showers, toilets and offices. The engineering and supply assets were situated in the old Renault garage that had bugger all. We arrived in the Renault garage in Vitez where the REME was to be located for the foreseeable future. I was immediately bathed in the splendour of the facilities.

No water, no electricity, no heating (in November!) only two showers for 150 men and women and three toilets that worked occasionally at first, but after a few days never worked again. Immediately we set up some rough and ready latrines using the bucket and chuck it technique into a hole we had dug.

The sleeping arrangements were tents on the garage shop floor or in the vehicles. I could feel straight away that this tour was going to be a luxury, which is if I were a sadomasochist with schizophrenic tendencies.

As mentioned, the battalion moved into the local school area. Needless to say, this had full facilities which did not cause any irritation to us at the garage at all! After stowing our kit and checking that all my company's Warriors were mechanically sound, we fell asleep in the vehicles as they were still warm from the engine heat created during the journey.

The next morning, I took in the sights and smells of this new location and thought what a pity this beautiful land is spoilt by the war. All the mountains were snow-capped and the winter flowers were out, the only thing not affected by this war was nature itself. Vitez is situated in the river Bosna valley with high mountains on either side. It has a very picture postcard-type atmosphere with all the little villages standing out from the mountains in the sunlight.

We were in this location for three days before our first humanitarian aid convoy arrived. We set about the task of escorting the HNCR (United Nations

High Commissioner for Refugees) aid convoys, as this would be our main priority for the next six months. Each convoy required a minimum of four Warrior infantry variants and a Warrior repair and recovery variant to escort them, although some of the larger convoys required a whole company.

The distance travelled could be as short as 20 miles and as long as two hundred miles depending on where the aid was needed most. After a period of time, we came to realise that only about half of the supplies that we delivered were actually received by the ones who needed it. Each link of the chain took a little out for themselves to give to their families or to the soldiers in their area.

Therefore, depending on which enclave we were supplying aid to, we were indirectly supplying one or more factions with food and blankets. This we had to accept as we did not have the time or the ability to deliver each load to each separate house and had to use the supply system dictated by UNHCR.

One of our first tasks was to go into Vitez and help the Zagreb Zoo move a brown bear into a cage. The bear had been a pet for a garage owner who had now fled the war and left the bear to starve to death and was kept in a large cage. The owners had now left the area a few days before and the bear was now hungry and angry at the strangers messing him about.

Eventually, we managed to get the bear some food and after that, he was quite placid. We then had to break open the cage to allow the zoo rescue people to do their stuff. Everything went quite smoothly and it gave us another tale to tell our kids.

At first, we were allowed to go where we wanted, but slowly over the next few months, the local commanders began to realise that we were neutral and we were not going to fight for their cause. The restrictions to our free running were slowly tightening and it would not be long before we had to flex our muscles and take command of the situation.

At this point, sniping at our vehicles whilst driving on convoys and other diversions became part of daily life. It was expected that a harder line had to be taken by the U.N. but nobody could sanction the use of force to deliver the aid. As the UN involvement in peacekeeping in this area was still early days, no orders were issued apart from the basic ones and we were left to approach each situation using our own common sense.

For example, if we came across a checkpoint with only a few local soldiers guarding it, we would try and force our way through by just shouting at them. However, if they still were adamant, we could not pass. Occasionally we would just crash through the barriers. Sometimes, however, it was obvious with the tension in the area that if we did this it would not take long for the guard force to get reinforcements and become aggressive.

This did not bother us but we had to think of the civilian lorry drivers in their soft-skinned vehicles that we were escorting, and slowly but surely our hands were getting tied as so often happens with United Nations missions.

At one checkpoint, whilst trying to convince the chap at the road barrier to let my convoy pass, a Serbian guard actually fired his weapon at my armoured vehicle to vent his anger at us. This was all well and good until some of his rounds actually ricocheted off the vehicle and hit another Serbian guard standing in the vicinity. The injured soldier then promptly lost his temper with the other guard and returned fire hitting his assailant in the legs.

So, there I was with two Bosnian soldiers bleeding all over the place trying to give them first aid for numerous bullet wounds and trying to explain to their fellow soldiers who suddenly came running to the disturbance, that they had shot each other and I had not done it.

Whilst they were running about looking for an ambulance, I just lifted the barrier, got back into my vehicle and escorted the convoy down the road leaving them to it. I reported the incident when I arrived back in Vitez and was told not to worry as they were always shooting each other either by accident or over some other trivial matter.

Most of the opposing forces on both sides were not very well trained and had only become soldiers a few months ago. They had been given a uniform, a gun and some ammunition and told to go and report to a local commander and he would tell them what to do.

The only rules of contact we had was if we were cornered and there was no chance of escape could we open fire, but if it was at all possible to drive out of the situation without showing aggression then we were to do so. Generally, when in an armoured tracked vehicle, it is possible to extract yourself out of a situation just by battening down the armoured hatches and simply driving away.

Providing you are not in charge of civilians travelling in soft-skin vehicles this was regularly done. However, extraction took a lot longer if civilians were involved as we could not just drive away and leave them.

The Bosnian's rules of contact seemed to be, that if the target was white with a blue UN flag flying and UN painted on the side, they could shoot at it any time they wanted. Time and time again over the next few months we were shot at by the Bosnians, Croats and the Serbs. With everything from small arms fire to artillery, mortars and tanks not to mention the mines they would purposely put on the roads.

We also had to keep an eye out for the kids firing ball bearings from catapults. Several vehicle commanders who had to sit in the turret with their heads sticking out were hit in the face with ball bearings. It did not take long for most vehicles to jury rig a transparent plate to look through and give protection from both catapult ammunition and the biting freezing wind chill that turned our faces blue in minutes.

This did, however, keep us on our toes and I did not have any problems with constipation for the whole six months I was out here.

There were times I must admit that I had had just about enough of these people, but once you leave the hostile soldiers and see how the civilians are struggling just to live, it is possible to see how frustrating it is for the soldiers in each of the factions. Knowing that their family may be starving or being ethnically cleansed, whilst they are somewhere else freezing cold, hungry and trying to protect the front-line.

Initially, the sight of starving humanity was very off-putting and we would throw our personnel rations from the vehicles as we drove passed. This was to try in our own little way to help stop the suffering, even though we knew that we now would not be eating ourselves for the next 24 hours.

This in the end had an adverse effect as once we were further into the tour the civilians were expecting this and so they would walk for miles to a road we would use regularly, in the hope of the odd ration pack thrown their way. The powers that be, quite rightly I suppose, ordered that this practice must stop.

Unfortunately, by now this was expected of us by the refugees and when we refused to give them anything, we were quite often pelted with stones and generally abused.

A run to Sarajevo was conducted every few days with medical supplies, food and blankets being required throughout the blockade. Warriors were only allowed to go so far as they were deemed to be too aggressive looking for a peaceful mission. For that reason, we had to stop about 10 miles out of the city and wait for the armoured personnel carriers to drive into the city, drop off the supplies and return.

This left us very little to do whilst waiting a few hours for their return. One day the lads parked up by the abandoned Sarajevo Winter Olympic village. Off they went to explore as they had a few hours to kill. Within 30 minutes, there was a call for a medic as one of the REME guys had broken his ankle.

The reason being that he had gone down the Olympic ski jump in a bin bag. Surprise, surprise you couldn't make it up! He could not understand how it had happened as lots of his mates had already done it quite safely.

I never did find out how far he jumped!

Of course, I never attempted anything dangerous on icy mountains. Well! There was that one time when I made a sledge from an old Swedish-style settee in Germany and used the tubular chrome framework to make a four-man sledge. We then transported it in a minibus with some mates up into the Harz mountains for a bit of fun.

It was only when it disassembled itself on a black-graded ski slope at 60 miles per hour did we considered that this was not the brightest thing to do. However, nobody broke any bones and it was mega fun up to the point everything went wrong. The German Ski slope people did not have a very good sense of humour and refused to see the funny side.

The slope had to be closed for an hour as the safety people had to go on the slope and remove the remains of the sledge that had a crash site about two hundred meters long. Needless to say, we were asked to go away and not return again. Ever.

Several times, I went on reconnaissance or escort missions where we would jump into a Land Rover and visit the small enclaves where there were some of our REME guys working on broken-down vehicles or recovery jobs. On one occasion, the workshop Recovery Warrior was called out. A vehicle had broken down on a mountain about 60 miles from Vitez and needed assistance. We led the way as an escort for the Warrior.

When we finally arrived after several hours of driving due to the icy road conditions and the very bad tracks for the Warrior to travel down. We found that the vehicle had not broken down but the commander was too scared to drive down the icy track in his 10-tonne vehicle! Here we were driving a 40-tonne vehicle up the same track to rescue them. Needless to say, a few choice words were said to him.

He then very sheepishly commanded his vehicle back to Vitez behind the Warrior. On the way back, we took a detour through a village and from the top of the hill we watched 50 or 60 prisoners of war being marched along the road after a town had been liberated by one side or the other. The borders shifted daily and it was hard to keep track of where the battle lines were.

We generally travelled with two or three vehicles but occasionally only one vehicle with two people. Greater numbers gave us a higher element of safety but generally, once out of the built-up areas, it was quite safe to travel. Anyway, I was used to working alone from when I was in Northern Ireland.

Chapter 20
Enniskillen/Armagh Border, 1979

On one tour of Northern Ireland, I was employed in a covert information gathering role. For this role, I had been allowed to grow my hair long and wear civilian clothes, not army uniforms. The tasks involved driving around Northern Ireland in a standard car dressed in civilian clothes picking up supplies for the small detachments dotted around the area the battalion was responsible for.

The other part of the job was dropping off the special forces chaps or our intelligence guys and then finding a quiet place to lay low until they were ready to be collected again. This was usually in the early hours of the morning down a country lane. When this happened, I would park the car in a hidden location and then walk down the track a few hundred yards and find a ditch to wait in.

At the time, the IRA were also patrolling the border areas so it was a good idea not to draw any attention to the location you were waiting. Although I carried a rifle and pistol, it certainly kept your mind focused whilst waiting for the rendezvous (RV) time to come. There were lots of wild animals and birds making noises in the hedges and long grass which kept me on my toes and also sometimes let my imagination give me some very bad scenarios.

After six months of doing this, I was quite knowledgeable of the shortcuts to many locations within Northern Ireland. At the end of the tour, the store's staff sergeant asked me to guide two trucks full of soldiers and weapons to a certain location. We set off and as I knew the route, I didn't look at my map. It was only after about 50 miles I realised that I was heading for the wrong location. I wasn't lost. I had just taken the troops to the wrong place.

Well never mind, what could possibly go wrong with taking two trucks loaded with weapons through the heart of Bandit Country? Once we reached Bessbrook mill I made a quick phone call telling them we had been delayed and would be at the correct location in an hour.

Hopefully, nobody would find out providing none of the guys in the trucks and escort rover said anything. Needless to say, when we returned to our home location, I was the laughingstock that night in the bar.

Another time I was driving a Sherpa van disguised as a builders van with a six-man squad in the back. Rather than take a long way around from Armagh to Enniskillen I knew a shortcut through Southern Ireland that did not have a checkpoint on the border and would save an hour of driving.

We had only just come back over the border into Northern Ireland when three Armoured Ford Granada's pulled us over and with rifles pointing at us told us to get out of the van. The Garda thought we were a southern Irish crew running illicit guns or bombs over the border. With a sheepish face, I told them I was a very naughty boy and I was on their side and had to promise I would not do it again.

On a more serious note, I was free running on my own one night in a Dodge van and broke down at Five-mile town between Enniskillen and Armagh, which at the time was quite a dodgy border town place to be. I knew there was a police station in the middle of the town so I coaxed the van coughing and spluttering (the van not me) to their front gate. When I arrived, the police station was closed and the van was now dead and wouldn't restart.

The radio was dead and we didn't have mobile phones in those days to make the situation worse, I also could not find a public phone. I found a dark unlit area to wait whilst I figured out how I was going to get out of this mess. Luckily an Ulster Defence Force Land Rover patrol had been sent from the next town to see what was going on.

The CCTV camera on the police station had picked me up loitering around the station area with a suspicious van that in reality could have been a proxy bomb. I have never been so relieved to see a friendly face. They towed me to their local UDR camp and I waited until morning for an army tow truck to take me back to St Angelo Camp in Enniskillen to get another van. This was not my finest hour.

Towards the end of the tour, we had to move from Portadown, Craigavon to an old police station in Kinawley, Enniskillen. The police station had just been a victim of a 1000 lbs bomb courtesy of the IRA and therefore was a bit of a mess. Whilst still in the covert role, part of my job was also to keep the platoon vehicles roadworthy. I required an area to work on the vehicles that was dry. The garage area was just a mess of twisted metal, wood and bricks due to the bomb.

Over the next few months, every time I went out on patrol, in my Sherpa van, I kept my eye out for any bricks, scrap wood or metal sheeting. After a few weeks, I had a garage-sized shelter to work on the vehicles and keep them dry.

Cushty.

Chapter 21
Vitez (Continued)

A Warrior repair and recovery vehicle is a 31-tonne armoured tracked vehicle with a crane and a winch fitted to allow every type of maintenance and recovery to be carried out in the field. To accompany the winch is a huge spade that mounts on the rear of the vehicle and to assist the crane is a stabiliser leg and lockouts to keep the vehicle on a level plain when lifting up to 6.5 tonnes of weight from the side using the crane.

During one convoy run, the hydraulic stabiliser leg mounted on the back of the Warrior recovery vehicle slipped out of location and was 400 mm proud of the side of the vehicle. As we passed a parked VW Golf GTI the offending leg hit the vehicle on the rear right-hand side and shunted it about 20 meters through a hedge.

We stopped to check if anyone was in it, which luckily there wasn't, as there was no one about to witness the incident we just secured the leg into the correct stowed position and carried on our merry way. In the current climate, stopping and finding out who owned the car could have enhanced the already heightened aggression we were subject to from the locals in this area.

It was safer all around to disappear before tensions were made worse, plus the fact that most cars had now been commandeered for use on official business and would not have been insured anyway.

The OC had the unenviable task of trying to keep the peace between all the different warring factions. One day, I went with the OC's party to visit a Croat commander. As his group walked down into an old factory cellar, they noticed that all the factories had explosives strapped to the building uprights made ready to explode in case the Bosnians attacked.

In the dark cellar, the cigar smoke was thick and as the new members for the meeting arrived, they all kissed a portrait of Marshall Tito that was hanging on the wall. It was just like a scene from The Godfather.

The commander had just finished talking about how professional his men were when one of his soldiers squeezed his trigger by accident. The rifle fired as the safety catch had not been applied. In this confined area, this was like a cannon being fired.

After the initial reaction thinking, we were in a shooting situation, our OC just sat there without saying a word and waited for the unfortunate soldier to be dragged out of the meeting whilst receiving several kicks and punches from every Croat in the room. At no point did we comment, as no words paint a thousand pictures. The majority of these soldiers were just local farmers who had been given guns.

As well as the tense times there were good times also and I will always remember the first time we managed to reach the town of Maglaj, this was a town that had been under siege for months by the Serbians. The look on the children's faces who had been living in the cellars for a year when they realised that the vehicles we had brought were full of food and warm clothing.

It was a very uplifting feeling at the time knowing that we were the only help they had received for months, knowing that the food and medical supplies we were bringing were actually saving countless lives.

On reflection, it was always depressing when returning to base, thinking that these people we were leaving behind, especially the women and children should not have been placed in this predicament by their own countrymen in the first place. How they were still living in the cellars again waiting for a more peaceful time.

Maglaj is about 100 miles west of Vitez and at the far end of the British sector of operations. At the checkpoint, just before Maglaj, I spoke to some of the locals who told me that they were quite happy living in a mixed community but now because they were in fear of their own lives, they were ordered to carry out ethnic cleansing of their friends and neighbours.

As they were telling me this, they were pointing to one graveyard saying this was a Croat graveyard, then to another graveyard saying this was Serbian, Muslim, Christian and so on.

Nothing is clear cut here because for many years the community has lived together and there is a lot of interbreeding between Muslims, and Christians both

Croatian and Serbians, so when the war arrived at their doorstep, they had to decide which side they supported, as there were no neutral areas to retreat to. The all-powerful HOSS roamed the hillsides and if there was any doubt at all, they would carry out immediate executions on the spot.

All around the country whether in Croat or Bosnian Muslim areas, when a HOSS Member walked past everyone from little children to grown men would lower their eyes and once the threat had gone, they would spit on the floor. They will get even one day and probably start off another civil war as this is the reason this one started, with the Serbians getting even for the atrocities carried out by the Croats years ago.

An orphanage was situated across the main bridge in Maglaj, all the residents lived in the cellars. This was to protect them from the artillery attacks and also the constant sniper fire. Although the snipers were firing across the valley, the snipers could guarantee a hit on a stationary target at one thousand meters.

The snipers could tell if a person was walking or running by using uprights of the bridge structure, acting as aiming points, just how far to aim off to hit a moving target. This was yet another place where we were to be accused of ethnic cleansing when evacuating people, even though we were just moving people to a safer place.

Orphanages were local aid drop-off points throughout our sector and we regularly dropped off food and blankets at their locations. I remember seeing a video of our guys visiting one during the Christmas period. All the soldiers who had been hardened by all the cruelty they saw in this country were now handing out loads of toys and presents to the children who had lost everything.

There was not a dry eye in the place. When aid was dropped off only a small portion made it to the actual people who needed it as much was syphoned off by the soldiers handing it out as their families were starving or poorly supplied also. At least, on this occasion, we hoped the children would be able to keep the toys we gave them.

Chapter 22
Kladanj

After six weeks located in Vitez, we were ordered to secure a base in a town called Kladanj. Kladanj is in the north of the country and our task was to act as a staging post for the convoys going to Tuzla. Tuzla being the main city in our northern area of operations. The trip to Kladanj involved going over yet another range of mountains and was about 150 miles northeast of Vitez. Visoko was about 40 miles from Vitez and was the main route through the mountains.

Initially, the journey to Visoko town was very pleasant, we were following the road along the bottom of the valleys and above us were the multi-coloured trees and bushes on the surrounding mountains. Once through Visoko, we started to climb severely and it was obvious that we could not continue on this route for much longer due to the worsening conditions of the icy roads. Many of the vehicles had had close encounters with the falling kind.

It is hard to explain the sensation one feels when the vehicle begins to slip and there is nothing anyone can do until the vehicle slams naturally against the bank overhanging a horrendous drop. One day, the banking will give way and someone will be killed. It was at this point we decided to turn around and after a few more dangerous moments trying to turn around on this narrow track, we then headed for Breza in search of a safer route.

We soon found good roads free of ice with only a few Bosnian checkpoints that waved us through. Unfortunately, this route took the convoy close to Sarajevo where the Warriors were not allowed to travel due to its aggressive appearance and as there was a noticeable build-up of troops in the area, we had to be very cautious not to cause an incident.

Between Visoko and Breza, we drove within three miles of the Serbian gun positions and it was apparent by all the shell craters that we were well within the artillery's range. However, they must have been on a tea break as we passed through this area without any incidents.

This shortcut was regularly used in the next few months as it cut out about 30 miles of mountain track. We just had to run the gauntlet of the artillery and hope we could pop through this area that was about half a mile long, whilst the Serbians were having a cup of tea and biscuits.

On arrival at Breza, it was obvious that an artillery barrage had indeed just finished as there was a large amount of commotion and ambulances rushing about everywhere. Due to the atmosphere of the crowds and the presence of many soldiers, we carried on through the town without stopping so as not to aggravate them further. Just lately it seems no matter which side was being shot at; it was always the UN's fault for not stopping them.

The next point on the journey will be Olovo which was the start of the real mountain passes and our confidence was at a low ebb due to the detour we had already made on basically sound roads.

The thing that really annoyed me was that we had to travel over all these mountain dirt tracks due to the fact that the perfectly serviceable roads ran in and out of Serbian-held territory, I am sure that as we were supposed to be helping both sides keep the peace, we should have been able to secure a safe route through and not put our lives at risk needlessly every day.

Passing through this normally quiet town of Olovo the atmosphere was pleasant as the locals had not seen our Warriors before and I suppose in some way this offered the inhabitants a thread of hope to cling on to. It was a beautiful day; the sun was out and the frost on the trees glistened in the sunlight.

The convoy entered the main tunnel through the mountain which was about six hundred meters long and we reappeared into a winter wonderland of ice and 10-foot snow drifts. Again, it was time to practice the 30-tonne sledge technique as the Warriors slipped and slid along the drastically narrowing and climbing tracks.

The journey so far had been relatively quick apart from the one minor diversion that had wasted two hours, but we were now again travelling at a snail's pace and were being hampered even further by the civilian traffic trying to get up these narrow mountain passes without snow chains or any tread on their tyres.

We continually waited for a jack-knifed or ditched civilian vehicle to be recovered and when looking down to the base of the mountain we could see the valley floor littered with the wreckage of all types of vehicles' previous attempts to scale this route. All around these wrecks were locals seeing if anything was salvageable or if indeed someone had overlooked any food that may still lay hidden from the countless eyes that had already scoured over the area.

Most of these tracks were single traffic only and without any traffic control, it was not unusual to meet a convoy coming the other way and have to start the slow process of deciding who should give way first. The problem being the fact that any vehicle pulling over to let the other one pass stood a chance of pulling onto infirm or icy ground and ending up taking the short route down the mountain at one hundred miles per hour.

By the time we reached Milankovići, it was nightfall and whilst driving down the road I noticed what appeared to be artillery illumination flares high in the sky. It was only after a few minutes when my brain clicked into gear and I realised that these flares were not floating down from the heavens, but were in fact, the headlights of the first vehicles in the convoy driving over the top of the mountain two thousand feet directly above me.

The journey to the top of the world had started and I was not at this present time very impressed. The track was narrow, icy and steep with a switch back bend every hundred meters or so. At each switchback, I had to do a neutral turn to get around it. At the time I had a broken-down Spartan (Nine-tonne light recognisance tracked vehicle) in tow due to an earlier breakdown that could not be fixed immediately.

A neutral turn is done by allowing one vehicle track to go forward and the other backwards, thus, spinning the vehicle around on its own axis. The application of a neutral turn actually induces a skid and only served to aggravate the already major problem of sliding about on the ice, every few degrees we turned around we slipped back a few inches.

The problem then came that with every inch we slipped back the more momentum we built up and we regularly contained the skid with part of the vehicle overhanging a shear drop of hundreds of feet. By now, the crew in the back of the vehicle were walking up the mountain as I could foresee in the very near future my own or one of my fitter section's vehicles would be plunging over the side.

With only Butch and I in the Warrior just in case we did go over the edge, we continued up this road into the clouds. I was adopting my now infamous position crouched on top of my cupola prepared to jump at the shortest notice, much to the amusement of my crew on the ground.

Sorry driver but this captain ain't going over with his ship. Also, sod the snipers, this was a more imminent danger. Butch my driver had his driver's seat safety harness undone and the driver's protective armoured hatch fully open just in case he had to jump also.

Milankovići was the crossroads of various routes we would take over the next few months. As well as being a rallying point for the local militia. It was a place, although a very small village, that all traffic in the area had to pass through. This in turn made it a place where tempers were regularly tested due to the frustration of small single-track roads and masses of traffic needing to use it.

This is because all the main roads that normally snake in and out of the valleys are now out of bounds due to the new front-line borders and No-Go enclaves, where a hostile response is given to anyone who is not known by the local militia. Every major bridge had mines strewn across it with machine gun posts at every junction. On top of that, the local militia can be as young as 14 and had no training on the weapons they have been given.

Milankovici was nicknamed Bon Bon village as Bon Bon is the Bosnian name for sweets and initially, all the kids would run out to the side of the road and stop vehicles shouting for sweets, Bon Bon. Bon Bon, which of course all the squaddies gave them.

After a while, it became a real hindrance and a danger as the kids would just run out of nowhere and risk life and limb trying to pick the sweet off the ground that had been thrown out of the truck windows before the next truck went thundering by. On one occasion, a Dutch female soldier was directing traffic when a child ran in front of her, she tried to grab the child and they both went under a truck killing them both.

During one move on the mountain above Milankovići, a Warrior lost control on the switchback track section and plunged several hundred feet down the side of the mountain, jumping over the switchback track several times. The vehicle commander jumped off the vehicle but left his headset on.

The headset strap got caught on something on the vehicle and he went most of the way down the mountain bashing against the side of the Warrior until the strap broke and deposited him on the hillside. Luckily, not under the vehicle tracks.

Inside the vehicle, the crew were obviously panicking because they didn't have a clue what was going on. The Warrior careered all the way to the bottom of the valley and jumped a stream at the bottom of the valley, burying its nose in the opposite stream bank and coming to an abrupt stop. Luckily the Warrior had been slowed as it ploughed through 10 or 20 large pine trees and had not rolled.

The driver and crew were bruised and beaten but after getting over the shock carried on with the tour but were not very keen to sit in a Warrior driving over the switchback tracks on the mountains again.

As we approached the top of the world, we came across a problem as one of the Warriors had tried to get around a broken-down lorry and had slipped slightly over the edge, being stopped from falling all the way down by a large tree stump. After trying every method of recovery possible, we had no option but to drag the civilian driver from his cab and push the lorry down the mountainside to gain access to a good towing position.

Even so, there were a few moments during the recovery when I thought that the Warrior was going to slip down the mountain dragging me with it. We finally reached the top of the world, and although nighttime, it was obvious due to the lights below that in daylight this would be a marvellous view.

In the months to come, I would stop here on many occasions whilst travelling between Tuzla and Vitez. Sitting here so high. On top of the world, admiring the scenery and the absolute tranquillity and silence with just the snow dropping off the trees. It was ironic that sometimes in utter silence I could actually watch a war unfold beneath me without hearing hardly a sound.

The view took in both Serbian and Croatian positions up to 30 miles in each direction and I would watch artillery firing and landing from both the warring sides, with small puffs of smoke and a flash followed by a faint muffled bang 10 or 20 seconds later.

I could hear the shells screw through the air sounding like a Catherine wheel firework, until at their zenith directly above me they would stop climbing, pause in mid-air and then drop down the other side of the mountain, making small halo shaped clouds in the air as they cut back into the warmer air causing a vortex. Death was being dispatched and arriving in almost complete silence as if in a dream as all noise was dampened by the trees and the snow.

This stretch of the mountain was maintained by a little old man whose sole task in life was to keep a fire burning 24 hours a day so that the hot ashes could be put under the lorry tyres to give them some grip and to allow them to carry on with their journey. I often passed him and gave him cigarettes, coffee and food etcetera. Over the next few months, I got to know him quite well, although we did not speak each other's language.

From what I could gather using my pigeon Croat, he had lost all three sons, a wife and his daughter in the last year due to the war, but even so, every time I saw him, he gave me a large toothless grin and carried on with his task in hand.

One day, I drove passed him and as I was in a hurry I didn't stop and just threw him a packet of cigarettes and a wave out of the Land Rover window. In the rear-view mirror, I saw a young Croatian soldier come out of the woods, push him to the ground, and proceed to steal his newly received gift.

At this, I reversed the Rover back up the track, dashed out of my vehicle and after first taking the cigarettes off him grabbed the soldier by the scruff of the neck, threw him roughly to the ground, and gave him a boot up the arse for good measure. Before he could retaliate, I placed the old man into my vehicle and drove him a couple of miles away to a safe area, where he could wait until the young lad had cooled off and he could have a smoke in peace.

It was quite refreshing driving between locations in a Land Rover once snow chains had been fitted, it was easy to negotiate even the worst tracks and country lanes. Sometimes with the Warriors, we would have to cross bridges rated at three or five tonne whilst we were a 30-tonne armoured vehicle often with the tracks hanging over each side or actually up on the ramparts.

If the route included several of these bridges then to get four or five Warriors any sort of distance could take hours. The humanitarian aid we were escorting would get very frustrated as they wanted to get to their destination and back as soon as possible, but if they wanted our protection then they would have to wait for us. This obviously raised the frustration levels on both sides.

We arrived at Kladanj at first light and were surprised by the fantastic facilities we had managed to secure during our short visit. Yes, you are right. No water, heating or electricity, how unusual!

On top of all this luxury, the place was literally riddled with shrapnel and bullet holes, which did not fill me with the correct amount of confidence I would have enjoyed. Each bullet hole could be traced through three rooms as the walls were just made from plasterboard. We immediately started making ourselves a more secure area to give ourselves at least some protection.

The fitter section was allocated an area in an old factory hanger but, as there was no electricity and the roller doors were jammed permanently open, this would have proved acceptable in summer but with the outside temperature at minus 20 degrees a vehicle could come in for work on it and leave three days later still covered in snow.

All around the factory floor were lathes that had been manufacturing parts of artillery shells that had been earmarked for local manufacture within the factory. These parts were just rolling around on the floor among the remnants of the explosive charges that were intended to go in the shell cartridge. Although these would not explode, it was a massive fire hazard, and the whole factory had to be made safe.

We lived again in a tent, set up on the shop floor and worked outside during daylight hours to try and get at least a little heat into our frozen bones from the weak winter sun. A brazier was made from an old 50-gallon oil drum and was set up just outside the hanger door. This was being constantly fed with scraps of wood so we had somewhere to go and thaw out our bodies. It was also a good meeting point for a chat and a cigarette.

If we had been on convoy duty that day, some of the crew would sleep in that vehicle during the night. Due to the massive fuel tank being inside the vehicle it still radiated the heat the fuel collected as it had passed through the engine fuel system before it returned to the fuel tank. Once the vehicle had been running for several hours the interior of the vehicle was toasty warm.

As I had been poking out of the cupola for five or six hours in minus 20 degrees Celsius, I would strip down to my underwear and fall asleep immediately onto the horsehair mattress I had permanently mounted on top of the fuel tank. Several hours later, I would wake up frozen as all the latent heat had left the fuel tank and I would quickly get inside my sleeping bag to try and warm up again.

During one of the first nights, whilst sleeping on my camp bed in the tent, I was awoken by something crawling over me and in panic turned my torch on in the attempt of bashing what I thought must be a rat. In the torchlight, I could see the tiny face of a little kitten who had hardly any fur due to having been in a fire of some sort. It had woken me trying to cuddle up for some heat.

For the rest of the night, I broke off small bits of corned beef and fed it. In the morning, we had an official fitter section meeting and we adopted the kitten into the section as an honorary member with the name of Tiddles. Well, nobody can say we aren't original as I am sure nobody could have thought of that name for a cat before. The cat's name was changed to Kladanj once we moved back to Vitez.

At the bottom of the compound was a slaughterhouse where any animal of any kind, alive or dead was brought for dismemberment. From natural death and road kills to an unfortunate cow, sheep, dog or deer that had been caught in the crossfire of a local skirmish or had wandered into a minefield. There were hundreds of minefields around and not one minefield was marked.

This would cause major problems in the years to come whether the war ended or not. This is quite apparent when seeing the news from Cambodia or Vietnam and seeing the pictures of the thousands of legless casualties still appearing after so many years. Princess Diana would later visit Bosnia and become famous for her campaign to ban land mines.

The locals were not proud when it came to what they ate as far as meat was concerned. Meat was one of the main substances that they were missing. The first sign to indicate ethnic cleansing had taken place as we approached a new village was the dead cows and sheep in the field. The attacking group always killed any livestock they found.

We often used to see horse-drawn carts of all descriptions dumping off load after load of various animal remains into the slaughterhouse and in a matter of minutes moving off with bags of freshly killed and cut-up meat.

Just outside the other corner of the compound, there was an orphanage holding about 20 children who would wander around the compound scrounging or stealing anything they could lay their hands on. Needless to say, with one blink of their eyes they could secure a meal from some soft-hearted squaddie any time day or night.

We were constantly being told to stop feeding the kids as we were running out of rations, but nobody cared and we fed them until the day we left. One of the boys was aged about 12 and was deaf and dumb due to a psychological shock he had suffered a few months ago.

This had not subdued his character, however, and if any kids were fighting or caught stealing, nine out of 10 times he was involved. I am calling him a boy, but we must remember that at 12 years of age, he will be a soldier in a year's time if the fighting continues.

Directly over the nearest mountain and down in the valley are the Serbian positions and they are in plain sight of the company when we take the southern route out of Kladanj or more importantly the company is in plain sight of their guns.

To reach Tuzla or any town northeast of the camp, we have to travel down a stretch of road that is directly in line with the Serbian artillery. For a stretch of two miles, the road was named Bomb Ally as every time we drove down it, we were either shot at or mortared. A Warrior is a fast vehicle but when climbing up this icy hill we had to slow to 20 miles per hour and this is when the buggers had their fun.

At this point, all the soft-skinned convoy vehicles accelerated and left us to face the music. I cannot say I blame them. The crash barriers on this section were completely riddled with shrapnel and the few houses on the side of the road had long since been bombed out, although the Serbs still used them as ranging marks for their guns. The mortars did not bother us too much as only a direct hit could damage a Warrior, but I could still have done without this activity twice a day.

Over the next six weeks, the officer commanding the Company held many talks with his opposite Serbian number across the valley and every time we were promised that they would not open fire on us. After lengthy negotiations, it was decided that if we drove over only at night they would not aim at our vehicles, but they did. They informed us that they did not know it was U.N. vehicles as it was dark.

Then they said if we drove over at night but with our four-way hazard flashers on, they would not open fire, but they did because they said that they could not resist such an easy target. Eventually, we had had enough of this and so we assembled a counterattack group and unofficially drove to the top of the bomb ally where we parked up in plain sight. The Milan anti-tank crew drove onto a separate hill and set up their missiles.

Once the mortars had started arriving in our vicinity, the Milan crew reported spotting three targets and applied to the United Nations HQ in a town called Kiseljak if we could open fire, but they said not if we could retreat in safety. We then decided that our hands were tied and that it was pointless giving the Serbs target practice and so we started to manoeuvre to return to base.

Just then with a cloud of exhaust fumes a T55 Russian-made tank came out of the opposite woodlands and fired a shot just above the vehicles. Now! Two-inch anti-personnel mortars are one thing, but 105-millimetre armoured piercing shell is another, and the pace of our withdrawal sped up just a touch. The Milan crew were informing Kiseljak of the new situation, but still, they were not allowed to fire.

Suddenly, we saw the tank commander and gunner jump out of the turret that was gushing smoke and there was a mighty explosion and the tank turret blew about 50 feet into the air. We immediately reported this fact. Kiseljak were screaming we had caused an international incident and we had not been given the authority to engage the Serbians with cannon fire.

It was only once they had calmed down and it was explained that we had not fired but it had blown up due to an internal breach malfunction of its own making, once they understood this, the radio traffic calmed down. Even so, we still had to account for our rounds once back at base.

The Serbians were convinced that we had blown up the tank and could not be convinced otherwise, or perhaps it was very convenient for them to have this ace in their hand. All our rounds were correct and so it couldn't have been us.

Could it be?

During one night there was a knock on the main gate and a chap from New Zealand was standing there asking if we could give him a hand. He was on his own and was taking food to an enclave about 50 miles north of Kladanj. His Bedford truck needed the clutch replacing and he would not make it over the mountains with his current worn-out clutch plate. He had the spare but no tools.

As we were in a good mood, we brought him into the compound and through the night changed the clutch for him. This chap had just finished qualifying as a lawyer and before starting a job for his father, he wanted to see the world. He showed me his business card and had his profession down as an adventurer. In the morning, we gave him breakfast and then he went on his merry way. He was quite a character. Never to be seen again.

Opposite the main gate was a brothel and throughout the day there were many comings and goings of the locals visiting this establishment. Obviously, the girls sat in the front window showing off their wares. I found this shocking and it was annoying how I had to keep averting my eyes.

In the end, I gave up and just had to look.

The whole compound we were living in was surrounded by wriggly tin that we could not see through, and more importantly, the locals could not see into and take a potshot at us. I have never known so many people volunteer for guard duty where they could see the outside world or more importantly, see the tourist sites across the road. Typical squaddies.

Our days in Kladanj were brightened up with the prospect of the daily shower run into town. The local hotel manager had told us that for a small charge, he would let the company have use of the facilities within the hotel between 1800 and 1900 hours every night. We thought that this was brilliant as heating up hot water every time we needed a strip wash took hours as we only had a lazy man boiler.

The boiler worked using the following method:

When we wanted hot water, we had to pour a bucket of cold water in and we would get a bucket of warm water out. Unfortunately, the colder water that was put in the colder the water that came out.

As we generally did not finish work until after midnight, all we wanted to do then was go to sleep and not have to go through this rigmarole every night.

What we did not realise until we arrived at the hotel was, that the reason we were given these times to shower was because the rest of the population were hiding in the cellars. This was the time that the nightly artillery bombardment commenced. Every night we embarked on the hotel with flak jackets, helmets and shower gel and enjoyed a lovely shower whilst all around the hotel windows were being blown out and buildings in the town were being reduced to rubble.

Throughout our stay here, this practice continued and we managed in the end to run from the transport to the hotel, undress, shower, dry ourselves, dress again and be back on the transport back to the base within five minutes, which is a record Linford Christie would have been proud of.

The hotel also managed a laundry system of sorts, where we could hand in our dirty clothes and if we were lucky, we sometimes got them back. This was due to the fact that the hotel owner was also a member of the local militia and if he was short of any clothing for his troops the British Army could supply it. Needless to say, after lots of reports of soldiers' clothing going missing, this facility's contract was soon terminated.

Later, during my stay in Kladanj, there was a shooting incident and as my fitter section was in the near vicinity on another task, we were asked to give first aid to an injured Bosnian soldier. The casualty turned out to be one of the hotel owner's friends.

Whilst treating him one of my company soldiers shouted out, "He's got my combat jacket on. He's got my bloody combat jacket on."

I do not know why he wanted it back as it was now full of blood and bullet holes but get it back he did, with a comment, "I don't know why you are having a go at me. I swapped him some bandages for it, didn't I?"

After 20 years in the army, I still have never come across people with such a brilliant sick sense of humour and no matter how depressed I felt at times throughout my career there was always someone to bring me back to reality with either a comment or an action that was so ludicrous that it made my problems seem trivial.

As mentioned earlier, when leaving the compound to escort the convoys we had to climb a steep hill traversing around the mountain overlooking our base before entering Bomb Ally. We then crested the hill and went down the other side of the mountain, where there was a bend in the road halfway down the hill.

On one occasion, we were following a Warrior and as it negotiated the bend, slipped on the ice and sat stationary broadside, so we could not proceed down the road in our vehicle until the crashed Warrior righted itself. The Serbians across the valley saw this and thought this would be a good chance to practice shooting at us. For several minutes, we were stationary waiting for the Warrior in front to sort himself out.

All the time we were stationary, the incoming fire was getting more accurate. The Serbians had just got our range when the Warrior managed to get itself pointing in the right direction and moved down the hill after the rest of the convoy and we followed rapidly behind him. I was quite happy that they did not have a T54 tank anymore.

"Karma!"

Throughout our stay in Kladanj, we always knew when the convoy was returning from the day's task via Bomb Ally as we could hear the small arms fire and mortars exploding around the returning vehicles. This noise was always a sign to put the kettle on and welcome the troops back home.

Whilst driving in a convoy, the vehicle commanders and drivers always made sure that they kept their heads below the cheese cutter wire guard. The cheese cutter was a piece of angle iron mounted just in front of the vehicle commander's head, with a notch cut in it that would cut any wire that was strung across the road to try and garrotte anyone that had their head above the vehicle cupola.

There were also attacks from youths who would practice the art of using catapults to fire ball bearings to amuse themselves. This was something we just had to be aware of as there was no way we could stop a convoy just to chase a youth and apprehend him. There was no law enforcement out here to do anything about it and we couldn't shoot them as they were just kids amusing themselves.

There were a few vehicle commanders that were hit in the face with catapult ammunition and it made quite a serious injury. Most vehicle commanders rigged up a Perspex guard to protect us from a catapult's ammunition and these also helped cut down the wind chill. The Warriors in Afghanistan have all got official ballistic screens fitted now. These also protect from bullets.

One of our regular tasks was to escort a group of workers home after they came out of a mine they had been working in. Halfway through loading them into the back of the Warriors, we came under artillery fire from the Serbians on the other side of the mountain. Once the all-clear was sounded, we quickly drove from that area.

On return to camp, at the debrief, the sergeant major said it was probably to mortar fire. At that point, one of the lieutenants produced a dud artillery shell and on placing it on a table said no. Definitely Artillery. We all moved away from the shell as these can slow burn for 6 hours. The lieutenant was politely advised to take it to a safe area.

Tiddles the cat is now a fully-fledged member of the fitter section and comes on convoy runs with us even though he is not impressed with the U.N. beret we make him wear, this has to be done otherwise he may get mistaken for an infiltrator and be arrested for supporting Chairman Meow!

I have tried to explain this to him on many occasions but I think he has a problem grasping the situation he has found himself in. He puts up with all the petting and pestering he gets; I presume this is because he has never slept in a warmer place nor had as much food as this to eat in his short adventurous and very mobile life.

As Kladanj is a staging post for all the aid convoys passing through I met all the weird and wonderful people who inhabit them. These ranged from sisters of mercy spreading the word and delivering first aid and mental support, to rich eccentric yuppies delivering well-intentioned clothing, food, tents and a number of other things needed in a war zone.

The latter genuinely thought that taking aid to these dangerous places was jolly good fun and quite a wheeze, but after one run down Bomb Ally, their minds were soon changed as they were brought back to reality with a bump. In fact, more of a krumppfh with nasty fast-flying, sharp, hot and smoking bits of metal from the mortar rounds that were landing all around them. The yuppie element usually only did the run once and were never seen again.

Others did a daily run, time and time again. Considering that their vehicles had no protection whatsoever, this required a steady nerve and a strong belief in what they were doing. Quite a few were injured over the time we were there and I did admire their courage and determination.

On the other hand, however, there were some who obviously knew better than us and ignored our warnings when certain situations developed or the atmosphere of the locals told us that there was a degree of unrest. These types always got themselves into dangerous situations and expected us to get them out, which of course we did, but we were not impressed by their attitude of that's what we were there for, which we weren't.

Day after day, we went out on the convoys. Sometimes, only 10 miles sometimes a hundred. We would drive down a Muslim Valley and the Serbians would shoot at us as we were giving aid. We would then drive down a Croat valley and the Muslims would shoot at us because we were helping them. We could then drive down a Serbian valley and Muslims and Croats would shoot at us because we were helping the Serbians.

The HOSS went around and shot at everyone. At one point, I had climbed down into the passenger area of my armoured vehicle to grab a mug of tea. This area whilst nice and warm was also very noisy due to its location next to the running engine. Whilst within the interior of the vehicle I noticed white fluffy stuff coming down from the cupola hatch. I presumed it had started snowing as it was about minus 15 degrees Celsius outside.

When I climbed back into my commander's cupola position to carry on the journey, I noticed that the kapok cushion padding on the cupola hatch lid had been strafed by a machine gun fire and ripped to bits. I had not heard anything over the vehicle engine noise. At this point, we evacuated the area fairly smartly.

Our period at Kladanj was nearly over as A company were about to take over our duties here for the next six weeks. This would give us a bit of a rest back in our base camp in Vitez. We were looking forward to the change even though we had to drive back through the mountains in the icy conditions.

Two days before we left Kladanj, one of the Warriors slid off a mountain track and finished off upside down in a shallow river, luckily no one was hurt apart from minor bruising and a few battery acid burns to the driver. The Warrior driver's normal practice was to have a bergen (large kit bag) behind him with all the personnel possessions he may need on the journey.

On this occasion, he now found himself upside down in a stream and could not get out via the escape tunnel, as his bergen was jammed between the seat and the vehicle bulkhead. It was lucky it was only a shallow river into which they had rolled into. If it was a deep river, it would be a different story.

My recovery crew had been immediately behind the Warrior when it slid and rolled into the river and before the vehicle had stopped rocking, they were gaining access into the vehicle to get the crew in the rear of the vehicle out. They had managed to access the vehicle interior and spent five minutes trying to get the bergen out of the way and rescue him.

Whilst this was happening the driver was panicking as he had battery acid slowly dripping all over him, as the six large vehicle batteries were located under the driver's seat which as the vehicle was upside down were above him.

After holding up the traffic on this single file mountains track for about four hours, the vehicle was tipped the right way up and recovered back onto the track and back to base.

In Bosnia, when we have to hold up the traffic, it is not as simple as it seems. Nothing is simple in this place. The traffic on these mountain tracks were either aid convoys which is not too much of a problem, or soldiers trying to reinforce certain areas and this is where the problems arise.

There is nothing worse than trying to do a task with an irate Bosnian ranting and raving about needing to get past. At times, tempers flared to the point of aggression being used from both sides and at times it nearly came to shots being exchanged. This was really annoying as at the end of the day we were here to help these people and we were the target of their abuse and frustrations.

I suppose in some cases, it was justified but generally when the militia were involved, it was because they were used to getting their own way with the civilian population by using bully-boy tactics. When they tried that with us, it usually had a reverse effect, as we went out of our way to show them that we were in charge.

Chapter 23
The Recovery to Vitez

Two days after the overturned vehicle incident, we headed back to Vitez. With tears in our eyes, we left Kladanj on New Year's Eve. Christmas had passed in the blink of an eye whilst we were on a convoy to some village delivering aid and we had not even noticed. Looking back over the years I had spent three Northern Ireland tours, Gulf War I and now Bosnia away from home at Christmas. Not the best record for family life.

On top of this, the normal practice when back at camp in Germany is to let the single soldiers return to the UK and their families whilst married personnel are used to carry out the camp guard duties. So again, no Christmas Day at home.

My vehicle was towing the same Spartan vehicle I arrived at Kladanj with, as spares were still not available to carry out the much-needed repair. 24C was towing the recovered but very poorly Warrior that had slipped into the river. After 20 miles, we started to climb the hill leading to the top of the world, this time from the opposite direction. We immediately had problems with the sheer weight of the dead vehicles we were towing on the icy tracks.

Every mile we had to pull over and let the long trail of vehicles that had built up behind us pass. The tracks were getting steeper and we were constantly slipping either sideways or backwards which was quite disconcerting when only a few feet from a four-hundred-foot drop. No matter what the driver does the vehicle keeps slipping until it hits a solid object and finally comes to rest.

As we approached the Top of the World, it was obvious that 24C could not gain any purchase whatsoever, so I took my vehicle and my lighter Spartan casualty vehicle that was on my tow hook to the top of the mountain and dropped it off. I then had to reverse back down the mountain for about half a mile and hook up to 24C so we could do a tandem pull on his towed vehicle. This we did and after a few hairy moments, finally arrived at the top of the world.

This whole process took over an hour and by the time it was completed a large trail of vehicles was now stuck both in front and behind us with us stuck in the middle. In true Bosnian tradition, after we pulled out of the way, both lines of traffic decided they had priority and tried to get over the single-track mountain pass together. Only after a traffic jam that stretched for a mile either way came to a stalemate, did the shouting stop and nobody could move either way.

This did not bother us as we were going nowhere important anyway, so we spent our time making fun of the local commander of the Bosnian army who if he had listened to me in the first place would not be in this fix. He finally vented his frustration by grabbing hold of me by my shoulders and throwing me against the side of my vehicle. He then fell over very quickly holding his mouth and I think he also had been struck very suddenly with the infamous mumps bug.

Later I was questioned about this action as he reported me and I explained that this must be brought on by something in their diet.

I was told that I was treading on very dodgy ground, to which I replied, "I know I was four thousand feet up an icy mountain."

The pun fell on deaf ears as battalion headquarters obviously did not pack their sense of humour for this tour, and would not know a joke if it jumped up and bit them on the bum. We often find the people who lock themselves away in a headquarters and never leave their nice warm safe building, lose touch with both reality and the ability to communicate on a one-to-one level, and have to rely on, I say, so you do management. (Sad people)

Slowly, the traffic jam cleared and the news from the village of Milankovići at the bottom of the mountain was that another convoy was moving in soon, so now was a good chance to come down off the mountain.

Coming downhill was even more dangerous than going uphill as the full weight of both vehicles was trying to push us off the mountain. We inched ourselves down the steep passage, keeping one track in the inside drainage ditch to act as a guiding rail and hopefully to stop the vehicles slewing across the road, and with all the warning lights on the vehicle driver instrument panel telling me that the engine, gearbox and brakes were overheating we plodded on knowing that this was the last time we would see this bloody mountain.

The brakes on a Warrior are housed within the gearbox and if the gearbox overheats the brakes fail totally. This meant that if the brakes did overheat, we would have to batten down and take our chances going over the side of the mountain with the only things to slow our headlong charge being the trees if we were lucky. We had heard of this working before but not with another vehicle in tow and to be honest I did not fancy my chances.

Whilst all our problems were taking place, down in the village tempers were flaring even more. Weapons had been pointed at the British troops and the locals alike. As this was supposed to be our overnight stop for the night, we were warned by radio not to pull into the village with our slow awkward party and instead find an alternative route.

The alternative route we now had to take meant navigating down even steeper and narrower side tracks than we had been down before. We did not know the condition of the ground or if they were actually passable. After two hours, we reached the bottom of the valley and a safe rest place for the night. We all climbed out of the vehicles white-faced and shaking. We sat on the floor and lit some cigarettes just looking at each other without saying a word for 10 minutes.

Each of us knew that we had probably completed the most potentially dangerous task we would complete for the rest of our lives. Suddenly, the grins started to appear and everybody started making fun of each other, recounting the last few hours of our very exciting, adventurous and stressful lives. A cup of tea was produced and biscuits were passed around. Things were back to normal again, let's see what tomorrow brings.

We arranged a sentry system so people could get some sleep whilst still remaining safe. During my stag, I sat in my vehicle cupola with an umbrella up so nothing entered my cupola and the snow silently fell around me. It was a very tranquil night after the excitement of the day. Every so often, I would traverse the cupola and check through the night sight that no sinister actions were taking place in the fields around us.

I suddenly found that I had a huge smile on my face sitting in all this silent tranquillity with the snow falling around me thinking about the total opposite position I was in a few hours ago. All this and I get paid for doing it as well, I wouldn't swap it for anything.

At first light, we set off again but this time only the drivers were in the vehicles. The rest of the crews were walking in front with spades preparing the roads with any grit or old branches they could find that would allow the vehicles to pass without slipping. This was a physically draining task as everything was frozen solid and one small bend could entail 20 minutes of work.

Branches, fence posts and anything else we could get our hands on were used time and time again. We were soon joined by Lieutenant Murdoch and his

Scimitar vehicle crew who had been sent back to give us some protection if we required it, as the rest of the company had carried on to their destination of Vitez.

The day went slowly on and by the last light we came upon a switch back corner that try as we might we could not get around due to the gradient on which the corner was situated. It was at this point, I called a halt as we had been walking and shovelling for 16 hours and to put it politely, we all were shattered.

After a meal, whilst I contemplated our problem, I decided that the only way we would get up this next hill was a tandem pull again, but first, we would need to take off the rubber track pads to allow the steel tracks to dig into the ice. Each trackpad was secured to the pad by two bolts, these over the months had become either rounded or were clogged with hard stones that would take 10 to 15 minutes to remove each bolt.

A Warrior has 82 track pads on each side and two bolts on each pad, times that by 15 minutes and needless to say in minus 20 degrees temperature it was the best part of 14 hours before we were ready to try and get up the hill again. Whilst we were in this location, we heard a commotion in the forest and suddenly about 20 Bosnian militia came out clutching bottles of brandy and hugging and kissing each other.

My initial reaction was to grab my rifle for protection but then thought, What the hell's going on here, it soon became apparent that there was no threat to us as they could only just stand up themselves.

It soon became clear what the celebration was for once they started shaking our hands and offering us drinks. It was New Year's Day! And we had completely missed it, as it was now quite late in the evening.

Back to the problem at hand and the continuation of the saga of the man versus the mountain. Initially, we thought we had cracked it but as we negotiated around the bend the tracks started to slip and in no time instead of rubber track pads we had ice pads, the result being a very scary slip of one hundred meters backwards finishing up about five feet from the original resting place and a waste of 14 hours hard graft of sweating and cursing.

The only way we were going to get up this bloody hill was to wait until the ice went away. Suddenly, with a spark of inspiration, I decided that this could be possible as we carried 50 gallons of petrol between the three vehicles and so after tipping a few gallons of fuel over the vehicle tracks, I lit the blue touch paper and retired. With an almighty whoosh, the petrol caught fire and immediately started melting the ice on the vehicle tracks.

As the ice melted, the melted water took the burning fuel down the mountain and started melting the ice on the ground. After 15 minutes, the whole mountainside was on fire and it was, to say the least, quite spectacular in the dark of the night but I don't know what any passing Bosnians thought about it.

During this exercise of setting the road on fire several times and then driving up the track for a hundred meters and then repeating the exercise, my Commanding Officer Colonel Bob Stewart turned up out of the blue. He spent 10 minutes with us checking we were all happy in our task and then after giving me some choice words of abuse he buggered off again.

Four hours and half a dozen soul-destroying attempts later, we finally made it up the last section of the mountain and rested for a couple of hours to tackle the next range of hills, however, the worst was behind us and we could finally see the light at the end of the tunnel. Or had I just lulled myself into a false sense of security? The light at the end of the tunnel is usually some bugger with a torch bringing me a wheelbarrow full of more problems.

By now, we were getting short of rations and even worse, short of cigarettes. Each army vehicle that passed us was summarily raided for food and drink and we begged borrowed and stole any cigarettes that were available. The lad's joke of the day was that I could only last one week without food, two weeks without water and three seconds without a fag in my mouth.

Morale was high now that the worst was behind us but a few lads were now having problems with frostbite and we had to stop regularly to dry out boots, clothing and generally warm up. Due to the extreme exertion, we were constantly sweating and in this temperature the sweat was turning to ice and we all looked like a picture from the Antarctic explorer's expeditions with icicles hanging from our few day's growth of whiskers.

Luckily, it was so cold that our clothes were staying relatively dry. The ice on the outside was acting as a barrier to the elements and it was only the extremities i.e. nose, ears, hands and feet that were actually being affected. As we could not see our own faces it was up to the rest of the crew to say when ears and noses had turned a shade passed blue and it was time to get into a vehicle and thaw out.

When we first heard we were going to be deployed to Bosnia and would not be issued any cold weather kit apart from gloves (as it was classed as Northern Europe climate), most people went out and bought warm gear and good winter boots as the issued army boots were useless in the cold for insulation properties.

During this whole adventure, the only person in my fitter section who suffered frostbite on his toes was my corporal, a Scotsman who would not buy boots and so wore army-issued useless boots. I myself still have bald patches at the corners of my mouth where my moustache was constantly an icicle and the hair follicles for my moustache have been burned away.

Again, we set off. Finally, we could actually get back on the vehicles and rest whilst the drivers continued the slow climb up the last range of mountains. We had to stop occasionally as by now the engines had had enough and the track links were slowly deteriorating and required replacing therefore needed tensioning every few miles. A slack track can be dangerous and may be thrown off the wheels easily.

All of which was now taking longer and longer as tiredness set in and with the freezing conditions things were becoming brittle. Care also had to be taken as we had long since stopped feeling our fingers. As well as being numb from feeling/touching objects, we also did not realise that we had injured ourselves until the next thawing-out stop when the pain came with a vengeance.

With one last crest to climb, we were a little bit too enthusiastic and instead of using the tried and tested technique to get around a switchback bend for some reason one of the drivers decided to try and power around. The result was both Warriors ended up at 45 degrees in a ditch with both tracks being thrown off the vehicle doing the towing.

The driver, realising what he had done, locked himself in the driver's compartment and would not come out until we promised we would not kick the hell out of him. Like an idiot, he believed us. (fool). Again, we started to repair the impossible by using techniques we would not have dreamt of before this adventure.

Using ground-mounted Tirfor winches, we hammered these into the frozen ground and dragged the vehicles one pull at a time back onto their tracks. We had both Warriors back on the track within six hours and it was time to allow ourselves the luxury of a few hours' sleep.

The following morning, we crested the last hill with no further problems and to celebrate we took an hour off for a good meal and to experience the sheer delight of what as a team we had accomplished.

Straight away, the lads realised that pretty soon we would find ourselves back into the humdrum life at Vitez garage so decided to let their hair down a few minutes by sledging down the mountainside in black bin bags and generally having a good old all-in snowball fight or should I say a good old all-in fight that included the odd snowball.

As everybody was tired out, we settled into an enormous all-in stew and with a bottle of Bosnian brandy to wash it down, our noses slowly turned from numb blue to smiling glowing red.

It had taken the team three and a half days to recover this single vehicle 45 miles, all the time this was being completed, the dead Spartan vehicle had to be relayed to the next section and dropped off before we could return and carry on with the task of hooking up in tandem and continue towing.

This recovery story was a main feature article in our Corps magazine 'The Craftsman' 25th-anniversary special edition as the longest single-vehicle recovery in REME history.

Luckily, we had Lieutenant Murdock and his crew to guard us. Throughout the whole operation, he kept a vigilant eye on the surrounding area and although they were not needed to give any covering fire, it was very reassuring knowing he had our safety as his main priority. This also meant we could carry on with the task without worrying about perimeter protection.

Throughout the whole time, he had a bemused look on his face and later I found out that it was because he could not believe what we were actually achieving. Every problem that was thrown at us, he thought was impossible with the manpower and facilities we had, but we just accepted that the vehicle needed to be recovered back to base and there was not an alternative way of doing this but with brute force and a bit of ingenuity.

I myself had a great feeling of achievement even more so when I thought of the amount of people who had passed by the team whilst we were working on this recovery and after assessing the situation, had shaken their heads and disappeared into the distance with the only comment, "Rather you, than me."

But we had persevered and now we were returning from mission impossible and our thoughts were aimed at a nice shower and a warm bed.

Lieutenant Murdock wrote me a glowing report that he gave to my officer commanding and I later placed it in my CV for when I went looking for a job when leaving the army.

Bill

Having spent 5 long days with the C Company fitter section in rather adverse weather conditions, I feel I have seen them working under a unique type of pressure.

I feel that it has to be brought to your attention how much I was impressed by their abilities. They had to work exceptionally hard throughout the five days.

Their ability to adapt, improvise and eventually overcome was truly amazing.

They also managed to look after me and my crew who did not have any facilities as the Warriors.

The humour too, made things much more tolerable also. Please pass on my congratulations to SSGT Flower and the boys for a successful mission.

Lieutenant Mike Murdock.

Figure 7: A collage of photos from my Bosnia tour currently on my study wall.

Figure 8: The path the Warrior cleared through the trees jumping the switchback track four times on the way down.

Figure 9: Myself Posing in Vitez in front of the Recovery Warrior 24C

Figure 10: Typical single-track mountain road with very few pull-ins and a shear drop to the side. Note the rain gully on the right. On the narrower tracks, I would place a Warrior track in there so it did not slip over the drop.

Figure 11: SSGT A.L. Flower BEM—Vehicle Commander.
Note: This was at the start of a convoy as I was not covered in frost yet.

Figure 12: The recovery crew, me second from right.

Figure 13: 24C on its side halfway down the valley.

Chapter 24
Vitez the Sequel

We had been away from Vitez for six weeks and as we drove closer to the town limits it was apparent that the hostilities had increased in this area, as the once beautiful villages were now mostly burnt-out shells and the Bosnian army presence was quite apparent.

Whereas, before we only used to see groups of a dozen or so, now they were walking around in company-strength formations of one hundred or more. This indicated that the front-line of the war zone was rapidly approaching our base location.

All three vehicles from the recovery adventure arrived back at the garage, to the general abuse I was expecting from those who lived there. It is against all REME policies to congratulate someone for doing a good job, so it is normal to measure your achievement by the amount of complaining people do about the length of time it took us to do a task or the state of the vehicles we returned with.

By the amount of slagging off we received from our workmates, we were finally convinced that we had achieved the highest accolade, especially when we were presented with some beers and told that we would not be needed for 48 hours.

As we were still on an operational footing we were only allowed two beers per man a day and I had to explain to the barman who was accounting for the beers that there were 57 men in my crew. In that way, I could ensure that all my eight tradesmen involved in this task could get well and truly blasted. Which we did and all on the garages expense account.

Vitez had been greatly improved in our absence. We now had hot water and more toilets, albeit a bucket with a bag in it and we now had the luxury of a torn sheet of hessian between the buckets for privacy. The outside area had doubled in size and hard core covered the walkways and parking area, so we were not dragging mud into the living accommodation areas all the time.

Porta cabins were being brought in but we would not be allowed into them as they were for the next battalion that would be replacing us in a few months' time. This really wound up the guys who had roughed it for four months through the winter.

When I visited the school area in Vitez where the main battalion was based, there was a makeshift sergeant mess where I could get a beer and chat with some of the battalion senior ranks from other companies and swap stories about what to watch out for in various locations we may visit. The Bandmaster had brought all the band's instruments with him in case there was an opportunity to do a parade whilst in Vitez to win over the hearts and minds of the locals.

I had my guitar with me so I often used to go up to the school and have a jam session with the bandsmen. They were actually over in Bosnia acting as medics to bolster the medical staff and to go on the convoys as medical backup, as we often collected injured refugees on our travels.

There was a large dining room in the school and the food was slightly better than at the garage. We had a few sergeants mess regimental dinners in this tent which we combined with the officers whenever a Kate Aidie or Martin Bell type person was around. During these meals, we would be fed all the latest speeches by visiting generals and members of parliament.

It was all very good for morale but we did not take any of the promises they made seriously, as we had been let down so many times in the past. One good thing that was promised, was the tour that took over from us for the summer tour was going to be issued a cold weather kit so they would not have to buy their own.

"Ya couldn't make it up."

Although Vitez was presumed to be a safe area, there were several hostile incidents around the camp. Billy Welsh had his office in a tent within the compound and after a mortar attack on the garage complex, he found a crater by the tent's front door and several shrapnel holes in the canvas. Luckily he was not in the tent at the time. We also had the odd local person taking potshots at the camp.

On one occasion, we were queuing for lunch when for five minutes some Croat was shooting several times over the perimeter fence in our direction. We sent out the quick reaction force to sort it out as we did not want our lunch to go cold.

As I looked around, I noticed a young soldier standing on top of a vehicle looking over the perimeter fence and shouting, "I can see him. I can see him."

Now obviously, if he could see the shooter then the shooter could see the young idiot, so with a few choice words I encouraged this pillock to get out of the line of sight, "Stupid boy, Pike."

It's the simple silly things that get people killed when they switch off and don't think about what they are doing.

Over the next few days, the convoys were grounded due to an increase in hostilities in the war situation in our local area. We now had time to bring all the company vehicles up to a decent standard again, this made a nice break as it meant we only worked 10 hours a day and in our free time could watch television which had recently arrived in the location.

Wives and girlfriends would send out videos of films and family shots for the soldiers to watch. This was our first and last token of appreciation from the system.

The Bosnian civilian translators lived at the school and they were always needed to help smooth the way between the local leaders who constantly argued with each other. One day, as the translator had not turned up for her shift, the convoy leader went to the house where the translator lived which was within our camp perimeter. When she didn't answer the door, he went into her flat and found her dead on the balcony.

She had been shot by a sniper whilst hanging out her washing. With this news circulating our camp area, most of the civilian staff we hired for the cook house and general cleaning duties, left that day not to return whilst we were in Vitez.

During the early hours of the morning, we were awoken by the sound of machine gun fire in the near vicinity. With the thought of us being caught in the middle of the conflict, we headed for the protection of our bomb shelter, which was a large vehicle servicing pit on the garage floor covered with railway sleepers and sandbags.

It was only when we were all crammed in like sardines that I noticed that the first people down here were a coupler of chaps from the compound guard force. After a few kicks and punches, they finally vacated this safe area to find out what was going on and more importantly to give us the protection they were supposed to provide in the first place. Needless to say, no Victoria crosses were awarded to the guard that day.

The reason for the incident was that a few Bosnians had decided to give a firepower demonstration by shooting a machine gun through our roof. Probably not known to the Bosnians, we had 50 people living in the loft who luckily were fast asleep and all lying down so nobody was hurt. Unfortunately for them, our compound machine gun protection group saw them shooting at the garage and so gave them a firepower demonstration themselves.

Straight through the vehicle they were driving. After a casualty count of what was left of the people in the car, the Bosnians decided that it was not a good idea to have done this and this episode was not repeated during the rest of our time here. It had, however, made our presence felt and they now realised that we were not to be trifled with. It also ensured that our relationship with the local Bosnian government forces was at an all-time low.

Our only casualty had been one of the protection group who had a cut and bump on his forehead. He told the doctor he fell over and knocked himself out but could not remember what happened at the time of the incident. After being examined by the finest trained doctors who are employed by the British Army, he was given a clean bill of health and told to resume normal duties.

Three weeks later, whilst on his two-week rest and recuperation(R&R) back at home in the UK that everybody gets if, on an operational tour of more than four months, he visited a casualty ward in England and complained of a constant headache. At this point, they x-rayed him and five minutes later removed a bullet from his forehead.

Thank God, he didn't have anything seriously wrong with him in the first place. After that, the medical centre was flooded with squaddies with bullets sellotaped to their heads asking if they could have some aspirin and did the doctor knew why they weren't feeling well.

Chapter 25
Kakuni

One of our missions was to take the UNPROFOR (United Nations Protection Force) advisers into all the trouble spots that were springing up all over our sector in an attempt to stop ethnic cleansing. Whilst our main task was to try and smooth things out among the opposing sides, the most we usually managed to do was to at least stop the fighting between the factions on the same side.

As I have explained before, the only time the Muslims and the Croats stop fighting each other is when they join forces to fight the Serbians. It is not unusual to have one battle with four independent sides shooting each other, this tends to make it quite difficult to control especially when the HOSS are present and they are shooting anyone who does not have black coveralls on. Which is their standard dress code.

As well as mercenaries on both sides, we have Muslims from the Arab states on the Muslim side and Russian advisors on the Serbian side. The few mercenaries I have spoken to, are completely schizoid and they are generally soldiers who could not make it within their country's professional army as they were of the wrong temperament or just plain useless.

Countless numbers of mercenaries had been killed here due to the fact that if the side they were fighting on felt that there were traitors in their midst, the first execution was usually the mercenary.

Whilst towing a Warrior along a steep mountain pass during a convoy move, I could hear over the headset one of my crew talking to someone. This was a bit strange as he was sitting in the back of a vehicle on his own.

When I asked who he was talking to, he replied, "There's a lad here from Bradford."

He had actually offered a mercenary a ride up the hill. I politely asked the mercenary to get out of the vehicle and then explained to Phil why he should not do this again, as we could be seen helping in Bosnian troop movements. I seem to remember I explained this quite loudly with quite a lot of very rude words.

On another occasion, the Company's colour sergeant had just resupplied us and somehow got around to talking to some mercenaries who needed a lift over the border in his Bedford truck. Being a thick git, he had said yes. As soon as he had crossed the border, the mercenaries jumped out of the truck and started shooting at people.

The mercenaries were quickly captured and led away to face their fate and the embarrassed sergeant was captured and luckily held prisoner until he was handed back to our guys. He quickly found himself on the next plane home. Later, demoted for causing an international incident. It wouldn't have been out of character for the Croats to have shot him on the spot, along with the mercenaries.

Part of our remit was to tour the countryside and visit with an interpreter or a UNPROFOR (United Nations Protection Force) group on the local farms and try to gather some local intelligence about the area we were operating in. We had been asked to escort some UNPROFOR people to a small farming village to talk to the local commander.

They required a show of force from the Warriors as the last time they were in the vicinity they were just driving Land Rovers and they were greeted with a volley of gunfire. As we approached the farmhouses down a small icy track, one of the Warriors slid off the road, it slipped down the side of the hill and did a complete somersault, landing again amazingly on its tracks.

The driver naturally panicked and got out of the driver's compartment as quickly as he could but forgot to put the hand brake on. The result was 30 tonnes of armoured fighting vehicle slithering down a further four hundred meters to the bottom of the mountain completely out of control and crashing through the undergrowth at the bottom, before finally coming to a halt.

Luckily, there were no troops in the crew compartment as they had de-bussed moments earlier to secure the perimeter area.

At this point, there had to be an assessment to look at the possibility of recovering the vehicle from six hundred feet back onto the track. It was decided that it could be done. As the Recovery Warrior 24C had moved forward to a position where the winch could be deployed the tracks of the now stationary vehicle started to slip due to the heat of the trackpads warming the ice beneath them.

In a second, that vehicle was also on its way down the mountain, turning over three and a half times and ending up on its side two hundred feet below. The crew who had luckily disembarked from the vehicle rushed down and managed to get the driver out who was badly bruised and rapidly going into shock.

The UMPROFOR seeing this promptly did an about-turn in their Land Rovers and buggered off as it was apparently quite a dangerous place to be and it was time for their tea break. Cheers mates.

Luckily for us, the local farmers who we were visiting had seen the incident and ran down to us to give assistance. As they did not have any transport, one of the locals offered to guide us towards Busovača about five miles away where our nearest checkpoint was. However, he could not go all the way, as if he was caught he would have been killed by other local militia.

The crew set off on the journey carrying a gibbering driver between them and leaving the original casualty Warrior crew behind to guard the vehicles. After what seemed like they had climbed over every mountain track in Bosnia, the guide left at the limit of his safe area.

The crew headed to the checkpoint delivering our casualty to a confused checkpoint platoon commander. He had spoken to our UNPROFOR people three hours ago but they had not told him of the rolling Warrior incident or more importantly of our casualty.

Leaving the driver with the platoon commander, the crew walked five miles back to the stranded vehicles. The next morning, we set about recovering the two vehicles.

The Company had sent 7 Platoon to provide protection who were now setting up a cordon around the recovery area. The first recovery was relatively easy as the first Warrior was already at the bottom of the mountain and had actually crashed through a lot of bushes and crossed a tree line and the river at the bottom of the valley.

After a few hours repairing damaged axle arms and taking the broken track off one side of the vehicle (call sign 13) we were ready to start the recovery to the top of the mountain.

A Foden-wheeled recovery vehicle turned up at the location with Billy Welsh and a Land Rover and after driving around to the other side of the valley and placing the anchor blades down on the recovery vehicle we started the casualty

Warrior engine. Using the engine power and the one remaining track to assist, we managed to winch it up the opposite side of the mountain.

Once it was recovered to the level standing at the crest it would be possible to work on it and make it battleworthy again.

There were quite a few locals gathered around the recovery vehicle whilst we were busy with the recovery task. It was only noticed a few hours later that there were a number of items that were strapped to the sides of the vehicle that were now missing. There were also a lot of footprints disappearing through the snow into the forest never to be seen again.

Some of the items were 20 kilograms of hydraulic jacks. Another lesson learnt:

When you are in a country where the locals have nothing. They will steal what they can to trade it for food and weapons.

A major and his driver had a road accident and their Land Rover went down the side of the mountain. Luckily, neither was injured but by the time they had walked to the nearest village to call for help and returned to the scene of the accident eight hours later with some assistance, the Land Rover had disappeared and all that was left was a lot of horse hoof prints and some block and tackle marks on the nearby trees.

The locals really are resourceful or maybe we are just spoilt by having access to modern equipment.

My Repair and Recovery Warrior was another matter as it was on the wrong side of the river, on its side, only halfway down the mountain and completely unserviceable. The first problem was to get it back onto the tracks again without sending it down to the bottom of the valley.

This was done in several stages by employing turfer winches to coax it back on its tracks and securing it so it would not also career to the foot of the valley. Once this was done, we had to attempt to bring it up the mountain onto the original icy track it had slipped off initially. With this in mind, I tasked a group of engineers and they came to our location to cut away the banks with power tools.

They also had to get rid of the steep gradient by talking away tonnes of earth and to ensure that the camber of the road was modified so that if we did slip again, we would slip towards the bank and not over the side again. The locals all thought this was highly amusing. Each morning for the next few days, they would come from all the nearby farmhouses and watch the unending struggle to recover this unrecoverable object.

This did not cause any problems as they kept well out of the way and did not bother us at all apart from the fact that if we put anything down for more than two minutes it would be stolen. With a good track to base the recovery vehicle on, the Warrior extraction exercise started.

Although the initial turning of the Warrior back onto its tracks did not cause a problem, after a brief inspection we found out that three axle arms were broken and therefore it would not be possible to give assistance to the recovery vehicle by driving out of the valley. By now, it was nighttime and we decided to leave the next step until morning.

Rather than have to start feeding ourselves. I decided to walk up to the farmhouse with a box of rations for 10 men and explain to the local farm owner, who was also the local militia commander, that if his wife cooked us enough food to feed six men they could keep the rest. Normally, I stayed clear of small enclaves as they have a tendency for being volatile.

But over the last day, I had set up quite a friendly banter with the locals and thought that it was justified for me to push my luck on this occasion. When I reached the farm, I realised that there were only the womenfolk about apart from the grandfather of the family.

I put my proposition to him in sign language and in the true Bosnian way he could not make a decision without first consulting a bottle of home-made brandy, the deciding went on for almost an hour, by which time I was three parts to the wind due to the fact that it may have caused an offence not to partake with him.

He told me that my offer was acceptable.

When I asked him where all the men were, he told me that since we were here protecting our vehicles, we were also protecting the farm complex so it was safe to leave the women guarded by us from attack. Also, if we wanted to we could stay for as long as we liked because as long as we were here they could send all their men out at night to fight in Busovaca.

I could not help but smile at the fact that everybody's misfortune is someone else's gain. What I would like to know is why it was always my misfortune.

I finally rolled down the hill numb of the face and wobbly of the leg to find that my crew had also found out about the Bosnian home brew and at midnight we sat down to plum brandy and a stew that was to this day one of the most tasteful things I have ever tasted.

The next morning at sunrise, we started again and for the first six hours, we only succeeded in turning the Warrior around and around on its own axis. We then attached another tow rope to try a double pull. The reason we had not done this before is that there was no room for a decent purchase and if the Warrior slipped any further down the mountain it could drag the recovery vehicle down with it.

Slowly the Warrior started to move and inch by inch it came up to the top of the ridge until it reached a point where we were going to have to disconnect it and pull at a different angle. The vehicle was choked so as not to roll backwards and enough slack was given to disconnect the tow rope.

Whilst the recovery vehicle was being re-positioned the Warrior and the chocks all decided that they preferred it where they were and promptly slid back down to the original resting site. (and now for my next trick).

The task was started again and this time was successful until we butted up to an object under the snow. This turned out to be a huge tree stump and after digging about five feet down into the frozen ground we finally uncovered it. Apart from dynamite, nothing was going to shift it. At this point, the crowd on the hillside were actually taking bets on the time we would have the recovery finished.

I think it was due to the fact that one man's time was running out, that he suddenly appeared with some chainsaws and then set to work himself cutting the stump level with the ground.

After general friendly abuse from the locals, we started again and the Warrior flew up the last few feet and balanced itself sweetly on the edge of the rim, it then buggered off back down the mountain again. Completely disillusioned we decided to sack it for the day and would try something else tomorrow.

That night, I ordered two lorry loads of hardcore to arrive in the morning as we did not have any options but to fix the broken bits on the Warrior and try and drive it out, this was a very dangerous job as we had to have people on and under the hull and at any time it could have started to slip again.

All the trees in the vicinity had been systematically plucked out of the ground over the past few days in an attempt to drag the vehicle up the slope using a block, tackle and winches. There wasn't any other position we could use to pull from that would still be relatively safe.

I decided then to call up the Royal Engineers Tracked vehicle (CET) and to bury it into the mountain and use it as an anchor. Luckily Billy Welsh had stayed with his Land Rover and so we had somewhere warm and dry to have our meals and spend the night.

First thing in the morning, the hardcore and the CET turned up and within three hours the hardcore was poured onto the icy slope and the CET dug a massive hole on the opposite side of the track and buried itself in it to act as an anchor. The Warrior was recovered up onto the track in one single winch pull.

Why hadn't I done this at the beginning?

"Because I did not want to. Alright!"

We still could not tow a vehicle along the track and so various bits had to be swapped about to allow this to happen. First of all, we got the engine going which in itself was no mean feat, as it had been upside down for 24 hours and had sheared all the engine mountings as well as covering everything in oil. The only thing keeping the engine in place was the driveshafts.

It was also a fireball waiting to happen, as the whole thing was swamped in diesel and spilt engine oil. As soon as all our military observers (who just happened to be passing on this little track 20 miles from nowhere) saw the vehicle was recovered they all disappeared back to Vitez leaving only my two vehicles in location and allowed the final touches to be made. After all, it was only 20 miles away and nothing could go wrong, could it?

That was when the blizzard started, covering the tracks in freezing snow. The only safe way to guide the Warrior down the track was for me to walk in front of the vehicle and use hand signals. As if that wasn't bad enough, whilst we were edging our way along a ridge line a few snipers located in the surrounding hills decided that it would be good practice if they made me dash between safe areas whilst trying to guide the vehicle down this icy section for four hundred meters.

I decided to humour them as it seemed a good idea at the time. My driver who was driving my Warrior in a battened down safe and secure position, spent the next few minutes having a good laugh at my expense watching me sprint 20 meters then dive into a bank before guiding him towards me, then sprint again for another 20 metres and dive into the next banking.

This continued until we were around a bend and out of sight of the snipers. The track improved and we continued down the track until we reached the road from Kakuni to Busovaca.

As we came to the junction, we could see in the distance two British Army Land Rovers. As we drew near, I recognised my boss who was the captain in charge of the workshop and Martin Craig the ASM who was standing by the road with piping hot food and mugs of coffee. After my four hundred-metre belly crawling and sprint dashes this went down like God's ambrosia.

Life is not that bad after all, is it? After our lunch, we headed for home, escorting the first broken Warrior we had repaired. We both limped back to Vitez very slowly as 24C had two wheels missing and no engine mounts securing the engine so that was jumping about in the engine compartment every time we tried to accelerate or brake.

Call sign 13 had three wheels missing and a turret that we had to tie in place as the turret lock was broken so the turret spun around on every bend we drove around.

The next few days were taken up with a spot of rest and generally sorting out what damage had occurred to both the crashed vehicles. Martin Craig who was my immediate boss both here in Bosnia and also when I was in the Gulf War I, asked me if I would go with him to Split and pick up a new Warrior repair and recovery variant as a replacement for my broken one. The roll down the mountain had damaged the vehicle's hull and it could not be repaired at our location.

This was a chance that I jumped at as we had been friends for a long time and it was ages since we had had a quiet meal and a drink and generally good time together. I could not wait to go as there were no restrictions in Split and I had not had a night on the town for four months.

We set off in the morning and throughout the journey, Martin had a smug grin on his face, it was only when we met a Warrior repair variant on the mountain above Tomislavgrad did he tell me that plans had changed and they had agreed to bring my replacement vehicle this far.

He obviously took great delight the night before watching me pack some decent civilian clothes and abusing everybody who would not be able to come with me for a meal and a beer or six in downtown Split. I would now have an egg on my face when I return to base. Martin obviously found this greatly amusing as he did not stop laughing at me for ages and for a long time after he would call me on the radio and ask if I wanted to go downtown.

I did get my own back on him later when his dog was knocked down and killed by a passing car. The dead dog was brought to him by a soldier who had been on guard at the main gates. He told Martin what had happened and left the dog outside the Control Point truck which Martin used as an office.

Whilst Martin went into the back compound to dig a grave for the dog, bugger me if the dog's body didn't disappear. When he came back in to collect the body all he could see was a small area that had white tape all around it and a chalk outline of where the scene of the crime dead dog had laid. To his credit, he saw the funny side of it. After a few weeks!

Winter seems to be taking ages to come to an end. Every morning, we wake up and check to see if the early morning frost has gone because frost down in the valley means that there is still ice in the mountains.

In early February, I was called out to a recovery task at the Zeneca flyover. During the night, one of the 7th Armoured Workshop's recovery vehicles had skidded on the black ice and flown, complete with an eight-tonne truck on tow, through the crash barriers on a flyover and plummeted into the river below, with the towed vehicle landing next to it. Again, it was yet another miracle that nobody was killed. We certainly have been lucky on several occasions on this tour.

The problem still arose of how were we going to recover it. Eventually, we managed to borrow two huge cranes from the Dutch UN contingent and coupled with two Warrior winches we managed to lift and pull, lift and pull, lift and pull both the vehicles out.

Due to the 25-tonne weight of the recovery vehicle falling that distance, the chassis was completely wrecked and very few items were salvageable. However, the wreck still had to be recovered to Split at the cost of thousands of pounds.

During this task, Colonel Bob Stewart turned up and gave me the general abuse I expect from him, as every time he has seen me lately, I have been involved with some unique recovery task. He does, however, seem to appreciate what we are doing for his battalion and often stops and talks to the boys on the task.

This is more than can be said for some high-ranking officers, whose delusions of grandeur include thinking they could do a much better job themselves and only when interfering once too often do they realise that yours truly is about to take full verbal vengeance out in their general direction. Unfortunately, I am generally so sarcastic they usually miss the point completely, but I usually feel much better for it.

Chapter 26
Tuzla

Our six-week stay in Vitez is again nearly over and we are about to find out where we are going next. The rumours are rife but due to the fact that the winter is still with us, I reckon wherever we go we will have to climb some more horrible icy slippery mountains.

Where is Tuzla? About 60 kilometres north of Kladanj. And how are we going to get there? Over the top of the world, again (my, my, how fortunate I am). The date that we are moving to Tuzla has slipped due to the bad conditions on the top of the mountains and that suits me fine, even though the officer commanding the company has changed and the new one is keen to prove himself to his boss the commanding officer.

As far as I am concerned, he can prove himself all he wants so long as he does not bother me, or my section.

Just prior to moving to Tuzla, the company went out to Turbe to do a refugee exchange. During these exchanges, we were given set times when we could pass through certain Serbian-controlled areas safely. If we extended this stay, we could be considered a legitimate target and the Serbians could and would open fire. Just as the OC's Warrior entered the template the driver's instrument panel on his Warrior had an electrical fault and burnt out.

My electrician jumped immediately onto the problem but as all the wiring was burnt out, he had to do a major rewire job as fast as possible. This was certainly an eye-opener for the new OC. The electrician worked frantically to get the job done before the safety deadline but in the end, they had to connect the Warrior up to the Warrior recovery vehicle 24C and tow him to a safe zone, to be fixed later.

Whilst this was going on one of the Warriors was parked up giving protection to the OC's vehicle. As the heavy armoured back door of this vehicle slammed shut the main 30 mm armament fired off straight down the high street hitting the town hall. The vehicle commander could not understand what had happened, so he ordered the door to be opened and closed again.

Sure enough, the gun went bang again sending another round straight down the high street and into the town hall again. With that fact noted he unloaded the gun and would have to get the problem fixed back at the Vitez School compound by one of my armourers.

It is a sign of the warring factions and the times that they were living in that no one complained about the accidental firing of the weapon. The locals were so used to gunfire in close proximity. They probably thought the Warrior was shooting at someone to protect them. If this had happened in an English town, there would have been a full safety investigation with several HSE panels and the national papers and news channels involved.

Throughout our tour, the refugee exchanges took place frequently. This was one of the main reasons we were based in Vitez so close to the front-line. As the buses of refugees came into our area, the Serbians would occasionally open fire on the buses. These buses were full of refugees with their only possessions being what they could wear and carry.

There were always a lot of casualties on the buses, either injured prior to boarding the buses during the ethnic cleansing or during their journey across the borders. The passengers were mainly women and children as the buses had been stopped previously and all the men were escorted off and sent to PoW camps for the foreseeable future.

The whole time we were assisting the authorities to ensure the safe passage of the refugees, we were being accused of ethnic cleansing by various political parties within Bosnia and Herzegovina. Later, during the tour of the battalion that replaced the Cheshire battalion, the UN patrols found a lot of mass graves where genocide had taken place, so this was the possible fate of these refugees who thought they had at last found a safe haven.

They had ended up the same as so many others who had been captured whilst attempting to flee the war zone. Captured by whichever warring faction happened to be in that area at that moment in time.

The next day after breakfast, we received the order to move to Tuzla. The journey as far as Olovo went without incident but on entering the tunnel we knew that as soon as we cleared the tunnel exit, we would start to have the same problems as before in the winter wonderland.

As the first vehicle exited the tunnel, two words floated down the radio like wildfire into everybody's earpieces, they were the two most beautiful words in the world, "No ice."

Overnight, the temperature had risen and this had caused the last of the ice to melt. Of course, there were masses of freezing cold meltwater gushing down the tracks and some of the roads were being washed away with the snow melt, but this was only a minor problem and we did not mind doing detours up and down the side of the mountains as we had grip and when we pressed the brakes we stopped.

When we turned the steering yoke, the vehicle turned as well, all that worry and depression about this journey for nothing. A man just does not know where he stands any more, does he? (bloody nature). I had been building myself up for a nervous breakdown for days now and I was looking forward to it and now I am expected to have a nice drive through the countryside without a care in the world (typical).

The whole journey passed without incident. We drove through Kladanj shouting abuse as we passed a platoon of A company who were now in the location at the factory where we had spent Christmas. Even Bomb Alley was quiet and the company arrived in Tuzla on schedule and immediately started the handover procedure from the remaining platoons of A company who had taken over from us in Kladanj.

Tuzla camp was a training camp for the Bosnian Government Army and we had been allocated a small section of land about four hundred meters away from an airfield where we hoped the aid would now be arriving as well as the refugees being moved out of Serbian-held enclaves. Initially, the Bosnians begged the UN to help the people who were trying to leave Serbian-held land.

As soon as the UN started laying on relief convoys and airlifts to help the refugees leave, we then were again accused of helping the Serbians with ethnic cleansing. We are very rapidly entering a catch-22 situation and whatever we do to help one side, the opposing side complains.

The fact is that there is no way to give relief without being looking to favour one faction or the other, I am beginning to wonder why we bother.

The work in Tuzla is very slow and for the first time in four months, we can actually plan what we are doing tomorrow. Only a few convoys run past here as most relief columns' final destination is Tuzla. From then on, it is purely up to the Bosnian government who make the priority list of who needs the supply of food most urgently. Every week we were resupplied with food and fuel.

The fuel tanker turned up on one occasion and told us we could only have half a tank of fuel for each vehicle. This was unusual but we let it ride. It was only when someone was driving through Tuzla that and noticed a line of civilian traffic parked up behind our tanker. The operator had set himself up a nice operation.

He gave us half a tank of fuel and was then selling the remainder to the locals. Clang. Mind your fingers. You're nicked. If this had happened in Germany, he probably would he been slapped on his back by his mates for having the balls to do it. Out here running out of fuel could cost someone's life.

The other exciting event we had daily in Tuzla was that the airfield was subject to artillery fire which landed within one hundred meters of our operations office block. In the corridor, we had built a bomb shelter, which was a room strengthened by strong planks of wood the size of railway sleepers, whether or not it would protect us from a direct hit on the building we never found out.

The barrages were quite regular and usually went on for 30 minutes. The airfield received about 20 shells each day, systematically destroying the army camp we were based in.

Tuzla is the focus of attention for the world's press. Every dignitary who visits Tuzla visits our operations room. Kate Aidie is usually skulking around in the background and pushing her nose into everything, which is probably what she does best and why she gets so much recognition for the job she does. However, I did not get involved with her in the Gulf and I am not going to now.

On one occasion, I was leading a convoy back to Vitez and had arranged to meet her at a set location at a certain time if she wanted to jump on the end of my convoy so we could escort her party safely down the route to Vitez. When the time came, she was nowhere to be seen and not wanting to be late into Vitez we set off down the road.

Suddenly, there was the sound of horns blowing and her little convoy came flying around the bend. Skidding to a halt she jumped out and tried to give me a hard time for leaving her behind. It was my fault completely as I did not realise that the whole British Army came to a shuddering halt every time Kate bloody Aidie clicked her fingers.

Reporters came and reporters went, all trying to get the biggest story and not caring how many soldiers they were putting at risk just by the fact that we had to escort them into these dangerous areas, However, there are not many men in Britain who can say that they have entertained Kate Aidie and Bianca Jagger at the same time. This happened one early morning when they were visiting our operations room.

I had grabbed my guitar and was entertaining a captive audience within the building. My musical tones reverberated around the accommodation corridors prior to our daily routine starting. All this happened before I was politely asked to shut the F*%k up as the officers were trying to give a briefing. This was all done in the best possible taste. No bawdy songs were sung that day. Bianca Jagger was there as part of a Save the Children contingent.

Tiddles (the cat, not the recovery mechanic) had been left in Vitez for this period as he has been quite poorly. Every night he jumped on my bed and snuggled down and then later in the night went into the main hangar and got fed by the guard force. On this one night one of the sergeants grabbed hold of him and made him settle down on his bunk as he had been prowling around meowing loudly.

It wasn't long before the contented sound of him purring in this sleep filled the room. It was that night that Tiddles had a miscarriage and we found out with a shock that he was she. Unfortunately, she had made quite a mess on the sergeant's nice new sleeping bag and although she was recovering slowly, it was some time before she would recover fully. The same could not be said for the sergeant and his sleeping bag.

Tuzla camp is overrun with two packs of dogs and the main characters were a big African ridgeback dog and his mate a half wolf half Alsatian bitch who had just had nine pups. Seven of which would survive, for a while at least. One day, the Alsatian nicknamed Linda Gray (after Linda Gray from Dallas because she was a bitch as well), was knocked down and had her front left leg broken.

After a few days of trying to put a permanent pot on her leg, it was decided that we must find a vet. The puppies continually nibbled the pot so it was always soggy and not doing its job. Later that day, we drove into Tuzla and started the search for a vet but to no avail. It was then decided that we should commandeer a doctor, so we waited outside the main hospital and hijacked a doctor who was walking through the car park to his car.

For a hundred German marks, he put a pot on that was no different to the one we had been putting on. She broke it or the pups chewed it off within the day, but the thought was there.

Thinking back to that time I wonder, what that doctor thought about these mad British soldiers who, when all around our area people were being killed daily, his normal day's work was removing bullets and shrapnel from people, here I was with my dog with a broken leg and at that precise time that was my main priority. However, he did take my money conscience or not.

Over the next few weeks, she started to learn to walk with one leg flapping uselessly beside her and day by day reacting less and less to the pain. If anybody had told me that I would have been sitting next to a semi-wild dog with a very protective mate within biting distance, bending and twisting her broken leg to get it to heal normally, I would have told them they were mad.

There was no mistake that they were wild as quite a few stray dogs from the other pack of dogs within the airfield complex found out. When these dogs strayed into our area unlike domestic dogs who would just chase an outsider away, these dogs attacked for the kill as this was their next meal.

Slowly but surely, one of the packs disappeared whilst the other grew fatter. For the rest of our time in Tuzla, Big Red and Linda did not leave my side whilst I was in the tank park.

Although I said that we were not very busy whilst in Tuzla, we did have a few moments when things got completely out of control. One of our companies accompanied a peace mission and spent three days in the Cerska Pocket surrounded by hundreds of Muslims who would not let the vehicles move out of their village once we had dropped off the aid package. The Serbian army was on the next hill and as soon as we moved out of the area they would attack.

The translator with our company was a British Army officer and although British was also half Serbian. He was threatened by the Muslim army on numerous occasions but still stuck to his story that his grandmother was Croatian even though he did speak with a Serbian accent. Almost hourly the leaders and their henchmen would march down to our group and threaten that if we drove away, they would shoot us.

Driving away was possible but was not to be seriously considered as the Muslims had placed all the women and children around and under the vehicles to stop any vehicle movement. This aggression towards us went on for three days and all the time the Serbians were sending messages that if we did not move, they would attack anyway.

An UNPROFOR vehicle was parked about 30 metres away and I do not think that the occupants got out during the whole episode. On day three, the company was just settling in for another day of haggling and arguing with the Muslims. Telling them to leave the village and them telling us that we were helping the Serbians to ethnically cleanse the area.

The UNPROFOR members had finally left their vehicle and were wandering around the location taking notes on the situation here, when suddenly their vehicle took a direct hit from a Serbian artillery shell.

From that point on, things were just a blur as more and more rounds fell in close proximity and everyone dived into a ditch or behind walls making themselves as small as possible but with nowhere to go in reality and certainly not enough protection if a round landed within 20 metres. As it was, individuals were deafened by the explosions and bodies were buffeted by the concussion of the exploding shells.

In Canada, the safety area is a thousand meters away from exploding shells during the firepower demonstration, providing that the observers are under a shelter, here we had shells landing within 40 or 50 meters and the shock waves were making ears and kidneys ache.

The artillery stopped and everybody slowly extracted themselves from whatever protection they had forced themselves into. All around were blown-up bodies of men, women and children some dying, some screaming and some already dead. One shell landed killing a child as the mother was running for cover with the child in her arms. Other children had their legs amputated by the explosion.

In all, there were 25 people killed and 30 or 40 with injuries. Although this was an ideal opportunity to get out of this place, we forced ourselves to stay behind to administer first aid and after we had done as much as we could, the leaders of the Muslims came to our vehicles and thanked us and told us that we could leave if we wanted, but they were still staying.

Two of our vehicles, soft-skin vehicles including our Foden recovery vehicle had sustained damage and had to be left behind as well as the UNPROFOR rover of which none of that team had been hurt or showed their faces until after the show was over.

With a final look over their shoulder, the company drove away to leave the Muslims to prepare for their final battle and even as we drove away the next artillery barrage started again. Over the next year, Cerska would be in the news for all the wrong reasons. Ethnic cleansing, massacres and uncovered mass graves.

Throughout our time in Bosnia, various information-gathering groups of our military organisation turned up to extract information from us about our experiences and our actions in certain situations. One day, two Marine commandos turned up at the Tuzla camp to do a recognisance of the area.

After an initial debrief, they were told where they could and could not drive, including where all the Serbian front lines were and why they should have respect for the agreements which we had in place with the Serbians concerning go and no-go areas. This information was taken in with a pinch of salt.

Within 10 minutes of leaving the safety of our camp, they decided that they knew better and decided to see how far they could drive into Serbian-held territory before being stopped. Well, the answer to that question that anybody could have told them if they had asked, is about three to five inches. They had totally ignored our safety advice with the attitude We are royal Marines and we can go where we like!

As they drew level with the border crossing, not realise that the Serbians had had them in their sights for the last six hundred meters as they travelled through no man's land.

As soon as they entered the Serbian-held territory, an RPG7 anti-tank missile slammed into the front of their Land Rover and again gifted by some God only minor injuries were inflicted. The completely deflated and panicking Marines managed to get away from the vehicle but were still caught in no man's land, where they had to sit in a nearby ditch whilst the Serbian snipers systematically shot their vehicle to bits.

We were completely unaware of this situation unfolding as the sound of gunfire from the border area was commonplace and was just normal background noise to us. It was about an hour later when the Serbian commander called our operations room on the radio and said if we wanted to come and get these plonkers he would let us into no man's land without firing upon us.

The Marines were rescued, removed back to camp, had their injuries attended to and then were helicoptered back to Vitez where they got the rifting of their life. They were then helicoptered to Split for yet another bollocking before finally being flown back to Plymouth where someone was to make the decision on the rest of their short careers. The whole episode took less than two days from arrival in Split to their departure.

The airfield was used from time to time to evacuate the refugees from various enclaves around the area. The refugees were supposed to be women, children, old men and wounded soldiers. It was amazing how many wounded soldiers got off the helicopters and then made a miraculous recovery within minutes and were then picked up by previously arranged transport and shipped to another area that required reinforcements.

Throughout this winter tour, the Warriors have proved their worth, although I personally would have preferred to use armoured-wheeled vehicles when driving over the mountains. In fact, to even consider tracked vehicles for a role in this terrain, in winter was ludicrous.

It was now time for me to consider taking my two-week rest and recuperation. As everybody else had had theirs I had to take the last allocated dates and so when our weekly ration drop came in, I jumped on the transport and headed for Vitez.

I was not looking forward to the journey over the mountains stuck in the back of a Bedford, so when an opportunity came to actually drive down there myself with the ASM In a Land Rover, I jumped at the chance. Saying goodbye to the lads whilst accepting their general abuse, I set off on a trouble-free journey to Vitez.

The next morning, we headed back to Split and as we entered Gornji Vakuf, which I hadn't visited for quite a few weeks, I realised that the beautiful town that I had driven through only five months ago, was now raised to the ground. There was also the pitter-patter of shots from sniper rifles echoing around me but thankfully not at me today, for a change.

It was in Gornji Vakuf that Sean Edwards had been shot and killed by a sniper whilst driving a Warrior over the main bridge at Gornji Vakuf, not many days before. This incident had been very saddening, not only because he was the first British soldier to be murdered in Bosnia, but because Sean and I had known each other since the Gulf War and although not my company, I knew him to be very good at his job.

When asked to do something, I could always rely on him to do an excellent job. Later, a plaque was placed on the bridge in memory of him. This tour had turned out to be so much more than a peacekeeping mission. Every day, we seemed to be in the firing line or the brunt of some frustrated foreign soldier's anger.

The journey progressed until we finally reached Split. Once there, I was shocked by the hard life the 7th Armoured Workshop had to endure, hot showers, good food, electricity, and the real problem they had was that they had to be back from town by midnight, after getting a good meal and half a dozen beers. It's a hard life, isn't it?

The following morning, I set off for sunny Germany and was met by Ursula my wife at the airport. I won't tell you about the rest of my rest and recuperation as it was very rude and you probably wouldn't enjoy hearing about it.

After two weeks of rest and recuperation, I arrived back in Split and should have begun our slow move back to Vitez. Billy Welsh had jacked up some transport for us to travel in and so I told the Bedford truck driver to tell my ASM that I would be arriving a day later in Vitez. Billy was going to be my new boss when we arrived back in Fallingbostel as I was posted into his unit, the 7th Armoured Workshops.

It was, therefore, decided that I should meet the new team I would be joining and we could do this on a night out in Split town centre bars. We had a very good night with copious amounts of food and beer and I was looking and feeling my best as we set off on the 150-mile cross-country track to Vitez.

Chapter 27
Tuzla (The Return)

Once we were back in the mountains, after passing through Tomislavgrad, we settled down into the routine of driving around the sharp and steep mountain tracks. I could only admire the work that the Royal Engineers had put in. What a difference there was in the condition and width of the tracks by comparison with the state they were in during that horrific initial journey over the mountains when we first arrived in Bosnia.

New bridges had been built and all the boggy areas had now been firmed up with hardcore. All the negative cambers had been reversed so that even in bad weather a vehicle would slip into the mountainside rather than off the track and down into the valley floor. The trip was uneventful and as we approached the surrounding areas of Vitez, I noticed a significant build-up of militia troops.

This usually means that something has happened or was about to happen. This became apparent as we reached Vitez and saw that this once beautiful town had been completely flattened in those two short weeks that I had been away.

On arriving back in Vitez, I was greeted by a very disgruntled ASM Martin Craig and officer commanding workshops who hadn't been told I was staying an extra day in Split and thought I had missed my flight from Germany. I explained that I had sent a message back to them and I could not miss the opportunity to meet my new platoon. I would soon be managing when we returned to Germany. I forgot to mention that I had not seen one of them as Billy had dragged me downtown as soon as the transport disappeared.

Ahmići is situated on a hill overlooking Vitez. It is one of the many villages that had a tall minaret mosque tower and a beautiful white wall around it. This tower had been destroyed along with most of the buildings in the village. Ahmići village was soon to be a worldwide name for the atrocities carried out there in the near future.

The whole world saw Colonel Bob Stewart looking at the burnt remains of children who had been ethnically cleansed, some had been shot prior to being set on fire, but many had just been thrown into the house cellar and burned alive. The attack had started at 0500 hours with a mortar bombardment followed by snipers shooting everyone who ran out of the houses.

The Croat commander then attacked the village with 70 soldiers with orders to shoot all the men and teenagers. Then shoot the women and when the buildings were burning throw the children into the inferno. The most shocking thing of it all was that Croats that lived in the village also started shooting and murdering their neighbours that they had lived with for 20 years.

All the cattle, dogs, cats and horses were also killed. The Serbian commanders later were sentenced to 25 years in prison by the War Crimes Commission. All this happened within five miles of the Vitez camp, whilst we as UN forces were not allowed to intervene.

As we walked around the garage on our return from R&R, we were immediately the brunt of all the jokes about deserting them when the fireworks started and the whole of Vitez had been shooting at each other, not to mention all the eyewitness reports which were very interesting but once I had heard the 99th version, I decided it was time to move back to Tuzla.

With tears in our eyes, we set off into the sunset in a northerly direction heading for winter wonderland and wondering what could be thrown at me in the remaining four weeks of this tour.

Arriving in Tuzla we were greeted by a sight, not of intense activity which was the normal way of life when we left, but one of peaceful tranquillity. Apparently, the day we left the daily shelling stopped and all convoy runs were made without escorts as the main body of the warring factions had moved down to reinforce the battle for Vitez.

The lull in convoy runs had left my lads all the time they needed to repair maintain and service all the company's vehicles, which was brilliant as we only had three weeks before we all moved back to Vitez. Hopefully, all the ice will have melted for good by then and enable us to travel back without any major incidents.

Our replacements have been arriving and making themselves familiar with the daily routine. The last few days have been spent going through all the procedures and possible incidents that they could expect to be confronted with.

The new unit is a Canadian infantry unit that decided that the way we do things is not the Canadian way so they will do their own thing. This is their prerogative, so I wished them well and hoped that ignoring our proven and tested ways, that we performed for a reason does not backfire on them.

As the company slowly moved out of location those that could, looked back at the town and around the area wondering when would be the next time we come back, as it was pretty obvious that there was no end in sight for this conflict. It is possible that this war could last for another five years at least.

Although the news reports still refer to this as a conflict, to the hundreds and thousands of Yugoslavians who have lost loved ones or indeed been injured themselves it is a full-blown war. All right, it does not have the modern-day technology nor are there air raids anymore, but due to the close proximity of their enemies, it is more personal than anything I encountered in the Gulf.

Later, the British Army's United Nations role was to be changed to one of UNPROFOR and with that change in role, the vehicles changed from the White of the United Nations to Green of an aggressive army and the berets changing from blue to black. This meant the British Army had the power to intervene in humanitarian rights matters. This would have simplified things if we had these powers from the start, instead of advising the warring parties that they should not do things to each other and then letting them carry on with the atrocities anyway.

The move back to Vitez went ahead without as much as one breakdown and with all the snow and ice now melted it was hard to imagine how it took my crew so long to recover that single Warrior. The tracks were now firm and only looked like slight gradients which the vehicles ate up without even straining.

When these tracks were covered with ice, our vehicles were slipping and sliding just under the force of gravity acting against them these slight gradients appeared to be steep gradients. The section that took us three days of blood sweat and tears recovering the Warrior, disappeared behind us in one hour and 40 minutes and the whole trip only took four hours. Throughout the journey, I took in the scenic views, knowing I would not be seeing this place again.

All the while, I was getting flashback memories of the things that had happened to me over the last few months, every bend, hill, or river seemed to have some hidden memory both happy and sad from the lads throwing themselves down the mountainsides in black bin liners for sledges to the sheer terror of a possible slip on the ice that would send us plunging down a mountain.

The drunken group of soldiers on New Year's Day. Or the remains of firefights we had come across, and the faces of the locals knowing they would have to carry on with their families getting smaller and smaller every day.

On our arrival back in Vitez, the new battalion was ready to take over the routine duties and could not envisage the problems we faced throughout that long hard winter but no doubt they would find problems enough during their operational tour. This country has a knack of lulling the occupier into a false sense of security for weeks and then scaring the shit out of him in a second.

Chapter 28
The Move to Split

The next few days flew past and finally, the battalion lined up for the long journey back to Split. If the trip goes as smoothly as the one from Tuzla, then we should be at Tomislavgrad by nightfall and from there we are to be transported to Split. Bish, Bash, Bosch. And it sounded like a nightingale.

Even before my vehicle left the location, I had notification of a breakdown two miles from the start point but that shouldn't be a problem as all the vehicles have been looked over these last few days and any major problems have been ironed out.

"Wrong!"

On arrival at the breakdown, we found out that one of my company Warriors had thrown its rear idler and track and as this was the first time we had come across this problem, no spares were available. The only thing left to do was take the tracks off, crane them onto the Warrior's roof and drag this useless 28-tonne lump of metal behind us for the next 150 miles, this was going to be a long day.

Surprisingly, due to the good state of the roads, we made excellent time although we are way behind the rest of the company, apart from one Warrior who has stayed with us for protection.

The trip continued with no other problems at all. We made our customary tea stop at the layby overlooking Prozor for one last photocall and then carried on the journey. It was now spring and the views from the high mountain pass were magnificent.

All the villages that were dotted on the mountains in the distance looked very picturesque even though I knew that if I drove up close to them they would all be pockmarked with marks from exploding shells and bullets and many houses would be burnt-out shells. Also, each village would have a field of newly dug graves.

As we traversed around the very last mountain bend before we dropped down to Tomislavgrad, I felt the rear of the vehicle give a slight kick sideways and then jerk violently to the left.

The tight bend we were navigating around was also on a steep incline and due to the rapid transfer of weight, the vehicles jack-knifed and in seconds were see-sawing over a precipice and whilst the drop of one hundred feet was not vertical, the downward slope was very severe, and with the casualty vehicle strapped on our back by holly bones, steering accurately down such a drop would be impossible.

Luckily, we still had the protection Warrior with us and with his help, we managed to drag the dead vehicle backwards and across the track enough to allow Butch to manoeuvre the vehicle around so at least we were pointing in the right direction. Meanwhile, I was stuck up in my turret cursing Butch for being the worst driver in the world and generally giving him a hard time.

Not that any of it was his fault, I just didn't believe that this could happen to me so close to the end of the journey. Finally, we started slowly down the last steep hill, which was about a 1 in 10 gradient for about three kilometres with the odd short stretch of 1 in 4 thrown in for good measure to keep us on our toes.

Luckily, the track was as straight as a die.

As we moved off again, the vehicles reached the safe towing speed of about 25 miles an hour which was fine for this gradient. However, we continued to speed up, and I started to get a very uneasy feeling that something not very nice was about to happen. I told Butch to slow down, however, our two-vehicle package was slowly gaining momentum. We were still picking up speed and so I then started to shout at him to bloody well slow down.

At this point, he decided to let me know quite calmly the vehicle brakes had overheated and he was struggling to check the increasing speed. After careful consideration of about three nanoseconds, I screamed at everybody in the back to batten down and strap up as tight as possible.

For the complete three-kilometre journey, we hurtled down the hill at over 50 miles an hour with Butch trying his best to brake and steer with the minimum assistance he could get from the mechanical system. Every time we seemed to be slowing down, we would hit another section of the track that was very steep and so the speed increased again. This could not be happening to me. We only had a day to go and our operational tour was over.

Eventually, the gradient started to level out and we slowly started to slow down. In front of me, I could see the track was level and even.

After about a kilometre, Butch spoke up with a smug, "That was brilliant, wasn't it, boss?"

I didn't answer as I was fumbling for a much-needed cigarette with very shaking hands and in the background I could hear the lads in the back laughing their heads off and whooping. It was alright for them they could not see where we were going, the steep drop at our side or how fast our two vehicles with a combined weight of 60 tonnes of metal could have flown off the road. We finally coasted to a virtual halt.

I told Butch to keep the vehicle going for the final half a kilometre which he did and we gently manoeuvred into line with all the rest of our company vehicles within the TSG Camp. All the driver's instrument panel warning lights were flashing on and off, alarms were sounding in our headsets and steam and oil belched up through the louvres.

At this point, Butch switched the engine power pack off and apart from a slow hissing and clicking noise of cooling metal, the engine fell dead, never to start again until a replacement could be found back at Fallingbostel.

Right then, let's get the brews on.

Chapter 29
Home in Time for Tea

There's not much else to say about the rest of this latest adventure as we now have to hurry up and wait whilst the military strategy practices the age-old techniques of on the bus and off the bus just to ensure that every poor sole no matter how old, new, borrowed or blue gets thoroughly fed up with the movements staff.

I often wonder about the fact that after countless years of moving troops in and out of hundreds of theatres and countries, the excuses given in any of these moves can be counted on one hand and usually with such conviction that the bearer of bad tidings seems to actually believe them himself.

How on Earth could the movement of over a thousand men be postponed for a day because one truck has a flat tyre, or we were not expecting you to arrive today? It had only been planned for the last six months.

We eventually moved into Split and straight to the airport, where a plane was waiting. We flew into Hannover where we were met by the press, the local dignitaries as well as every Tom, Dick and Harry, wanting to be seen on the newsreels. Finally, we arrived in Fallingbostel to be met by Ursula and the kids.

Hopefully, this will be the last time I will be away from them for a long time as with only two and a half years to do in the army, I personally think that I have done enough for Queen and Country and to quote the words of some infamous prophet, "I'm getting too old for this shit."

Chapter 30
Poetry Corner Part Three

THE GIRL OF MY DREAMS

Sometimes, I have some really vivid dreams, and I can recall parts of these dreams for days. Sometimes I have weird dreams that are really so weird I subconsciously think this is stupid and wake myself up. Sometimes, I wake up and think that was a weird dream but also a great dream. What I don't understand is how can dreams be so detailed and last so long when it has been scientifically proven that a dream only lasts seconds.

At some point, I think everyone has a dream where they meet the most fantastic looking person and for that briefest of moments everything is perfect.

Well! until the alarm clock rings.

These verses should be read in a Yorkshire accent.

I saw her she was standing there.
With her jet-black eyes and her raven hair.
She had just turned around and she looked at me.
Well, she must have thought I was quite a joke.
Cause when I tried to speak. I kind of choked.
I spilt my beer all over my new blue jeans.

I looked at her, and she looked back,
I thought I may as well have a crack.
So, I walked up to her and I said, "Howdy do?"
She said hello and then she smiled,
I suppose it took me quite a while,
To think of the next thing, I should do.
I asked her if she'd like a dance.

She shook her head and said no thanks.
She never danced with men whose jeans were wet.
I said stay there! I'll be back in a flash,
With my fingers crossed, I started to dash,
To my room where some clean jeans I could get.

Well, I broke every record for getting changed, And I ran straight back, for what remained.

Of the night with the girl of my dreams.
But when I appeared back on the scene.
I could not find that girl of my dreams.
I asked around but nobody knew her name. (Boo Hoo)

I looked all around and searched every block,
The last place I looked, I got quite a shock.
I found her drinking coffee in a cafe.
I said I thought I'd lost you then.
She laughed at me as my face was red.
What with the running and the looking, and the huffing and the puffing? And the beer.

She said she had the catch the last bus home.
But if I wanted to, because she was all alone,
I could wait with her until that last bus turned up.
Well, my smile must have been a mile wide.
Because she sat me down and looked into my eyes.
She said, "I'll go and get another cup, Chuck."

I said I don't normally act like this,
She leant towards me and gave me a kiss,
That's when my alarm woke me up. (Boo Hoo)
I was so disappointed I nearly cried,
I put on my shirt and I tied my tie,
And I waited for the ground to swallow me up.

I slowly walked to the end of the road,
Feeling bent over with the weight of my load.
I thought I'd go and get myself a beer.
Then I saw her she was standing there,
With her jet-black eyes and her raven hair.
When she turned around and she smiled at me.

(Yippee)

THE LOVER

Thank God, my courting days have been over for many years. I used to hate all the build-up to breaking up, and then the fumbling of making up again. Making promises that neither party had any intention of keeping. After all, we were young and could do what we wanted, and did not care about the consequences.

And whilst I watch the drops of rain.
Roll softly down upon your face,
Turning gently into a slowly flowing river.
And I consider just like before the beauty only time can cure.
And the raindrops are just like tears of sorrow.

I've seen love in many eyes.
It makes me want to sympathise.
But how can someone dare to leave a lover,
How can someone bear to leave a lover?

It's like the story we've all heard before.
I dare not think of another war with the one you love,
It only brings pain and sorrow.
And so, I close my mind and dream,
Of things that make people seem, to spend their days,
Wishing for a new tomorrow.

When I think of the things we've got,
Sometimes good, more often not.
But how can someone dare to leave a lover,
How can someone bear to leave a lover?

So, from now on, I will admit my fate,
And despise all of those I hate.
And the ones who laughed, and told me of you're leaving.
And I will continue to protest, to the ones who say,
"There's nothing left."
While I spend my time searching for a new beginning.

When I think of the things we've had,
Sometimes good more often bad.
But how can someone dare to leave a lover,
How can someone bear to leave a lover?

THE MAKER

I was very influenced as a young teenager listening to the lyrics of Bob Dylan. The song 'Masters of War' was a particular favourite of mine. Should I blame him for leading me into the army, instead of finishing my apprenticeship as a factory maintenance man?

These lyrics, written during my early days as a soldier are of a similar ilk. It's surreal that here I have now retired as a manager within a defence industry that manufactures all the things Bob Dylan protested about within 'Masters of War' all those years ago.

"Some things change but most remain the same."

Freely wheeling, turning, screaming, a death's head in the sky.
Throwing columns of mutilation side-stepping the golden eye.
Nothing can touch it; it can't be seen.
Only that electronic beam will say who will die.
The silver bird of inspiration, its maker safe at home.
Leaves only desolation, Blood and crumpled stone.

The rich man of an aged wealth is safe beside the fire,
Looking at the blueprints he drew himself and slowly he retires.
He sleeps well into the night, dreams of his untold might.
Of fire and flame, of blood and bone,
Oh! What a powerful man he has grown.
In the morning, he will try again to devise an invincible plan.
To stop the fighting and the pain to offer combat to any man.

Although he has no inclination He has no thoughts of annihilation.
Throwing columns of mutilation.
He has designed the extermination of man.

THE NIGHTINGALE

Arlo Guthrie's performance of the song 'Alice's Restaurant' held me spellbound for years, although the film was not that good. I saw him on YouTube the other day doing some other stuff and he was still very amusing.

In the 80s, I had been playing guitar with a friend and with the help of a couple of crates of beer we had been putting the world to rights. In the early hours of the morning, he stood up to leave. As he walked to put his guitar away in his guitar case, he started to pick the 'Alice's Restaurant' tune. Needless to say, we sat down for a few more hours whilst I learnt every tricky note.

With that said if you know someone who knows that tune. Or you may well know that tune. And if you know that tune: this song was written to that tune.

Let me tell you about a man, I met by a stream one day.
His coat was shabby, his shoes were scuffed,
And he looked like he had come a long, long way.
I asked him his name and he just smiled.
He told me he'd been here for quite a while.
He dragged a guitar from a leather sack and slowly started to play.

The face was cracked and the back was holed.
There were scratches on it from head to toe.
The frets were worn to the ebony root.
And the bridge was held on with half a dozen screws.

He sang a song about the prairie in fall.
He sang another song about the Berlin Wall.
But when he played, the trees they swayed.
And it sounded like a Nightingale.

I asked him, if I could have a go, but it didn't sound half as nice.
He said it takes a little while to know, but if you listen closely to my advice.
You can hit it hard, but stroke it kind, you can bash it about, it doesn't mind.
Put some new strings on now and again. That will keep it sounding sweet.

We sang and played for most of the night, and we talked of war and peace.
We talked about some countries afar, and we soon got around to his old guitar.
He said he got it given in 53, that's when an old man he gave it to me.
And he'd carried it all around for the rest of his life, wrapped in this leather sack.

He told he'd leave when the morning came. As he must be moving on.
I gave him all of the money I had, which wasn't much, but he'd get along.
I sat around and played for another hour, but I couldn't stop it sounding sour.
So, I pulled my blanket over my head and tried to get to sleep.

When the morning came, the air was cold and the old man was gone.
I walked back to my truck, I grabbed a coat and put it on.
Laying there on the passenger seat, was a note and the leather sack waiting for me.
The note said, "Play this, it will make you smile and then find a friend and pass it on."

I opened up the leather sack and slowly pulled it out.
The face was cracked the back was holed.
And there were scratches on it from head to toe.
The frets were worn to the ebony root.
And the bridge was held on with half a dozen screws.
But when I hit those strings it sure did sing as sweet as a Nightingale.
I went to Alice's restaurant and started to sing a song.

Officer Ogilvie came with his sirens on and told me to move along.
I put my guitar in the leather sack and threw that sack right over my back.
Then drove on out and down the road. Just me and my old guitar.
I cruised on out and down the road. Just me and my old guitar.
I mellowed on out and down the road. Just me and my old guitar.

THOUGHTS OF URSULA

Throughout my marriage, I have spent many a month away from home. This includes four Christmas periods when I was away on military operations. Six-month tours in Northern Ireland (3), Gulf War, Bosnia, Canada, and first-class upgrader course.

I have lost count of the exercises, courses and sports events that kept me away from home. Even as a trials engineer, once I had left the army, I still spent a lot of time living away from home in some hotel. Some were seedy and some were posh but none of them were home.

That may be the secret to our 48 years of marriage. The great constant in my life has been Ursula waiting at home for me to return. Watch out, darling, now I am retired and you can have me home all the time you lucky girl.

It's only a week, seems like a thousand years.
I see your face in the mirror on my wall.
I reach for your love, and though you hesitate.
My love penetrates your armour.

And when I reach out to touch, my hands just grasp the air.
Instead of your soft velvet skin, your long silken hair.
When morning comes, I'll be thinking of you.
When the night falls, I'll pray for you.

Your image has touched the region of my heart.
When will it reach my soul?

THE SUMMERS COMING

All through our lives we strive for things we think will be impossible to have. When after years of saving or persevering, we eventually reach the dizzy heights of having it, whatever it is. An expensive holiday to America, a four-bedroom house, a new Martin or Gibson Guitar, a promotion at work. a new kitchen. A new car.

After a few months of achieving that goal and having it. It doesn't seem that special anymore, is it time to set new heights to achieve or maybe realise that you were more content with what you had rather than the new heights you have reached.

Examples being: It doesn't matter if you drop a £50 guitar. What's the point of living in a big house if you don't like the neighbours? What's the point of owning something if you are scared of using it?

The story of a man looking for lost love, even though he doesn't know what to do if or when he finds her. What's the point of staying with someone if they don't want to be with you?

The summer's coming, April is going.
The spring has started to fade away.
She left me without me knowing.
I suppose there was something that she wanted me to say.
I looked for her but she wasn't there.
I looked for her but she was gone.
I looked for her, I looked everywhere.
I looked for her I asked everyone.

Have you ever seen her face? Have you ever seen her smile?
Have you felt her warm embrace? Or did she just stop for a while?
Have you ever seen her face? Were her eyes still sad and blue?
Did she still wear her hair so long? Did you ask where she was going to?

The summer's left now, and September's blowing.
The leaves in the trees will be falling soon.
In a day or so, I ought to be going.
I should be going but I don't know where to.

I've walked a hundred miles or more.
Over hills and far away.
But the only thing those strangers say.
Is yes. I remember she passed by this way.
Have you ever seen her face? Have you ever seen her smile?
Have you felt her warm embrace? Or did she just stop for a while?
Have you ever seen her face? Were her eyes still sad and blue?
Did she still wear her hair so long? Did you ask where she was going to?

The winter's here now, snow drifts are growing.
Over the fields, and through the town.
My money's all gone, so I'll be going.
Back to my home and settled back down.
I saw her once over a crowded room.
But I just froze and I turned around.
For if I had spoken and she had run away.
Would she ever come back to me one day?

Have you ever seen her face? Have you ever seen her smile?
Have you felt her warm embrace? Or did she just stop for a while?
Have you ever seen her face? Were her eyes still sad and blue?
Did she still wear her hair so long? Did you ask where she was going to?

TRANSPLANT

Wow. Imagine if you had a heart transplant and the heart was actually the soul. What if the recipient could feel all the thoughts and feelings the donor had? I wrote this song just after having two stents fitted in my own heart. That near heart attack brought me down to earth with a bang. A quick reality check and evaluation of the life I had been leading was needed. I had been working constant 12-hour days for months.

After this long week, I was then driving home on Friday night which could take six hours and returning to my area of work Sunday night. All this coupled with late-night meals in the hotel with a few beers. This routine now ended up with my body telling me to slow down.

I had already stopped smoking years before and now I had to watch my diet, cut down on drinking and start exercising again which had dropped off in recent years. In fact, everything I enjoyed doing had to be cut out of my normal routine and I had to train myself not to overindulge. Why is it everything we like in life is bad for us?

You gave me your heart and saved my life.
And rescued me from the years of strain.
A life so hard that each night you cried.
I know this for I feel your pain.
And all the time I talk to you.
About the world outside we knew.
Until you left your troubled life.
I was scared of living mine.

The paper said you took your life.
To end those bitter days of shame.
What were things really like?
And who were they to cast the blame?
And all that time I sat in line.
Waiting for that heart of mine.
Not really thinking of what cost.
Slowly running out of time.

Your family so absorbed in grief.
Mixed with the fear and hope of mine.
And when I found from where you came.
I loved your family just like mine.
And I found your daughters on their knees.
I gave them pride and helped them see.
That things aren't as they seem to be.
You made mistakes just like me.

So, here am I as good as new,
A whole new life in front of me.
My friends and family so relieved.
To see me here so fit and free.

And looking back as years pass by,
I think we know the reason why.
Every night I think of you.
And hope that you're now happy too.
And every night I shed a tear,
And I thank you from the bottom of your heart.

TROUBADOURS

I have and still do, visit quite a few folk clubs where the talent is very hit and-miss. Some artists get on stage and give a performance that will leave the audience in awe that they are not already professional players. Others get up and cannot sing, cannot play and for 15 minutes of their fame sound like fingernails on a blackboard.

Throughout the performance, the audience sits and grins wishing for the pain to stop. Afterwards, everyone claps which only encourages the person to come back next week and start torturing us all over again.

Nobody ever says, "For God's sake, you were terrible, don't come back."

At least, people are getting out and meeting other people and playing their music whatever the genre. I also know that some of the people are turning up just for the enjoyment of it all. They are probably far more talented than some of the multi-millionaire artists who had a good publicity agent and made a fortune with a couple of commercial tracks.

Although I play the guitar to quite a high standard, I don't ever think my voice would ever have placed me in that professional artist's category, although I have done a few paid gigs over the years. The money that comes with fame would be nice but I would not want the celebrity life to be traded for the life I have already led.

A sign of the times is that roots music. (The music that tells the history of our past) is now generally told and sung by an elder generation whose music and tone of singing cannot be tolerated by the younger generations as it does tend to be a bit dull and boring in the way it is presented.

I have always enjoyed stopping and listening to buskers in the street. Admittedly most are three chord specials out to make a quick buck but sometimes I come across the odd one that is really impressive. I will not even broach the subject of Morris dancers. I know a story about a circumcised man who couldn't join the Morris dancers because he wasn't a complete prick. But I'll tell that story another day.

Hey, do you know their coming?
Can you really hear them strumming?
Here come the troubadours today.
Now can you hear their voices?
Knowing that you've got no choices.
You've got to get along and hear them play.

Yes! You can hear them playing.
Now, can see them swaying.
Look at all the dances flying around.

Hey, do you know their coming?
Can you really hear them strumming?
The Troubadours are coming into town.

WHO WANTS TO BE A HERO?

Harvey Andrews wrote a song in the mid-1970s called 'Soldier'. It was about a soldier dying trying to save lives in a Belfast train station.

The lyrics, "Who wants to be a hero," were written in Northern Ireland in 1977. During a tour of Belfast, we had to deal with four street bombs in the city centre in one night. That was a fun night. Every time we found a safe place to set up an incident point another part of the street would blow up. It was almost like the IRA had planned this.

During this tour of Northern Ireland, the armourer's shop had to modify all the Self-Loading Rifles (SLRs) from wooden stocks and butts and replace them with plastic ones. I jumped at this enterprise as the wooden butts were getting thrown away. I rapidly set up a production line to turn the scratched and marked wooden butts into highly polished crib boards with shiny brassware.

This was quite an easy process that could be done relatively quickly with the exception of the 126 holes that had to be accurately drilled to very tight tolerances by hand. This took massive concentration and to complete this I commandeered a small room next to the armourers' bay.

It was whilst carrying out this drilling procedure that the armourer staff sergeant crashed into the room shouting, "Come on then."

On looking up from the crib board, I noticed my workbench was covered in mess and there was dust everywhere coming down from the roof. What on Earth had happened? Well! About a mile away Anderson Town RUC police station had been blown up by a proxy bomb.

The bang that I may or may not have heard was not a normal bang that we were subjected to in the workshop whilst working on vehicles, but the shock wave from the bomb. Needless to say, crib board production stopped as we dashed to the RUC station to dig people out of the rubble. It had been a 1000 lbs bomb and although many people were injured nobody died.

The words of this song have changed slightly over the years but they are within context no matter which theatre a British soldier has to perform his duty. During my other life in the army, I saw action in Northern Ireland and the Gulf Wars as well as peacekeeping and humanitarian work in Bosnia. Working at both ends of the spectrum from fighting enemy armies and capturing murdering warlords to saving starving child refugees.

These activities gave me a wide breadth of emotions to call on for inspiration. In every campaign, I saw the absolute best and absolute worst in every group of people I encountered, including the British and the rest of the civilised world. A lot of countries do plough their money into just causes and rightly so. Doing nothing is probably just as bad as backing the aggressors.

After so many years and meeting a vast number of ethnic groups, different religions and nationalities, I still have not decided whose God is the biggest and the best so I have decided to plod on through life ignoring them all.

> You can make the boys go out at dawn.
> You can wave goodbye they'll soon be gone.
> When the bomb blast leaves their bodies torn.
> Who wants to be a hero?
> There's a bomb blast in the city street,
> That shattered limb, just a piece of meat.
> Tattoo of death the drum will beat.
> Who wants to die lonely?

Gone are all the laws of war. My wounds are deep my body sore.
The human race is turned to gore. The politician said what a pity.
Now's the time to live or die, you do not ask the question why.
When the brass tells you that age-old lie.
You're fighting for the Queen and country.

And the grieving mother, she wails and weeps,
She's tortured in her shattered sleep.
Why does life become so cheap?
For 18 years, she fed she clothed she dressed him.

Disillusioned words they hit the mark.
The kids are playing in the park.
Gravitational pull and a white-hot spark.
Explode the bomb for freedom.

You can make the boys go out at dawn.
You can wave goodbye they'll soon be gone.
When the bomb blast leaves their bodies torn.
Who wants to be a hero?

And the grieving mother, she wails and weeps,
She's tortured in her shattered sleep.
Why does life become so cheap?
For 18 years, she fed, she clothed, she loved him.

Disillusioned words they hit the mark.
And the kids are playing in the park.
Gravitational pull and a white-hot spark.
Explodes the bomb for freedom.
You can make our boys go out at dawn.
You can wave goodbye they'll soon be gone.
When the bomb blast leaves your faith, all torn.
Who wants to be a hero?

WRITER OF POEMS

Probably, the first ditty I wrote after joining the army in 1974.

To think I joined the army to see the world.
To set everyone free from the enemy's grips.
I left all my friends and I left all the girls.
I dreamt all my dreams and decided to split.
But I wish that I had never done that now.
And now that I've done that I can't think how.
I once had a girl who thought a lot of me.
I'm not into loving, but I like kissing and cuddling.
But now there's no one to cuddle up to me.

So again, I'm a loser and an unhappy loner.
But I will always be a writer of songs.

Chapter 31
Fallingbostel 1993

Once we had returned from Bosnia to Fallingbostel I had to hand my duties over to my replacement and move across to the other side of camp to my next posting as the staff sergeant running the shop floor of General Service Company, the 2nd Battalion Workshop REME.

My first posting in Detmold in 1975 was to a large REME workshop and things had not improved in the manor that the administration was run by the regimental duties staff. Unfortunately, they were the ones who dictated the priority of the tasks the tradesmen were to complete. Even when we had a heavy workload, sweeping the camp took priority over fixing a truck.

A few months into this posting, Billy Welsh who was my immediate boss was posted and I was promoted to warrant officer class II to take his place. Even with this higher rank, I still had no sway in the priorities for work within the unit. This is because army thinking is that if everything looks tidy then everyone will believe everything is running smoothly even if behind closed doors it is a shambles.

There was a civilian workshop within our unit and if they were short of work then all the work we had been tasked to do was transferred to them, leaving my guys to sit and twiddle their thumbs and there is nothing worse than a bored soldier.

Chapter 32
Batus

I was therefore quite pleased when, after I had been at the 2nd Battalion for a year, I was offered the chance to do a six-month detachment to BATUS, Canada as the Battlegroup Maintenance Advisor. I went home and broke the news to Ursula, who would be left at home on her own again for six months.

Ursula by now had secured a job involving the selling of the rationed petrol coupons within the camp so at least her days would be filled with going to work. Jon was at school and Donna was a day boarder at a school and only came home at weekends.

Each time I had been to BATUS previously, I had seen the maintenance advisor (call sign 7X) on the area driving all over the prairie visiting the REME units on the ground and always thought this was a great job. Now, I was going to be that guy and I was hoping that it would be everything I had wished for.

Once in Canada, I settled down into the busy routine within the battle group training programme. The training was broken down into three sections.

Week one: All the units went to various parts of the area and completed low-level training within the unit area.

Week two: Each unit would join up with their respective battalion and practice manoeuvres with them.

Week three: The whole battle group meets up in the north of the area and over the next five days does a battle run for 50 miles to the south of the area. This move involves obstacle crossings, live firing, and night manoeuvres including a firepower demonstration which is quite something to watch.

During all these phases the range safety team of 20 to 30 vehicles, drive their red-topped vehicles all around their respective charges, shouting commands on the radio trying to keep the soldiers from shooting each other by accident or try and stop the armoured vehicles running over trench systems that have infantry soldiers in them.

Occasionally, this goes wrong and over the six or seven training periods the army has per year in BATUS, between five or six soldiers are killed, with twice that number being seriously injured each year. It is a dangerous game but all training has to be simulated as if it was a real situation.

The reason for this is, that if the balloon went up, the soldiers would not be taken by surprise when they found themselves on a full-blown war footing with a real enemy. They would know exactly what to do and know what all the other units would be doing at the same time.

I absolutely loved my role whilst I was in BATUS. Every day I had to go onto the prairie and visit each individual fitter section of the area. This involved driving perhaps 150 miles a day on rough dirt tracks. As I was free running, I had to constantly check where the live firing areas were each day so I did not stumble into a live firing template and get shot at. Once at a fitter section location, a brew would appear and we would sit down and have a chat.

I would get a vehicle state from the chap in charge, also check they were happy with their spares supply and discuss any technical problems they had with their company/squadron vehicles. Once all questions had been asked and answered, I would then set off 30 miles in another direction to find another fitter section and repeat the process.

Whilst driving around there was lots of wildlife to be seen and if I was in the north of the area I would stay out for a few nights and just camp on the prairie taking in the vastness of this land.

Obviously, it was not all sunshine and roses. I had a lot of reports to write on the vehicle states and pass these on to the officers in charge. I had to provide lectures on the maintenance of vehicles each time a new battle group arrived to be trained and be in charge of the final vehicle inspection team prior to one battlegroup handing over to the next to make sure these vehicles were fit for purpose.

There were about 50 main battle tanks (Challengers) and one hundred Warrior infantry fighting vehicles as well as one hundred soft-skin vehicles, so it was not a small undertaking. This had to be done every month when a new battle group arrived. I also had to inspect each vehicle that was involved in a serious incident if someone had been seriously hurt or killed.

For five months, I carried out this role and loved every minute of it. Obviously, there were times when I was cold and soaking wet and things were not going as planned with a vehicle problem. As normal, we forget about them and only remember the sunny days. I also haven't mentioned the swarms of mosquitoes the size of B52 bombers.

I have mentioned previously the amazing rest and recuperation five days I had on my own at Cyprus Hills and this was a nice finish to my BATUS tour and I was a bit disappointed to leave as I really liked being on the prairie.

It was a nice finish to my career and when I came back to Fallingbostel, I only had six months before I would be posted to England for my last six months of service.

Chapter 33
Civilian Life

My final few months in Fallingbostel went without incident and I moved back to Catterick for my final six months in the army.

I was not very impressed with the changes that were happening in the way the army was being reorganised, so, instead of volunteering for extended service or applying for a commission as an officer as many time-served warrant officers do, I decided that at 40 years old, it was a good time to leave as I was still young enough to make a second career in Civvy Street.

I had intended to settle in North Yorkshire and did some pre-release courses on Total Quality and Safety and Health, but these were very boring subjects, so I did not follow this route into employment. I had left the army with an Exemplary grade which was the highest award and so this set me up being quite employable. I had also taken the last 18 months studying and passing my NVQ level five in management.

The jobs I was offered prior to leaving the army were not that enlightening and seemed to be very routine jobs where there was no diversity in what I would be doing day after day. Try as I might, I was finding it hard to drum up any interest in what I might want to spend the next 25 years of my life doing.

A month before, I officially left the army, I had an offer to work for GKN Defence as a trial engineer in Telford and I jumped at the chance.

I was offered the job with GKN Defence as I was probably the most experienced man in the world who had worked on the Warrior vehicle in active war situations, and this was the company that produced nine-hundred of these vehicles. With all this knowledge, I was sent to complete trials on an eight-wheel armoured vehicle called a Piranha. I then worked with this vehicle for the next three years before finally being given some trials to do on a Warrior. What goes around comes around.

For the next 27 years, I would work on armoured tracked vehicles in the role of an engineer. In that role, I visited Saudi Arabia, Kuwait, Qatar, Finland, Belgium, Switzerland and Germany.

The accommodation ranged from a five-star hotel to a tent on a firing range and the temperature ranged from 45 degrees Celsius where I was fitting the Main Battle Tank, Challenger 2 with additional armour prior to Gulf War II on the Iraq border, to minus 20 degrees Celsius where I was completing deep snow trials in Finland above the Arctic Circle.

The finest accommodation I lived in whilst working abroad was when I was taking part in a mountain trial in Switzerland. My apartment was situated on Lake Thun just next to Interlaken. I had a heated underground garage to park my Land Rover in and a lift from the garage up to my hallway within the apartment.

The view from the balcony was overlooking Lake Thun and I had a backdrop of the Eiger, Monch and Jungfrau mountains about 10 miles away. I would lay back in the sunshine and take in the view whilst cooking my Bar-B-Ques and sipping a beer. I was there for six weeks and fully covered by my expenses allowance. It's a hard life.

Finland was a fun trial although quite stressful. We flew into Rovaniemi and made ourselves at home in the hotel. The next day we drove to the docks and picked up our two Warrior repair and recovery trial vehicles from the ship. After putting them onto the low loaders which miraculously arrived on time, we retired back to the hotel and prepared for the trials starting the next day.

On our first day at the trial area, the transport arrived and as the vehicles had been transported for the last 15 hours in minus 20 degrees Celsius it took quite a while and two cans of cold weather easy start to actually get the engines started. If we had failed to start them, then the whole trial was in jeopardy and so was my job so there was no pressure on me at all. Once the vehicles were unloaded, the transport drove away and we were left in the middle of a large forest area.

At this point, we found out we could not move off the perimeter track to the training area as the snow was three feet deep and we just sank into our waist if we moved off the track. The whole point of the trial was to see how the vehicles performed in snow and so this was not totally unexpected.

Our sister company who carried out a reccy on the area, said it was only a maximum of two feet at this time of year and not the three feet we had now discovered with 10-foot snow drifts. At this point, it was turning dark, so we secured the vehicles and went back to the hotel.

The next day, we arrived back at the trials area with snowshoes for all the trial engineers, and then once fitted, marking out the course for the two Warrior vehicles was a lot easier.

Moving over the snow wearing snowshoes was possible but it was very tiring. Whilst walking over the snow, if I trod on a small pyramid of snow, it would usually turn out to be the tip of a five-foot spruce tree that was hidden under the snow and hollow under the initial covering skin crust. The first warning of this was my leg disappearing into a hollow and then my body pitching forward.

My outstretched arms saving my fall would just punch through the snow and eventually, I would be flat on my face buried about two feet into the snow. I would, therefore, end up virtually upside down in a large snow hole and need help extracting myself. Of course, everyone thought this was hilarious until we had all done it half a dozen times and we were all knackered. Initially, this was quite amusing but after the sixth time, the novelty wore off.

Throughout the trial, we set different tasks for the vehicles to complete and the army vehicle crew we brought with us would set about driving the course, whilst I and the track engineers monitored the track performance. The ambient temperature ranged between minus 20 degrees Celsius and minus 5 degrees Celsius.

It was quite an eye-opener to find how differently the snow reacted throughout this range of temperatures, from billowing dust to clinging slush. No wonder the Eskimos have so many words that describe snow.

On the third day, we arrived at the trial area totally prepared. We had brought three hired snowmobiles with us and now getting about the area was great fun and made the trial a lot more bearable, being able to fly over the snow on 750 cc's of raging snowmobile. Needless to say, we had time to build a racecourse and do some rider training to make sure we could handle these beasts safely.

The trial consisted of two, 31-tonne recovery variants of the Warrior vehicle. Each vehicle had a representative from the track manufacturers and a team of five British soldiers to crew them.

We were in Finland for three weeks and really became experts on surviving in the snow. Every day, an Eskimo and his wife would turn up and feed us reindeer stew and crusty bread. This only cost us pennies and then once consumed, they would collect up the wooden bowls and cups and disappear over the tundra again.

Only to turn up the next day at lunchtime with more stew. Nobody organised this. It just happened. It must have been the Arctic equivalent of a jungle telegraph system. After three weeks, all the trials were completed successfully and we took the vehicles back to the docks and spent the last night in Helsinki.

I'm glad, it was only one night as the cost of the beer was unbelievable.

My five years as a trials engineer were my most enjoyable, I was working on my own with just the trial vehicle crews. I did not have too much input from the bosses back at the factory provided we kept within budget. The downside was I was always away from home during the trials, only getting back home on Friday night and heading back down south on Sunday night.

Some trials were five or six months long. The upside was that I was on full expenses and also had lots of overtime so we really managed to save some money over the years.

One of the proudest moments of my career was when I was asked if I would lead the 25th anniversary of the Falklands War parade through the streets of Market Drayton. I did not go to the Falkland conflict as I was in Northern Ireland at the time but had quite a few friends who had been there during the war.

I and a guy named Keith Gossage were given a vehicle from Alvis vehicles which was the company name where I worked at the time. The vehicle was a Simitar tracked reconnaissance vehicle that had been used in the Falklands conflict. Over the next few weeks, we stripped the vehicle down and repainted it. Everything on the vehicle was brought up to an A1 standard and eventually, it looked brand-new even though it was probably over 30 years old.

On the day of the parade, we drove it from Telford to my house as I lived close to Market Drayton and parked it in my drive until it was time to go to the parade. All the neighbours came and took pictures of it as it was the closest, they had been to a real tank. To me, it was only a small vehicle of 12 tonnes and I was used to working on the 70-tonne Challenger tank but they were overjoyed it was here.

When it was time to leave, we drove through the country lanes and once in Market Drayton moved into position at the forming up point in front of the Parade. When given the word, we moved off with all the pomp and ceremony of the military masses following behind. The parade marched through the town with hundreds of local people and visitors waving flags and clapping.

It was quite emotional, especially as I knew quite a few people who were at the side of the road. The parade came to a halt at the British Legion building where we dismounted and went inside for a meal followed by a lot of speeches. Keith and I were thanked by the military top brass and the mayor for giving up our free time for the occasion. Totally unexpected, one of our company directors turned up out of the blue who had nothing to do with the build-up for the parade.

He gave an impromptu speech about the company's involvement with the vehicles during the war. After the speech, he spent almost two minutes thanking Keith and me for the work we had completed on the vehicle and then he buggered off from whence he came with the little trinket that the parade organiser was going to give me for coming. Why am I not surprised?

The company changed owners several times and I went through the redundancy process for a few of these changes but I still managed to remain employed. I changed my role from trials engineer, where I spent most of my time away from home again but had the opportunity to earn lots of money, which really set up our finances for the rest of our lives.

I was then promoted to project engineer and lastly, vehicle fleet manager, where I organised the modifications and the improved maintenance of a fleet of nine hundred Bulldog-tracked armoured personnel carriers for the M.O.D.

Looking back from when I was a paper boy or helping the bread man, working on the farm and then the copper works prior to joining the army I have never been out of work throughout my whole working life, which in itself is quite an achievement in this day and age.

Throughout the whole period of time that is retraced within this book. Ursula has been the mainstay of my home life. Managing the kids and the finances. All the problems she faced whilst I was away, she dug in and sorted them out, even back in the days when we did not have two pennies to rub together. And for that, I am truly grateful. It would be amiss not to mention one experience she had with a ginger tomcat we owned. Whilst I was working away.

Ursula had not seen our ginger tomcat for a few days and had heard that the old chap in the house behind us had it in his house and was feeding it. Ursula promptly went around to his house and demanded the cat back from this lonely old man. She took the cat home and kept it indoors so it would get used to being in our home again. When I returned home after being away for a few weeks, she recounted the tale telling me that she had sorted this old cat thief out.

It was only when the cat jumped up on my knee, a few days later, did I say, "This isn't our cat."

"Of course, it is," she said looking at me as if I'd gone mad.

I said, "It isn't because we had our cat neutered and this one has bollocks."

Apparently, we found out later, that another one of our neighbours had found a dead ginger tom on the road outside her house and thought it was hers and buried it. The old man had pinched his cat and not ours. We still kept this cat until it died a few years later and I have retold the story many times and always get a good laugh at Ursula's expense.

Chapter 34
Prologue

I hope the pages that you have read, have awakened some of your innermost thoughts, or at least given you some time to pause, reflect and relate to some of the things you have done in your lives.

This exercise of writing down my thoughts on all these subjects I have covered has certainly laid some ghosts to rest and also awakened many more that had been buried in my long-forgotten past.

I do not expect you to agree with my philosophy in all cases as everyone has their own opinion about the many subjects I have covered. An opinion is always based on what you were brought up to believe, or what you believe is the correct way to deal with certain scenarios.

This book has just given a very brief snapshot into my life, and I know that I do tend to be blase about things that really do matter or that are really shocking. Perhaps that is my inner protection device that allows me to deal with emergency situations that would otherwise allow me to fall into the PTSD casualty category.

I deliberately stayed away from the subject of PTSD which affects thousands of ex-servicemen and women but seems to be conveniently swept under the carpet by the government. I know very little about the criteria to get help for ex-servicemen and women, but I know that the set of apartments set aside for ex-servicemen and women who have problems with civilian life near where I live, had several ex-servicemen sleeping rough around them.

Apparently, they did not qualify for help. For a long period, these apartments sat empty. Later, to closed due to no uptake in the need for them. Just saying.

On no occasion in my life did I really think too deeply about what could have happened if the wrong dice were thrown, or think about the sliding door scenario. In the heat of the moment if I stopped and thought about the repercussions of any decision I made, would the end result change or remain the same? Should we stop and think about what we are doing or walk on through our chosen doorway and carry on regardless?

I never relied on an outcome of what should have happened if everyone had been nice. I was always prepared, as unfortunately, there are a lot of not-very nice people about, who are prepared to take advantage of the one who hesitates.

I have always hoped for the best and was prepared for the worst.

The verses in the three sections of this book are just that. Verses. They are not really based on any facts. They are mainly just words that came along whilst I was picking a tune on a guitar.

I hope this book amused you and also awakened thoughts about the people you know and the state of the world we live in.

The world we live in is quite a hostile one. Since leaving the army in 1996 I have witnessed; 9/11 and then the Gulf War II. The invasion of Afghanistan and the ISIS threat. We are now witnessing the Russia/Ukraine war. And the latest conflict is the Israel versus Palestine conflict that has started recently.

Meanwhile, I will try and enjoy my retirement, not concerning myself about politics and the various political parties as they are all as bad as each other. There is not a damn thing I can do about it at my stage of life. I can actually tell when a politician is lying because I can see their lips move.

I think I am just going to try and be content in my little bubble of friends and acquaintances and just enjoy myself. I will carry on singing and playing and spend more time in the motorhome discovering this green and pleasant land, that is England.

Figure 14: Commanding the Scimitar armoured tracked reconnaissance vehicle leading the 25th anniversary of the Falken War parade.

Figure 15: The whole family Jon's family Laura, Sofia and Amber on the left. Donna's family, Shawn, Sonny and Jasmine on the right. My darling wife Ursula is in the centre holding the family together as always.

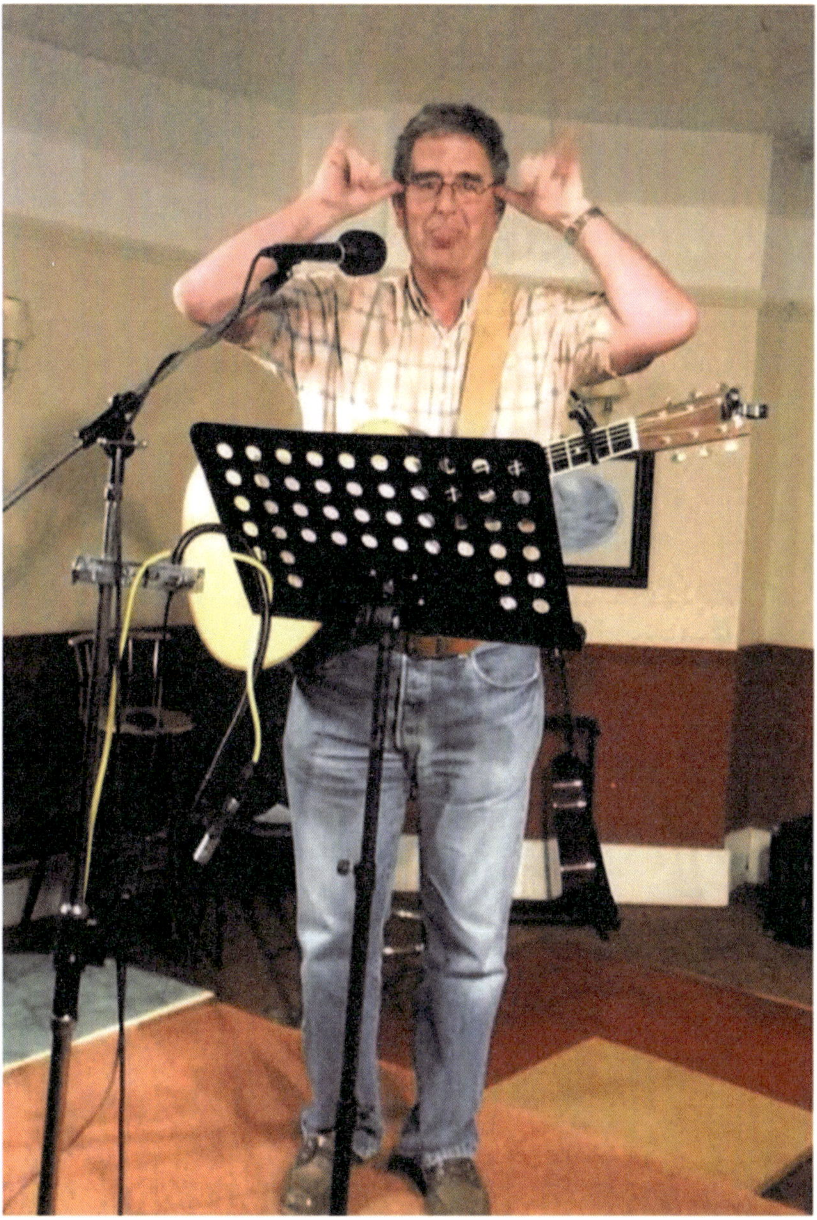